Patrick O'Brien, M.D., is a graduate of Yale University and The Johns Hopkins Medical School. He is Clinical Instructor in Psychiatry, Harvard Medical School at the Massachusetts General Hospital, where he has also been Associate Director of the Private Psychiatric Consultation Service.

THE DISORDERED MIND

What We Now Know About Schizophrenia

Patrick O'Brien, M.D.

A SPECTRUM BOOK

Prentice-Hall, Inc., Englewood Cliffs, New Jersey 07632

Library of Congress Cataloging in Publication Data

O'Brien, Patrick
    The disordered mind.

    (A Spectrum Book)
    Bibiography: p.
    Includes index.
    1.–Schizophrenia. I.–Title.
RC514.018   616.8'982   78-16079
ISBN 0-13-216465-5
ISBN 0-13-216457-4 pbk.

Quote on page viii is from Thomas Bernhard, *Gehen* (Frankfurt: Suhrkamp Verlag, 1971), p. 12. Reprinted with the permission of Suhrkamp Verlag, translation by Patrick O'Brien.

A SPECTRUM BOOK

Printed in the United States of America

10   9   8   7   6   5   4   3   2   1

PRENTICE-HALL INTERNATIONAL, INC., *London*
PRENTICE-HALL OF AUSTRALIA PTY., LIMITED, *Sydney*
PRENTICE-HALL OF CANADA, LTD., *Toronto*
PRENTICE-HALL OF INDIA PRIVATE, LIMITED, *New Delhi*
PRENTICE-HALL OF JAPAN, INC., *Tokyo*
PRENTICE-HALL OF SOUTHEAST ASIA PTE., LTD., *Singapore*
WHITEHALL BOOKS, LIMITED, *Wellington, New Zealand*

Preface

A Note to the General Reader: A summary section has been included at the end of each chapter. The summaries were written so that they would convey much of the essential information relatively independently of the chapters. I would advise anyone interested in a quick overview of our basic knowledge of the schizophrenic-type disorders to read Chapter 1, "Some Misconceptions," and then the summary sections at the end of each chapter. The chapters themselves may then be consulted for more detailed information.

A Note to the Specialist: Students of the social sciences or those involved in clinical work with individuals with schizophrenic-type disorders should consult the Notes on text at the back of the book for a further discussion of some important issues, and references to many of the more important articles on the schizophrenic-type disorders which have appeared in recent years.

Finally, in an effort to keep this a relatively short and practically oriented book, I have limited the discussion of some important topics (for example, the developmental theories of schizophrenia) and omitted discussion of some other important topics, such as the legal issues involved in psychiatric treatment (see Stone, 1977, for a recent discussion).

There are two areas which will probably strike some readers as conspicuous by their absence. The first is the subject of childhood schizophrenia. The incidence of such disorders, however, is relatively rare and their relationship to the adult schizophrenic-type disorders controversial.[1]*

The second subject involves psychological and psychophysiological research on the nature of the schizophrenic disorders. I particularly regret not including an extended discussion of this area of research, since it is an area I have been particularly interested in for years. However, such research is plagued by design and replication difficulties. A proper discussion of the results of such research would involve a long explication of research methodology which is beyond the scope of this practically-oriented volume. Further, the results of such research (for example, on "schizophrenic language" or "schizophrenic attention") have not, unfortunately, had much impact upon either diagnostic or therapeutic practice. While not containing a specific discussion of these areas of research, this book does provide a critical, practically-oriented frame of reference which should prove useful for further reading or research into the nature and causes of the schizophrenic-type disorders.[2]

PATRICK O'BRIEN
Cambridge, Massachusetts

*The reader should refer to the Notes section in the back of the book for detailed footnote information.

Acknowledgements

Many have been indirectly helpful in making this book possible. There are two groups of individuals, however, who are directly responsible for this book. The first comprises all those individuals with schizophrenic-type disorders who have shared their confusion and their anguish with me over the past ten years. The second comprises the editors at Prentice-Hall. In this and other books in the Spectrum series, they have demonstrated their responsivity to the needs (as opposed to the enthusiasms) of their potential readers. Special thanks are due to Lynne Lumsden for her assistance and encouragement throughout the writing of this book.

"The art we need is undoubtedly the art of bearing the unbearable. . . . It's obvious this art is the most difficult art of all." (Bernhard)

Contents

Introduction

You could multiply almost indefinitely the number of labels we use to refer to people who are acting or speaking in a way we find difficult to understand or tolerate. Behind the use of the words (*crazy, mad, insane, schizophrenic, lunatic, psychotic, paranoid, demented, deranged,* etc.) there is a vague conception of something called "mental illness." And behind the vague conception there is usually a very real fear, a fear of something unknown and terrible. Despite all the efforts in recent decades to educate the public as to the nature of mental disorders, very little has been achieved, especially with respect to schizophrenia. If anything really had been achieved, the public would simply find ridiculous the grotesque and absurd images of "madness" which the media continue to per-petrate. But for many people schizophrenia still evokes im-ages of berserk mass murderers, of demented, demonic "mad scientists," of deranged relatives locked away in dark attics, and of raving, wailing "maniacs." A little bit of educa-tion doesn't serve to dispel such images. They assail us again and again on television, in movies, and in books and magazines. The Madman is the familiar terror of our night-mares. We're educated to understand that individuals un-dergoing schizophrenic-type reactions aren't like this, but the fear and terror remain.

I don't think merely being told what, in fact, mental ill-ness in general, and the schizophrenic-type disorders in par-ticular, are like will eliminate such fears entirely. They touch upon some basic sense of dread that seems to be part of being alive, conscious, and human. The only way for some-one to become somewhat convinced that what I will call the Terror of the Madman has nothing to do with schizophrenia is to have had experience with a great number of individuals suffering from schizophrenic-type disorders. Then it be-comes absolutely clear that such people are sad, lost, often terrified souls whose plight should evoke neither terror nor fear but profound compassion.

But it seems even the knowledge of what a few indi-viduals who have undergone schizophrenic-type disorders are like isn't enough to dispel our fears. The Madman as Schizophrenic still lurks in the wings, as the Terrible Possibil-ity, either for ourselves or for those we hold dear. The Mad-man is simply not this particular "schizophrenic" (the pleas-ant young man on the TV show) or that one (the friend with his occasional "nervous breakdowns") but the Other One, the one you haven't met yet. The terror simply retreats be-hind our remaining uncertainty, where it rages unabated.

By dealing comprehensively with what the schizo-phrenic-type disorders are and what they clearly are not, hopefully this book will help divorce our images of the Madman from our conceptions of what someone undergoing a schizophrenic-type disorder is like. There are several popular books which do deal with schizophrenia. Some, such as Green's *I Never Promised You a Rose Garden,* are accounts of very atypical psychotic episodes; others, such as several of Laing's and Szasz's books, deal with very specialized and selective viewpoints. Still others are primarily one-sided panegyrics to particular—and as often as not, highly controversial—forms of treatment. The end result is that it's extremely difficult to obtain a balanced understanding. There are of course textbooks of psychiatry and psychology which attempt to summarize current knowledge, but they don't address themselves specifically to clearing up the enormous number of misconceptions concerning "madness" and schizophrenia currently prevalent in our society.

There is an extensive psychiatric literature on the subject of schizophrenia. Unfortunately, it's almost all contained in professional journals and isn't immediately accessible to the general reading public. There are a great number of articles published yearly on schizophrenia, but they are of such uneven quality, and in most instances deal with such limited issues, that unless you have a great deal of time to devote to the subject, you'll soon begin to feel overwhelmed. Instead of obtaining the desired critical and comprehensive understanding, you'll probably end up feeling more confused than ever. This is not to say that good summary articles dealing with one aspect or another of schizophrenia haven't been written. They have, and it will be one objective of this book to direct you to them should you care to inquire further (see the Notes section at the back of the book).

The primary objective of this book, however, is to clear up misconceptions—misconceptions as to the types of schizophrenic disorders and as to their causes and treatment. I'm primarily interested in telling you what we know currently, and, even more importantly, given the veritable explosion of *mis*information concerning the schizophrenic-type disorders which has occurred in the popular media in recent years, I'm interested in telling you what we don't know—what is a useful hypothesis, and what is pure speculation; what is manifestly misleading, and what is simply false. Hopefully the Myth of the Madman will be partially, if not entirely, dispelled by such knowledge and understanding.

THE DIAGNOSIS AND COURSE OF THE SCHIZOPHRENIC-TYPE DISORDERS

1

Some
Misconceptions

If the following list of forty misconceptions about schizophrenia seems long, be advised that I've only selected some
of the more popular ones. My purpose in this chapter is to
state each misconception and its refutation as concisely as
possible. In parentheses, I've listed the chapter or chapters
where the issues will be dealt with more fully. The list of
misconceptions follows the order in which I deal with them
in ensuing chapters.

    1. Schizophrenia is a single disorder.

  FACT: It's not known whether schizophrenia is a single
         disorder or a group of disorders with many dif-
         ferent causes. (Chapter 2)

2. Schizophrenia, like most mental illness in general, is a myth.

FACT: The label *schizophrenia* may refer to many different types of disorders. The fact of the disorders themselves, and the severity of the incapacitation they produce, is no myth. (Chapter 2; also Chapters 6 and 7)

3. Psychiatrists all refer to the same type of disorder or syndrome when they diagnose someone as schizophrenic.

FACT: There's a notorious lack of agreement among clinicians in diagnosing schizophrenia. A great number of individuals are carelessly and indiscriminately labeled schizophrenic because of the vague and idiosyncratic biases of diagnosing clinicians. (Chapter 2; also Chapters 4, 5, and 8)

4. There's a "special feeling" by which you can learn to tell whether someone is schizophrenic or not. Psychiatrists in particular have this special feeling.

FACT: You don't need special intuitions to decide whether a given disorder fits the descriptions of a schizophrenic-type disorder or not. Diagnosing by a "special feeling" has led to precisely the situation described in 3, above. (Chapter 2)

5. "Schizophrenics" live in a fantasy dream world.

FACT: The kind of elaborate delusional system described in *I Never Promised You a Rose Garden* or similar popular works is the exception. Individuals with schizophrenic-type disorders suffer from a disorganized and painful perception of current realities and not, in general, from an overabundance of escapist fantasies or nightmare visions of other worlds. (Chapter 2; also Chapters 6 and 7)

6. A schizophrenic-type disorder is similar to a mystical experience and may put you in touch with deeper truths about yourself and the world.

FACT: An acute schizophrenic disorder is certainly a unique and powerful experience, and everyone will make what they can of it. However, the main thing people who have undergone a schizophrenic-type reaction have learned is how to survive confusion, terror, and, at times, almost unbearable suffering and despair. (Chapter 2; also Chapters 6 and 7)

7. "Schizophrenics" want to stay "crazy." They don't want to live in the real world anymore. They don't want to be "cured."

FACT: This may have been true for some neglected chronic, backward patients. It is certainly not true for almost anyone undergoing an acute schizophrenic-type reaction, and it's probably not true for the vast majority of individuals with chronic schizophrenic-type disorders. (Chapter 2; also Chapters 6 and 7)

8. If someone has had a "nervous breakdown," this means he or she "went crazy" and is probably suffering from schizophrenia.

FACT: The term *nervous breakdown* is most often used to refer to acute anxiety or depressive reactions and other nonschizophrenic-type difficulties. It doesn't at all imply someone "went crazy" or had a schizophrenic-type disorder. (Chapter 3)

9. If there are times when you feel unreal or when it seems the world is unreal, that indicates you're losing touch with reality and are "going insane."

FACT: These phenomena—depersonalization and derealization—are related to depression and anxiety and occur in all of us. They are an indication of depression and anxiety and not of schizophrenia. (Chapter 3)

10. If someone is schizophrenic, that means he or she has a split personality.

FACT: Nothing could be further from the truth. Individuals with dual or multiple personalities (as in the books *The Three Faces of Eve* and *Sybil*) manifest a neurotic hysterical, or dissociative, type of reaction. Such reactions have nothing to do with schizophrenia. Dr. Jekyll was suffering from hysteria, not schizophrenia. (Chapter 3)

11. People who think they are Napoleon or God are usually schizophrenic.

FACT: Such individuals are not necessarily suffering from a schizophrenic-type disorder at all. Such grandiosity is as likely to occur in the manic phase of manic-depressive illness. In chronic schizophrenic-type disorders an almost whimsical grandiosity (as portrayed in films such as *The King of Hearts*) was more the result of years of backward social isolation and neglect than of any schizophrenic disorder per se. (Chapter 3)

12. Someone diagnosed as schizophrenic is prone to unpredictable acts of violence. Many of the great criminals of history (e.g., Hitler) were probably schizophrenic, and a fair portion of the violence today is caused by "crazy" or schizophrenic individuals.

FACT: The diagnosis of a schizophrenic-type disorder has nothing to do with proneness to violence. The great criminals of history almost certainly were *not* schizophrenic. (Chapter 3)

13. Many adults who sit around introspecting, meditating, philosophizing, and pondering the riddles of the universe are probably a bit "crazy" or schizophrenic.

FACT: Anyone may ponder the riddles of the universe. No one has demonstrated a greater incidence of schizophrenia among those preoccupied with the mysteries of life. (Chapter 3)

14. Hallucinations are an indication of schizophrenia.

FACT: Hallucinations may occur for many different reasons. They are not at all indicative of *only* a schizophrenic-type disorder. (Chapter 3)

15. Paranoid thinking is indicative of a schizophrenic-type disorder.

FACT: Schizophrenia *may* be defined to include many individuals who have paranoid ideas, but only at the risk of defining, for example, entire nations as schizophrenic (for example, China and the United States with their mutual paranoia in past decades). Psychiatrists distinguish between paranoid schizophrenia, paranoia, paranoid personality, and culturally based paranoid beliefs. (Chapter 3)

16. Drugs, especially hallucinogens such as LSD, can cause a chronic schizophrenic-type illness.

FACT: All of the evidence is simply not in. It's probably not the case that a single dose of a hallucinogen can produce a chronic psychotic disorder. It may be the case that repeated doses (for example, over a hundred "trips") can produce a chronic schizophreniclike disorder. (Chapter 3; also Chapter 11)

17. "Normals" never have schizophrenic-type symptoms.

FACT: We all experience schizophrenic-type symptoms.
        A schizophrenic-type disorder is characterized by
        the patterning, pervasiveness, and severity of
        reactions and experiences known to us all. (Chap-
        ter 3; also Chapters 2, 6, and 8)

18.   Schizophrenia is incurable.

FACT: Utter nonsense. (Chapter 5; also Chapters 6 and
        14)

19.   If someone is diagnosed as having a schiz-
        ophrenic-type disorder, there will certainly be re-
        currences and the person will probably end up
        permanently hospitalized.

FACT: As above, utter nonsense. (Chapter 5; also Chap-
        ter 16)

20.   Too much stress can drive you "crazy" and cause
        schizophrenia.

FACT: Individuals under great stress (for example, com-
        bat) may have many types of severe psychological
        reactions. Some may resemble acute schizo-
        phrenic-type reactions. The importance of severe
        situational stresses in producing chronic
        schizophrenic-type disorders is unclear and the
        subject of much debate at present. It is a well-
        known clinical fact that many schizophrenic indi-
        viduals react to acute situational stresses (for
        example, a fire or a severe illness) by becoming
        unusually sane and sensible. (Chapter 6; also
        Chapters 7 and 9)

21.   "Madness," like a heart attack, may come from
        "out of the blue." It may strike you down without
        warning and possibly leave you in a state of per-
        manent, incurable "insanity."

FACT: A schizophrenic-type disorder rarely appears "out
        of the blue." Where there are such acute psychotic

reactions there are almost always warning signals, and the reactions are almost always of brief duration. The individual almost always returns to his or her prior level of adjustment. If, for example, you had been severely maladjusted prior to the acute psychotic reaction, then, without further therapy, you're likely to continue so afterward. (Chapter 6; also Chapter 5)

22. "Borderline character disorder" is a type of schizophrenic disorder.

FACT: Their different characteristics, courses, and responses to various types of therapy indicate that the schizophrenic and the "borderline" syndromes should not be confused, though in practice they often are. (Chapter 8)

23. Schizophrenia is due to bad mothering (the "schizophrenogenic mother").

FACT: This is a simplistic statement of one among many speculative theories as to the "cause" of schizophrenia. What *is* known is that many individuals who undergo schizophrenic-type reactions come from apparently "normal" families. (Chapter 9)

24. Schizophrenia is due to "sick families" who need a "scapegoat"—the schizophrenic individual—to stay together.

FACT: This is another speculative theory and, as with most of the other theories, plausible with respect to a few individuals, implausible with respect to many, and still awaiting adequate investigation. (Chapter 9)

25. Schizophrenic-type disorders are very uncommon.

FACT: Schizophrenic-type disorders are very common. At one point approximately half of the hospital beds in the United States were taken up by individuals diagnosed as schizophrenic. Using a very narrow definition of *schizophrenia*, between 1 and 2 percent of the population would be so diagnosed at some time in their lives. This is an incidence similar, for example, to the incidence of diabetes. Further, a recent Research Task Force (1975)* study, using a very broad definition of *schizophrenia*, estimated that about one in twenty (or 5 percent) of all American children who survive beyond the age of fifteen will be diagnosed at some time during their lives as having had a schizophrenic-type reaction. (Chapter 10)

26. Society "drives people crazy" and causes schizophrenia.

FACT: The incidence of schizophrenic-type disorders is similar the world over in all cultures, technological or non-technological. There is no conclusive evidence that one society "produces" more schizophrenia than another. (Chapter 10)

27. Schizophrenia is a disease of the lower classes and is produced by the social conditions of life among them.

FACT: While schizophrenic-type disorders are diagnosed slightly more frequently in the lowest social class, there is no conclusive evidence that the conditions of life are the cause of this. (Chapter 10)

28. Schizophrenia is related to low intelligence and mental retardation.

FACT: Schizophrenic-type disorders have little if any relation to intelligence and no relation to mental retardation. (Chapter 10.)

---

*Parenthetical citations refer to works listed in the References section at the back of the book.

29. Schizophrenia tends to run in families.

FACT: Some families may have a somewhat higher incidence of schizophrenic-type disorders than would
be expected by chance alone. But it's absolutely
essential to understand the facts and not be a
victim of popular superstitions concerning "inherited insanity." (Chapter 10)

30. Schizophrenia is a disease, like diabetes or
epilepsy.

FACT: No organic cause has yet been found to validate
the medical-disease model, though this is not to
say one may not be found. We simply don't know
at present what the fundamental cause of the
schizophrenic-type disorders is. We don't even
know whether we should be looking for one fundamental cause or many causes. (Chapter 11, also
Chapters 6, 7, 9, and 10)

31. Schizophrenia is due to an allergic (autoimmune)
disorder.

FACT: This is one of a number of highly speculative
theories that provide research workers with leads
to investigate, but one which today remains as
unconfirmed and highly controversial as ever.
(Chapter 11)

32. Frontal lobotomy (brain surgery) is a recommended form of treatment for chronic schizophrenia.

FACT: Frontal lobotomy, or *any* brain surgery (there are
several variants these days), is an outmoded form
of therapy which most psychiatrists would never,
practically speaking, recommend. If such a procedure is recommended for anyone, he or she, or
family or friends (or a lawyer), should seek several
independent psychiatric opinions. (Chapter 12)

33. Shock therapy is often the treatment of choice for schizophrenic-type disorders.

FACT: Shock therapy is one of the most abused treatment modalities in the United States today. "Shock shops"—hospitals that use shock therapy indiscriminatly for any and all—abound. (There are good financial reasons for this.) Most schizophrenic-type disorders will respond to supportive therapy and appropriate medication. Shock therapy is not necessary. In some individuals, it may prove helpful where other approaches have failed to provide any relief from severe disorganization. (Chapter 13)

34. Valium, Librium, Miltown, and Thorazine are all similar tranquilizers.

FACT: Valium, Librium, and Miltown and other "minor tranquilizers" are quite different from Thorazine and similar "major tranquilizers." The two classes of drugs should not be used interchangeably. (Chapter 14)

35. If a doctor gives me a major tranquilizer such as Thorazine (or Stelazine or Haldol, etc.), then that means I must be "crazy."

FACT: Thorazine and the other major tranquilizers are frequently prescribed when they should not be prescribed—for example, as a drug of first choice for anxiety and depression. Further, the major tranquilizers are useful in disorders other than the acute schizophrenic-type disorders—for example, in mania, agitated depressions, and LSD reactions. (Chapter 14)

36. If I've had a schizophrenic-type disorder, I'll need to stay on medication for the rest of my life to prevent a recurrence.

FACT: No such rule can be formulated. Many will not need to take medication at all, some only intermittently, while others may find long-term maintenance medication quite helpful. (Chapter 14)

37.   Drugs like Thorazine are society's way of controlling the deviant. They are "chemical straitjackets" and not really for the patient's good.

FACT: Any practice is open to abuse. In general, the discovery of the major tranquilizers has been a major blessing in the lives of individuals suffering from schizophrenic-type disorders. They ease tremendous suffering and shorten drastically the period of disorganization and incapacitation. (Chapter 14)

38.   Megavitamin therapy with high doses of Vitamin B_3 (niacin and niacinamide) cures schizophrenia by reversing the basic biochemical defect.

FACT: In recent years, megavitamin therapy has turned out to be ineffective in at least three extensive double-blind studies. No one knows if there is a basic biochemical defect in the schizophrenic-type disorders, let alone what it is. (Chapter 15)

39.   Hospitalization is a necessary part of the treatment of schizophrenic-type disorders, and most of the time such hospitalization will need to be for a long time—for example, a year or more.

FACT: Hospitalization may sometimes be helpful. In most such instances hospitalization need only be for a month or two at the most. With many individuals, there is no need for hospitalization at all. (Chapter 16)

40.   If they could afford it, most individuals with schizophrenic-type disorders could be cured by several years of intensive psychotherapy.

FACT: Psychoanalysts and other psychotherapists in general have been quite pessimistic about the efficacy of their methods in treating individuals with chronic schizophrenic-type reactions. The question of the effectiveness of psychotherapy is quite complex and there are many issues remaining to be resolved. (Chapter 17)

2

What
Schizophrenia
Is

INTRODUCTION: CLASSIFICATION
IN PSYCHIATRY

In a recent, somewhat notorious, study by Rosenhan (1973), a group of investigators posed as patients seeking admittance to twelve different psychiatric hospitals. They complained of one and only one symptom—hearing voices, often unclear, that said "empty," "hollow," and "thud." Beyond this single symptom they reported no other difficulties and were presumably "normal." However, all but one of these pseudopatients had the honor of being admitted with the diagnosis of schizophrenia and discharged an average of nineteen days later with the diagnosis of "schizophrenia in remission." Psychiatrists are presumably taught that hallucinations arise from diverse causes and also that hallucinations are of only secondary importance in the diagnosis of schizophrenia. What happened, then? Why did these adventurous souls end up with the label *schizophrenic?* The answer lies in the extreme imprecision in the use of diagnostic labels in psychiatry. There are two reasons for this great imprecision. The first relates to the vagueness involved in dealing with psychological phenomena in general; the second relates to the laxity of many clinicians in applying the useful criteria, imprecise as they may be, which have been developed.

You may get a further idea of the extent of the arbitrariness involved in the diagnosis of schizophrenia from the results of a recent study comparing the diagnostic criteria of American and British psychiatrists, which found that

> those patients which inspired transatlantic disagreement were generally diagnosed as schizophrenic by the American psychiatrists; they received a wide range of British diagnoses, however,—especially the manic-depressive disorders, but also the neuroses and personality disorders. (Professional Staff of U.S.–U.K. Cross-National Project, 1974, p. 88)

Another study (Baldessarini, 1970) showed that at one hospital the number of patients admitted with the diagnosis of schizophrenia almost doubled over the two-year period following the discovery and introduction of the "antischizophrenic" drug chlorpromazine and, similarly, that the number of patients diagnosed as schizophrenic fell abruptly over the two-year period when the new effective "antimania" drug Lithium was introduced.[1]

I don't wish to sound unduly pessimistic. There are times when most psychiatrists would agree on diagnosing the presence of a schizophrenic-type disorder. But all too frequently there is marked disagreement. What one clinician considers a "schizophrenic disorder," another considers a "borderline personality disorder," "manic-depressive disorder," or even a "severe anxiety reaction." Why the ambiguity?

A great deal of it hinges upon the nature of the classification system in psychiatry. The diagnosis of schizophrenia is essentially one of exclusion. For a great many American psychiatrists, if you are sufficiently impaired in dealing with reality, and if you don't have various other syndromes (organic brain syndrome, manic-depressive illness, severe neurosis, or certain types of personality disorders), then you're called schizophrenic. It's like saying we'll call every tree in the forest that isn't either an oak, a maple, or a birch, an "elm." The diagram in Figure 1 will perhaps be helpful.

The kind of decisions most psychiatrists go through in deciding whether or not to call someone schizophrenic is, in a somewhat oversimplified form, generally as shown in Figure 2.

First it's decided whether the patient is psychotic or not.

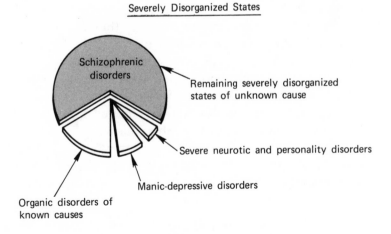

FIGURE 1

The American Psychiatric Association's official diagnostic manual (second edition) described someone as psychotic when "mental functioning is sufficiently impaired to interfere grossly with the capacity to meet the ordinary demands of life" (American Psychiatric Association, 1968, p. 23).* But everyone is going to have their own interpretation of what they consider psychotic. In any case, once you've decided that the person is sufficiently out of touch with current realities ("crazy," as one would popularly say), you've eliminated the categories of neurosis and character disorder. You're then left with only two more decisions to make. First, does the individual have a physical disease that's causing his or her mental difficulties (for example, hyperthyroidism)? Once this is ruled out, and it usually is fairly easy to do so, you're left with deciding whether the individual has manic-depressive illness or not. As manic-depressive illness has a fairly typical picture, it's not usually difficult to rule out.

Then what about all those other people, those great multitudes (variously estimated to constitute between 1 and 5 percent of the population) who have periods of being "sufficiently impaired" (i.e., psychotic) who don't have a manic-depressive-type syndrome? They're all called schizophrenic. If they don't have a medical illness to account for their gross disorganization and if they're not manic-depressive, then they're called schizophrenic. To elaborate upon our analogy: if you're a tree (very disorganized or psychotic) and if you're not either an oak (organic brain syndrome) or a maple (manic-depressive illness), then you're called an "elm" (schizophrenic)—no matter if you're a birch, or cypress, or mimosa, or weeping willow.

There's no way at present to know whether in this vast group of "leftovers" we're speaking of one disorder or many disorders with many types of causes. This statement will be

*From *The Diagnostic and Statistical Manual of Mental Disorders*, American Psychiatric Association, second edition, 1968, p. 23. Reprinted with permission of the American Psychiatric Association.

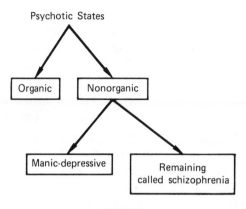

Psychotic States

Organic

Nonorganic

Manic-depressive

Remaining
called schizophrenia

FIGURE 2

repeated over and over in many different contexts through-out the rest of this book. It needs to be repeated because the basis of so many prejudices is that people think of all "schizophrenics" as the same, just as they may think of all "Commies," or everyone of one race or religion or country, as the same despite the fact that they are talking about all different kinds of people within each group. Some people label everyone by some outrageous caricature and proceed to treat them as though they were all the embodiment of their most extreme and lurid representative. So, for example, every "schizophrenic" gets treated in people's minds as though he or she were an embodiment of Hollywood's most vulgar and absurd portrayals of the "demented maniac" (e.g., *Psycho*).

Eugene Bleuler, who originally defined the schizo-phrenic syndrome as we know it today, spoke of the "group of schizophrenias," and there are many today who would prefer to speak of the *schizophrenic-type* disorders rather than of *schizophrenia*. The term *schizophrenic* should be used in a similar way to the term *sore throat*. It indicates that certain symptoms are probably present, but that many different causes may be possible.

It should also be clear why some writers have been able to go to the extreme of denying that "schizophrenia" is a disease or illness at all. They would tend to see "schizophrenia" as merely society's way of labeling people "sick" who don't think in terms of the same sort of realities as the majority (see Szasz, 1970, 1976; Scheff, 1975, 1976; and Laing, 1967). And of course, their criticism is justified to a certain limited extent. Someone who sufficiently distorts commonly accepted realities (i.e., who seems "crazy") and who's not medically ill or manic-depressive will, by current standards, be labeled schizophrenic. So Laing, Szasz, and Scheff and their followers have a point. But the fact is they don't know what causes *all* the schizophrenic-type disorders anymore than the rest of us do. Because some sore throats are caused by talking too much, for example, that doesn't mean they all are.

On the other hand, there are those who believe that schizophrenia is one specific disease. Once again, because some sore throats are caused by a virus that doesn't mean they all are.

WHAT SCHIZOPHRENIA IS

You may earn the diagnosis "schizophrenic" by either acting, talking, or feeling *very* peculiarly. Once known organic causes and manic-depressive illness are ruled out, you're considered a bona fide schizophrenic (acute or chronic, as the case may be).

A brief summary of the ways in which people end up being called schizophrenic would be the following:

   1. Acting peculiarly . . .

        a. with little if any spontaneous behavior (*catatonic schizophrenia*—if you're not clearly depressed or stuporous from a brain disease).

        b. with wildly excited or chaotic behavior (the relatively

rare syndrome of *catatonic schizophrenic excitement*—once an organic-brain-syndrome delirium and the manic phase of manic-depressive illness have been ruled out).

c. with other bizarre or very peculiar behavior (*acute* or *chronic schizophrenia*—once mania, organic brain syndrome, and various sensation-seeking or culturally-determined behaviors are ruled out).

2. Talking peculiarly . . .

a. with obvious delusions or hallucinations (*schizophrenia*—usually paranoid schizophrenia, once other causes of hallucinations—see Chapter 4—and of delusions—e.g., culturally-determined beliefs—are ruled out).

b. with very disorganized ideas (a *schizophrenic reaction*—once other types of disorganized thinking are ruled out—e.g., organic brain disease, mania, depression, or severe anxiety).

c. with severe disorganization and confusion (most frequently due to an organic brain disease, but once organic brain disease and mania are ruled out, the diagnosis is *schizophrenia*).

3. Feeling peculiarly . . .

a. with peculiarly strong and inappropriate feelings (a *schizophrenic reaction*—once organic brain disease, manic-depressive illness, and a few miscellaneous conditions—e.g., "explosive personality disorder"—are ruled out).

b. with a peculiar and inappropriate absence of feelings known as flat affect (*schizophrenia*—once organic brain disease and depression and a few miscellaneous conditions—e.g., "shell shock"—are ruled out).

I should add here that *disorganized thinking* is the dominant feature in most acute schizophrenic-type disorders and in many chronic ones. This, in fact, is much more common than hallucinations or elaborate delusions (which fit in more with the popular Hollywood version of "craziness"). You find that you simply can't get your thoughts together. They seem to be going off in all sorts of different directions at once. Or they seem to get stuck. They keep repeating themselves. Or your mind goes blank right in the middle of a sentence. You start talking about a problem at work and you end up talking about World War II or your father's funeral. You struggle to collect your thoughts but they keep wandering off. They go in starts and stops, or get all scrambled up, or seem to have a way of their own beyond your control, or they seem to grind to a halt altogether and you can't think of anything.

Most people undergoing acute, or chronic, schizophrenic-type disorders do not go off into some well-ordered fantasy dream world. They are dealing with fragmented or disordered perceptions of this world. We like to think of the "mad" as living in another world. Accounts which support this Alice in Wonderland (or Oz) notion of schizophrenia are often quite popular (Bergman's *Through a Glass Darkly*, or *I Never Promised You a Rose Garden*). But the construction of such alternate delusional worlds is *extremely* rare. It is, of course—like instances of multiple personality—from one point of view tremendously dramatic. It captures the public's fancy, and so the gross misconceptions continue to be perpetrated.

In the next chapter I point out that the syndrome of split or multiple personality is the very antithesis of a schizophrenic-type disorder, since it is characterized by hyperorganization and not disorganization. To a certain extent the same may be said about very highly organized alternative or delusional worlds. The Swedish mystic Swedenborg, the English poet Blake, and Castenada's Don Juan could all be adjudged schizophrenic by current popular notions of what schizophrenia involves. Swedenborg[2] and Blake in fact have been so diagnosed by some authorities. No one to my knowledge has conferred that honor upon Don Juan—yet. The official psychiatric nomenclature has reserved a special diagnosis for individuals with relatively stable and highly organized delusional systems. They are said to be suffering from paranoia. Paranoid schizophrenia is considered to be present only if there are marked signs of a generalized disorganization. So please, despite the media's best efforts to indoctrinate you, don't think of a schizo-phrenic-type disorder as primarily having anything to do with two personalities or two realities or two worlds going on inside one person. Rather, think of it as having to do with a *disorganized* personality and with *disorganized* perceptions of one world and one common reality. Think of it as having less to do with "other worlds" and more to do with this one world, which seems to be collapsing in ruins about the af-fected individual.

With most who are called schizophrenic what occurs is a kind of nondelirious confusion in which thinking and behav-ing seem to proceed aimlessly in erratic starts and stops. As the disorganization proceeds, the individual begins to seem more and more bizarre and more and more out of touch with obvious realities. But it is important to note that *there are as many ways of individually "falling apart" as there are ways of being an individual.* And, so far as we know currently, there are any number of different possible causes for such a falling apart (biochemical, hereditary, external stresses, inner conflicts, etc.)

I cannot emphasize too strongly that there is no *typical* way of going crazy, or of losing touch with obvious realities. What of course is typical is that individuals who are called schizophrenic by definition have lost touch with generally accepted realities in one way or another. So they'll have very peculiar ways of either acting or talking. In addition, they'll have various peculiar and puzzling emotional reac-tions (terror, rage, fear, panic, apparent amusement or indif-ference).

The label *schizophrenia* has been a wastebasket label used to describe all varieties of "craziness." In medicine, if one doesn't know what has caused a person's fever, it's labeled a *fever of unknown origin* (an "FUO," as it's referred to on the wards). In psychiatry, if one doesn't know what's causing a person's psychotic disorganized state, it's labeled *schizophrenia*. If it hadn't been a leftover residual category, there should have been some such category as "psychosis of unknown origin" which received wide usage. But there hasn't been. After listing the various types of organically caused psychoses and the manic-depressive and schizophrenic-type psychoses, the APA's second edition of the official diagnostic manual listed "Unspecified Psychosis" and instructed the clinician: "This is not a diagnosis, but is listed here for librarians and statisticians to use in coding incomplete diagnoses" (APA, 1968, p. 38). In other words, lacking evidence for organic or manic-depressive illness, you were instructed to call the disorganized individual schizophrenic. You almost never come across the diagnosis "unspecified psychosis" or "psychosis of unknown origin." This was one of the prime criticisms the Rosenhan pseudopatient study made of current diagnostic practices. The pseudopatients should have been diagnosed "hallucinations of unknown origin"; instead, they were all diagnosed schizophrenic, thus demonstrating the virtual equivalence of "schizophrenia" and "hallucinations of unknown origin" in the clinicians' minds.

SOME FURTHER COMMENTS ON THE MEANING OF SCHIZOPHRENIA

It should be noted that the term *schizophrenia* isn't a meaningless term. Just as the term *fever of unknown origin* is used to describe individuals who have certain symptoms, so the term *schizophrenia* (psychosis of unknown origin) is used to describe individuals who have certain symptoms (bizarre behavior, deluded or disorganized thinking).

It should be noted that calling certain types of disorders schizophrenic is neither unscientific nor immoral, as certain

critics such as Laing or Szasz might have it. Much knowledge
has been gained concerning this group of psychoses of unknown origin over the years. Use of the term *schizophrenia*, as
use of the term *fever of unknown origin*, has served to focus a
lot of productive activity in the area of understanding a very
extensive and glaring "unknown."

Szasz has argued that we have no right calling someone
who is out of touch with reality necessarily "ill" or "sick."
This is what he calls the myth of mental illness. It should be
noted, however—and his critics often miss the point—that
he's not saying mental illness or psychotic states don't exist,
but only that it's a myth to consider all forms of psychotic,
disorganized, or deviant behavior medical illnesses which
must be "treated," often against the person's will. The actual
state of affairs today is we don't know for sure whether all or
some of the psychoses of unknown origin (or schizophrenic-type disorders) are due to medical, or biochemical,
causes or not. That also means we don't know that they are
not caused by, for example, a biochemical disorder. *We simply
don't know.* And don't believe anyone who tells you they do
know. For some types of schizophrenic disorders we have
some good indications of what seems to be causing the
difficulty (e.g., some acute stress reactions), but that's about
as far as we can go currently.

What's important, however, is not to engage in
polemics and a war of half-truths. And this unfortunately is
the level of much contemporary discourse concerning the
psychoses of unknown origin.

Here I've dealt at such length with the description of
schizophrenia as a diagnosis by exclusion or as equivalent to
the residual category "psychoses of unknown origin" because I think it's fundamental to a balanced evaluation of the
knowledge that has been gained over the years. The message
you should be repeating to yourself throughout the rest of
this book is: this may or may not apply to any given individual who's had a schizophrenic-type "nervous break-

down." If I'm talking about genetics, or biochemistry, or bad mothering, or stress, you shouldn't assume this is why any given individual had his or her "nervous breakdown."

CONCERNING THE GLAMOURIZATION OF PSYCHOSIS

It should be remembered that people may have schizophrenic-type psychotic breaks for many possible reasons. It would be a grave mistake to reduce every person's psychosis of unknown origin to bad mothering, or biochemistry, or weak character, and so on. As Laing and other "antipsychiatrists" have so often proclaimed, for *some* people, losing touch with reality may be a sign of characterological strength, that is, of a refusal to accept an inescapable, unbearable reality.

The social philosopher Adorno has written, "In adjusting to the mad whole, the cured patient becomes really sick" (Adorno, 1972, p. 78). It should be emphasized, however, that while this statement may be true for some individuals, for most it simply isn't the case. If they find the world unbearable, it's because they have a tragic talent for setting up situations which make it unbearable. For one reason or another, such individuals are unwilling or unable to take the conventional sane escape routes from an intolerable existence. In this limited sense they may perhaps be considered courageous and possibly more heroic than some of us would be under similar stresses. But their courage is all too often the courage of someone trying to smash his or her way through a wall without noticing that the door behind is open.

Psychosis in general shouldn't be glamourized or glorified, as it so often is in contemporary writings, as any kind of victory. It is an expression of utter defeat and hopelessness. My point would be that it, as Laing might maintain, *may* be the defeat of someone with a sense of principle and integrity stronger than our own. We certainly must never look down upon anyone who has had a "nervous breakdown" as weaker than we are, as lacking in moral fiber or guts. Heaven knows how we'd react under such stresses, whether caused by an unbearable situation, a biochemical disorder, or whatever. Such individuals are being called upon to fight a battle we should thank our lucky stars we've never been called upon to fight. Ask many who've gone through a psychotic reaction and they'll tell you there's no mental terror or physical pain that comes even close to equaling that nightmare. To many it's like dying a thousand deaths, all of them terrible beyond description.

THE DIAGNOSIS OF SCHIZOPHRENIA

I have given my version of what is meant by *schizophrenia*. One of the major difficulties concerning the use of the term is that what one person means by *schizophrenia* is often quite different from what someone else means. The main problem, as will be discussed in Chapter 8, is that many who are not clearly "crazy" or out of touch with obvious realities may be considered, by some clinicians, to have a mild or insidious form of schizophrenia, so-called simple schizophrenia, or latent schizophrenia, or pseudoneurotic schizophrenia, all labels used to describe that other great residual category of "borderline" or not-quite schizophrenic-type disorders.

An important thing to keep in mind is that, especially in the United States, *many individuals have been called schizo-*

phrenic with the implication they are or have been psychotic ("crazy") when in fact they were never psychotic at all. Another way of stating essentially the same thing is:

Many have been told they have a mild or insidious or simple or latent form of schizophrenia (psychosis of unknown origin) when in fact we don't know whether they do or not. While it's theoretically possible that some maladjusted, inadequate, or simply eccentric individuals may have a mild form of some variety of psychosis of unknown origin, the truth is that we don't have any clear idea at all of what's going on with most of them, and certainly not that they have any one specific "illness." Nonetheless, especially in the United States, they are told they have an illness—"schizophrenia."

THE OFFICIAL DEFINITION OF SCHIZOPHRENIA

The "official" American definition for the diagnosis of schizophrenia is that given in the *Diagnostic and Statistical Manual of Mental Disorders* of the American Psychiatric Association. The third edition of the manual is much more than a revision of the second, especially in its section on the schizophrenic disorders. As noted in a prior section, the *brief psychotic reaction*, the *schizophreniform disorder*, the *schizoaffective disorders*, and the *atypical psychosis* are no longer classified as variants of a schizophrenic disorder; instead they are independently classified. The description of the schizophrenic-type disorders is much more detailed and it incorporates many of the results of recent research on symptomatology, diagnosis, typology, course, and prognostic factors which are detailed in this book. In addition, the new manual attempts to limit the rampant overgeneralization of diagnostic categories by specifying a definite set of "operational criteria" for each disorder. That is, the new manual specifies a "checklist" of fairly easily determinable features which are to be considered either present or absent. This has been termed by some the "Chinese menu" approach to diagnosis, but, in principle at least, it represents an enormous step forward over the current state of diagnostic chaos. (You must have read numerous accounts by now of how attorneys seem to have no difficulty whatsoever in coming up with psychiatrists to declare their client sane, or insane, as the case may be. The poor judge, who has just heard three psychiatrists testify that the defendant was insane at the time of the crime, and three other psychiatrists testify that the defendant was completely sane, must be left wondering about the sanity of the psychiatrists.)

You should also be aware, first, that many psychiatrists, out of force of habit, will continue using the amorphous, tremendously over-inclusive definitions of the earlier edition, and second, that most clinicians pretty much disregard, and will continue to disregard, other people's (including the American Psychiatric Association's) definitions; they will come up with one based on their own experiences. I'm doing the same thing in this book, but hopefully in a way that will clarify and not add further to the confusion. In any case, the *Diagnostic and Statistical Manual of Mental Disorders* introduces its description of the schizophrenic disorders with the following statements:

> The essential features of this group of disorders are: disorganization of a previous level of functioning; characteristic symptoms involving multiple psychological processes; the presence of certain psychotic features during the active phase of the illness; *the absence of a full affective syndrome concurrent with or developing prior to the active phase of the illness*; a tendency towards chronicity; and *the disturbance is not explainable by any of the Organic Mental Disorders*.

As defined here, at some time during the illness a Schizo-

phrenic Disorder always involves at least one of the following: delusions, hallucinations, or certain characteristic types
of thought disorder. No single clinical feature is unique to this
condition or evident in every case or at every phase of the illness, except that *by definition the diagnosis is not made unless the
period of illness has persisted for at least six months.* (APA, 1978,
p. C1; italics mine)*

You will note that the schizophrenic disorder, as now defined, must last at least 6 months. Schizophrenic-type disorders lasting less than 6 months are now classified as either
brief reactive psychoses or as *schizophreniform disorders.* Secondly, you will note that the schizophrenic disorders are essentially called "psychoses of unknown origin," that is, "not
explainable by any of the Organic Mental Disorders" (with
the added condition now that they are "psychoses of unknown origin lasting more than 6 months"). This is the first
step in formulating "schizophrenic disorder" as a diagnosis
by exclusion (see Figure 2). The second step, excluding forms
of manic-depressive illness, is taken by requiring, by definition, "the absence of a full affective syndrome." Further, if
there is a partial affective syndrome the disorder is, in most
instances, no longer to be classified as a "schizophrenic disorder," but as a separate "schizoaffective disorder".

This new diagnositc classification represents a great advance in our conceptualization of the "psychoses of unknown origin." However, it will take many years before it
becomes accepted common usage. In this book, when I refer
to the schizophrenic-type reactions or disorders, I am referring to the entire group of disorders which used to be called
"schizophrenia." When in later chapters I refer to the Acute
Schizophrenic-type Disorders, I am referring to what the
new classification would call a *brief reactive psychosis,* an *atypical psychosis,* or a *Schizophreniform reaction.* When I refer to the

---

*From American Psychiatric Association Task Force on Nomenclature and Statistics,
Diagnostic and Statistical Manual of Mental Disorders (3rd ed., draft 1/15/78),
Washington, D.C.: APA, 1978. Rerinted with permission of APA.

Chronic Schizophrenic-type Disorders, I am referring to what the new classification would call a *schizophrenic disorder*, or, in some instances, an *atypical psychosis* or a *schizoaffective disorder*. In any case, we are both referring to the same residual category of psychotic, or severely disorganized, states of mind, produced in the absence of known organic causes or the symptoms of an affective (manic or depressive) disorder (Figure 2). If the disorganized state of mind lasts less than one week, it is now called a *brief reactive psychosis*; if less than 6 months, but more than one week, it is called a *schizophreniform disorder*; and if more than six months, a *schizophrenic disorder*. But despite the refined terminology, the basic situation remains. We are still dealing with a residual category of all the disorganized or "psychotic" states which are left once we have excluded those produced by known organic causes and those related to manic-depressive-type disorders.

The Diagnostic Manual goes on to state the following concerning its definition of the schizophrenic disorders:

> The limits of the concept of Schizophrenia are still unclear . . . The approach taken here *does not limit the concept to illnesses with a deteriorating course*, although a minimal duration of illness is required because of the accumulated evidence that suggests that illnesses of briefer duration (here called Schizophreniform) are likely to have different correlates. The approach taken here also *excludes illness without overt psychotic features, that have been referred to as latent, borderline, or simple schizophrenia*. Such cases are likely to be diagnosed in this manual as having a Personality Disorder. Furthermore, *individuals who develop either a depressive or manic syndrome* before, or concurrent with psychotic symptoms, are *not* classified as having a Schizophrenic Disorder, but rather as having either an *Affective or a Schizoaffective Disorder*. (APA, 1978, p. C1, italics mine)*

*From American Psychiatric Association Task Force on Nomenclature and Statistics, *Diagnostic and Statistical Manual of Mental Disorders* (3rd ed., draft 1/15/78), Washington, D.C.: APA, 1978. Rerinted with permission of APA.

In the above you should note that even in redefining a Schizophrenic Disorder to refer to conditions which have lasted more than 6 months, the manual takes pains to explicitly deny that this diagnosis at all implies "a deteriorating course" (see Chapter 5 for a full discussion of outcome in these disorders). Further, you should note that "simple" and "borderline" and "latent" forms are not included. This is a great step forward, as the old classification essentially allowed a clinician to diagnose anyone as schizophrenic, arguing on the basis that the individual in question had simple or borderline, or latent schizophrenia, i.e. he or she was not "schizophrenic" but still was schizophrenic. It's of course possible there are mild, borderline, and latent forms of schizophrenic-type disorders (indeed it's most likely there are) but we have no way of specifying which individuals suffer from such mild variants and which individuals are simply withdrawn, peculiar, inadequate, or hapless for an infinity of other possible reasons.

In diagnosing the schizophrenic-type disorders the official criteria which the clinician should use, according to the Diagnostic Manual, are as follows:

1. *Diagnostic criteria for Brief Reactive Psychosis*

A. The symptoms in B appear immediately following a recognizable stressor that would be expected to evoke significant symptoms of distress in almost all individuals.

B. The clinical picture involves emotional turmoil and at least one of the following:

1. Incoherence, derailment, or markedly illogical thinking.

2. Delusions.

3. Hallucinations.

4. Behavior that is grossly disorganized or catatonic.

C. The duration of the disorder is less than one week, but more than a few hours. . .

D. The disorder may be superimposed on another disorder. . .

E. Does not meet the criteria for an Organic Mental Disorder, Manic Episode, or Factitious Illness with Psychological Symptoms. (APA, 1978, p. F4)

2. *Diagnostic criteria for Schizophreniform Disorder*

A. Meets all the criteria for Schizophrenia (see below) except for duration.

B. Duration of illness (including prodromal, active and residual phases) is more than one week but less than six months. (APA, 1978, p. F2)

3. *Diagnostic criteria for a Schizophrenic Disorder*

A. *Characteristic schizophrenic symptoms.* At least one symptom from any of the following 10 symptoms was present during an active phase of the illness (because a single symptom is given such diagnostic significance, its presence should be clearly established):

Characteristic delusions

1. Delusions of being controlled: Experiences his thoughts, actions, or feelings as imposed on him by some external force.

2. Thought broadcasting: Experiences his thoughts, as they occur, as being broadcast from his head into the external world so that others can hear them.

3. Thought insertion: Experiences thoughts, which are not his own, being inserted into his mind (other than by God).

4. Thought withdrawal: Belief that thoughts have been removed from his head, resulting in a diminished number of thoughts remaining.

5. Other bizarre delusions (patently absurd, fantastic or implausible).

6. Somatic, grandiose, religious, nihilistic or other delusions without persecutory or jealous content.

7. Delusions of any type if accompanied by hallucinations of any type.

Characteristic hallucinations

8. Auditory hallucinations in which either a voice keeps up a running commentary on the individual's behaviors or thoughts as they occur, or two or more voices converse with each other.

9. Auditory hallucinations on several occasions with content having no apparent relation to depression or elation, and not limited to one or two words.

Other characteristic symptoms

10. Either incoherence, derailment (loosening of associations), marked illogicality, or marked poverty of content of speech—if accompanied by either blunted, flat or inappropriate affect, delusions or hallucinations, or behavior that is grossly disorganized or catatonic.

B. During the active phase of the illness, the symptoms in A have been associated with significant impairment in two or more areas of routine daily functioning, e.g., work, social relations, self-care.

C. *Chronicity:* Signs of the illness have lasted continuously for at least six months at some time during the person's life and the individual now has some signs of the illness. The six month period must include an active phase during which there were symptoms from A with or without a prodromal or residual phase, as defined below.

Prodromal phase: A clear deterioration in functioning not due to a primary disturbance in mood or to substance abuse, and involving at least *two* of the symptoms noted below.
Residual phase: Following the active phase of the illness, at least *two* of the symptoms noted below, not due to a primary disturbance in mood or to substance abuse.

Prodromal or Residual Symptoms:
a. social isolation or withdrawal

b. marked impairment in role functioning as wage-earner, student, homemaker

c. markedly eccentric, odd, or peculiar behavior (e.g., collecting garbage, talking to self in corn field or subway, hoarding food)

d. impairment in personal hygiene and grooming

e. blunted, flat, or inappropriate affect

f. speech that is tangential, digressive, vague, overelaborate, circumstantial, or metaphorical

g. odd or bizarre ideation, or magical thinking, e.g., superstitiousness, clairvoyance, telepathy, "sixth sense," "others can feel my feelings," overvalued ideas, ideas of reference, or suspected delusions

h. unusual perceptual experiences, e.g., recurrent illusions, sensing the presence of a force or person not actually present, suspected hallucinations

Examples: Six months of prodromal symptoms with one week of symptoms from A; no prodromal symptoms with six months of symptoms from A; no prodromal symptoms with two weeks of symptoms from A and six months of residual symptoms; six months of symptoms from A, apparently followed by several years of complete remission, with 1 week of symptoms in A in current episode.

D. The full depressive or manic syndrome (Criteria A and B of Depressive or Manic Episode) is either not present, or if present, developed after any psychotic symptoms.

E. Not due to any Organic Mental Disorder. (APA, 1978, pp. C9–12)

4. *Atypical Psychosis*

This is a residual category for individuals who have psychotic symptoms. . . who do not meet the criteria for any specific mental disorder. (APA, 1978, pp. F4–5).*

Concerning the above definitions the following points should be noted.

---

*From American Psychiatric Association Task Force on Nomenclature and Statistics, *Diagnostic and Statistical Manual of Mental Disorders* (3rd ed., draft 1/15/78), Washington, D.C.: APA, 1978. Reprinted with permission of APA.

The criteria for a schizophreniform disorder are pre-cisely the same as those for a schizophrenic disorder, except that the disorder has lasted less than 6 months.

The diagnosis of a schizophrenic disorder (and there-fore a schizophreniform disorder) is made by first excluding the other two major types of psychoses, namely those due to organic mental disorder (Criterion E) and those due to a manic or depressive disorder (Criterion D).

While appearing to list a great number of apparently unique and specific "diagnostic" symptoms under Criterion A and Criterion C, with a little reflection, I think it can be seen that such a list can essentially be reduced to acting, talk-ing, or feeling peculiarly in an enormous number of different possible ways. In fact, if you have been acting, talking, or feeling extremely peculiarly for over six months, and there's no ascertainable "organic" cause for the way you seem, and no evidence of the presence of a manic-depressive disorder, then, even by the new refined definitions, 99 times out of a 100, you will be diagnosed as "schizophrenic," or suffering from a schizophrenic disorder (or a schizophreniform disor-der if less than six months, or a brief reactive psychosis or atypical psychosis if less than one week). Conceptually it remains a residual wastebasket category for the "psychoses of unknown origin."

The criteria for a brief reactive psychosis indicate that it must occur "immediately following a recognizable stressor." What if there is no recognizable stressor? Then according to the new definitions the brief psychotic disorder would need to be classified as an atypical psychosis, or a "brief psychosis of unknown origin." (See Chapter 6 for an extended discus-sion of the acute psychotic disorders.)

The new diagnostic category of atypical psychosis is a "residual" residual category. The schizophrenic disorder net is still cast so widely that most extremely peculiar states of mind (nonorganic and nonmanic or nondepressive) will fall within its criteria. But if a psychotic disorder should fail to meet the criteria for a schizophrenic disorder, the new diagnostic criteria allow you to fall back on an explicit baldfaced "I-don't-know-what's-going-on" category, the atypical psychosis. In the prior classification you were not allowed such a luxury. You had to diagnose "schizophrenia." According to the concepts outlined in this book most of the schizophrenic-type disorders, including the schizophrenic disorder and the schizophreniform disorder as outlined above, are essentially "I-don't-know-what's-going-on" disorders, and we would be as well off calling them all "atypical psychoses." This would cause a lot fewer misunderstandings, both within the profession and among the general public, than the use of such a "loaded" term as schizophrenic disorder, or even schizophreniform disorder. But having said that, it must be conceded that the new classification is an enormous conceptual step forward, and the formulators of this new classification cannot be faulted for retaining the old label "schizophrenia" with its implication that many or most of these disorders will turn out to be the result of a single disease process. That is certainly a possibility— though, based on many considerations, it seems a very slim possibility at best.

MANFRED BLEULER'S DEFINITION

In 1911 Eugene Bleuler wrote a book entitled *Dementia Praecox; or, the Group of Schizophrenias.* In it he defined a group of mental disorders which he called schizophrenia, or the group of schizophrenias. His son, Manfred Bleuler, devoted a lifetime to the treatment and understanding of the "group of schizophrenias." Recently he has summed up the results of his lifetime of investigation. Concerning the diagnosis of schizophrenia he has written:

> As you are well aware, the term "schizophrenia" is frequently misused: there are still some who use this diagnosis only for the most severe, incurable and deteriorating psychoses. Others use it in such a wide sense that almost all of us could be called schizophrenic. . . .
>
> The diagnosis of schizophrenia must be reserved for real psychoses. It entails an extremely severe alteration of the personality, at least temporarily. If we judge from our own everyday experience and that of our healthy fellowmen, we cannot understand the thoughts, feelings, and behavior of the psychotic. This does not exclude the possibility of an understanding during careful psychiatric treatment. People who are well-characterized, so-called originals, schizoids, psychopaths, nervous subjects and so on are not included in my diagnosis of schizophrenia. (M. Bleuler, 1970)*

He then goes on to give his criteria:

> What kinds of psychoses do we then acknowledge as being schizophrenias? Most important for diagnosis is the double life in the schizophrenic: behind or beside psychotic phenomena, signs of a normal intellectual life can be discovered. Furthermore, I have made the diagnosis of schizophrenia only if at least three of the following signs were present:
>
> **a.** typical schizophrenic dissociation of thought
> **b.** typical alterations of emotional expressions
> **c.** catatonic symptoms
> **d.** delusions or hallucinations of the sort usual in schizophrenia. (M. Bleuler, 1970, p. 212)

I might add when Bleuler says "typical" in the above definitions he is essentially saying: excluding those manifesta-

---

*Reprinted from *Behavioral Science*, Vol. 15, No. 3, 1970, by permission of James G. Miller, M.D., Ph. D., and the author.

tions which would be typical of manic-depressive or organic illness. For example, the typical schizophrenic thought disorder is characterized by Bleuler as consisting of disorganized thinking with a relative *absence* of flight of ideas, delirium, incoherence, organic labile attention, misunderstandings, confabulations, dreamlike states, and so on. What's left is considered "typically" schizophrenic.

PRACTICALLY SPEAKING

The above two definitions, the official one and Bleuler's personal one, are fine in theory. The question of primary concern to us, however, is what happens in actual practice? What actually happens is that different countries, and different medical centers within the same country, and different clinicians within the same medical center all use widely different criteria in determining whom they will call schizophrenic.

For example, two very-well-done studies compared the diagnoses of schizophrenia in the United States and Britain. One study by Gurland (1970) looked at diagnoses given to patients admitted to mental hospitals for nonorganic psychotic-type disorders. In one sample of patients seen in New York hospitals in 1967, 119 patients were diagnosed as having a schizophrenic-type disorder and only 13 as having affective illness (mania or depression). In another group of patients seen in London hospitals, 59 patients were diagnosed schizophrenic and 68 manic-depressive. It should be noted that the admitting symptoms of the two samples were comparable. The investigators concluded:

> The primary source of this difference was that the hospital staffs in New York tend to diagnose all kinds of patients (excluding alcoholics, drug addicts, and patients with organic

disorders) as schizophrenic, whereas in London some kinds
of patients are diagnosed mainly as schizophrenic and others
as affective disorder. (Gurland, 1970, in Cancro, 1971, p. 102)

Another British-American study was carried out between
1965 and 1970. In this study psychiatrists in Britain and the
United States were asked to review the same case records or
to view the same videotaped interviews with selected patients. The conclusions were as in the prior study:

> The paramount finding of the work reviewed here is that the
> American psychiatrists, in general, applied the diagnosis of
> schizophrenia to a much wider variety of clinical conditions
> than did their British colleagues.

In particular:

> The greatest disagreement was on patients whose main com-
> plaints were depressed mood, retardation, and/or anxiety,
> with or without additional psychopathology, including
> psychotic symptoms. In London the majority of such patients
> were diagnosed as affectively ill by the hospital staffs, while
> in New York, the majority were diagnosed as schizophrenic.
> Another important source of diagreement could be found in
> the cases diagnosed "manic-depressive, manic" by the proj-
> ect. These cases were almost invariably called schizophrenic
> by the New York hospital diagnosis. (Professional Staff of the
> U.S.–U.K. Cross-National Project, 1974, pp. 85–86)

I should remind you again that with respect to schizophrenia
we are dealing primarily with *definitions*. In the United States
we've obviously been using a very broad definition, while in
other countries a much narrower definition has been used.
It's important to realize that the definition is referring to
many types of disorders. These disorders may all have a com-

mon cause or many causes. They may constitute one illness, many illnesses, or no medical illness at all, but various unusual or deviant ways of dealing with unbearable realities. In the United States the broader definition means the term is used to refer to an *even greater number of disorders. Some may be psychotic. Some may not be psychotic. Some may be very closely related to manic-depressive-type disorders, others not. Some individuals may have a very mild disorder, others a very severe disorder. Some individuals may do relatively well, others very poorly.* The narrower concept tends to limit the use of the word to very ill psychotic individuals. As it is currently used in the United States, *no such conclusions can be drawn.*

What happens in the United States is that someone loosely diagnosed as schizophrenic ends up being treated as though he or she had a severe progressive mental illness. Consequently, as many American sociologists have pointed out, the label *schizophrenic* can tend to damn a patient in America as much as the diagnosis *leprosy* damned an individual in prior centuries. A little bit of leprosy, as far as the general public was concerned, was considered to be as bad as a lot, and, in the United States, a little bit of schizophrenia has been considered to be as bad as a lot. Leprosy, however, is a specific disease, while *schizophrenia* is no more than a label used to identify individuals with probably, so far as we know, a variety of disorders, or "problems of living" as Szasz might prefer to say. It is to be hoped that the new official diagnostic criteria detailed above will considerably lessen the current diagnostic anarchy. However, it will probably be a good while before many clinicians really begin to think in terms of the new classification. And even when they do, there will still be a great many individuals who will be labelled "schizophrenic" (that is, diagnosed as suffering from a "schizophrenic disorder") and who will still have to bear the unfortunate consequences of being so labelled.

SOME CONCLUDING REMARKS

If you're feeling a bit confused at this point as to what in fact schizophrenia is, I can only say you're sharing that feeling with a lot of psychiatrists. There are, to be sure, some individuals whom clinicians the world over would agree to diagnose schizophrenic. In terms of what I've been saying, there are some individuals concerning whom most psychiatrists would agree that (1) they *are* psychotic, and (2) they don't have an organic brain disease of known origin, and (3) they don't manifest primarily symptoms of mania or depression.

In order to bring some clarity to a chaotic situation, an International Pilot Study of Schizophrenia was undertaken in 1966 by the World Health Organization. One of their prime objectives was to obtain useful diagnostic criteria for the entity called schizophrenia. They intensively studied diagnostic processes in nine widely separated regions of the world (Colombia, Czechoslovakia, Denmark, India, Nigeria, China, USSR, United Kingdom, and the United States). They looked at patients in all these areas and derived a group they felt, by several different criteria, to be clearly schizophrenic:

The following psychopathological characteristics were noted:

97% of the patients were characterized by lack of insight;

74% had auditory hallucinations;

70% ideas of reference (e.g., they felt the man on the TV was talking about them, but didn't believe it);

67% delusions of reference (e.g., they believed it);

66% suspiciousness;

66% flatness of affect;

65% voices speaking to the patient;

64% delusional mood;

52%   thought alienation (e.g.,"this thought isn't mine");

50%   thoughts spoken aloud. (Sartorius et al., 1974, p. 31; comments in parentheses mine)

The above list of afflictions should give a fair idea of the types of things someone undergoing a psychotic nervous breakdown experiences. However, you should be aware that *many individuals in the United States who are called schizophrenic will not have had any such "typical" experiences.* This is because many individuals who are not typically schizophrenic are diagnosed as being schizophrenic in the United States, based, as often as not, upon the presumption that they have simple or latent or pseudoneurotic or borderline schizophrenia. Secondly, one should be aware of the fact that an individual with any of the above symptoms is not automatically considered to have a schizophrenic-type psychotic disorder. As discussed in the next chapter, someone with mania or depression, hysteria, severe anxiety, or various organic brain diseases may have *any* of the above symptoms. In the presence of such symptoms there are typically other accompanying symptoms which enable you to diagnose the above disorders. In the absence of those typical accompanying symptoms, the individual is considered to have typical schizophrenia, that is, a typical psychosis of unknown origin.

SUMMARY

1. Schizophrenia as currently used is basically a diagnosis by exclusion, as illustrated in Figures 1 and 2 in the text.

2. Schizophrenia is a residual category used to refer to those psychotic disorders which are neither mania, depression, nor caused by known brain disease.

3.   An individual is considered psychotic when he or she acts or talks or feels in a clearly inappropriate, unusual, peculiar, or incomprehensible way and seems to us in one way or another out of touch with obvious realities.

4.   Individuals may be psychotic and thus schizophrenic in an infinite variety of ways.

5.   Individuals diagnosed as schizophrenic may show primarily grossly inappropriate behavior, or obviously bizarre thinking (all varieties of delusions and hallucinations), or, as is most frequently the case, simply a great deal of disorganization.

6.   Individual clinicians vary greatly in their use of the label *schizophrenic.*

7.   In the United States, the term *schizophrenic* is often used to refer to individuals who have had no overt psychotic disorder (so-called mild, latent, borderline, or incipient schizophrenia) and to individuals who may have many symptoms of manic-depressive-type illness.

3

What
Schizophrenia
Is Not

We have dealt with the description of what the schizophrenic-type reactions are in the preceding chapter. The important things to keep in mind are first, in general, we don't know what the cause or causes of the schizophrenic-type disorders are, though for specific types of disorders we can make some fairly educated guesses; and second, in practice the diagnosis of schizophrenia is largely based on exclusion. Different clinicians differ in how rigorously they apply themselves to excluding other categories; consequently, some use the label *schizophrenia* to describe a lot of syndromes which more rigorous clinicians would never call schizophrenia.

At this point I think it will be most useful to discuss

those categories that most clinicians would exclude from their definition of schizophrenia, that is, to deal with what schizophrenia is *not*. This is quite important because, if clinicians are somewhat vague and confused in what they call schizophrenia, the general public is even vaguer and more confused and prey to an enormous number of superstitions and misunderstandings. In fact, there are a great many people who consider either themselves or someone else "schizophrenic" simply because they haven't been told clearly enough what schizophrenia definitely is not.

Consequently, the rest of this chapter will be devoted to discussing eight types of conditions that definitely are not schizophrenic-type disorders and several other conditions that probably have no relationship to schizophrenia.

THE SPLIT PERSONALITY AND OTHER HYSTERICAL REACTIONS

Eve in *The Three Faces of Eve* and Dr. Jekyll in *Dr. Jekyll and Mr. Hyde* were not schizophrenic. Multiple personality is a variety of hysterical or dissociative reaction. The splitting in schizophrenia (the term derives from the Greek words for "split" and "mind") refers to the disorganization of basic mental capacities. Thinking, willing, and feeling are all confused, "split up." Schizophrenics have trouble enough keeping their one personality intact. Such elementary confusion, combined with a sense of panic, doesn't allow them the luxury of elaborating a second, relatively well-organized and functioning personality as occurs in instances of multiple personality. A split personality is more an extension of those other selves (for example, the "social self" versus the "private self") that we all feel we are from time to time. Just as a hysterical person can hide so many things from himself (for example, "My mother was the most wonderful person in the world; I was never angry with her in my life"), so in the extreme he can hide one personality (for example, the Mr. Hyde who does the forbidden things) from the other (the Dr. Jekyll who is all kindness and consideration).

Similarly, amnesic syndromes have nothing to do with schizophrenia. The man in James Hilton's novel *Random Harvest* who woke up one day and couldn't remember who he was and wandered around for years fashioning a new identity handled himself perfectly well in current realities. Forgetting one's identity is akin to the multiplying of one's identities (after all, Dr. Jekyll kept forgetting he was Mr. Hyde) and is one of the human mind's more astonishing feats, even though it may not constitute the most efficient way of dealing with unpleasant aspects of oneself. Someone undergoing a schizophrenic-type reaction is too tragically disorganized to be capable of any such wonders. Very different, more primitive, ways of dealing with unbearable realities are brought into play.

Further, just as there are many people who react to extremely stressful situations by having hysterical seizures, so there are many who react to extremely stressful situations with hysterical psychoses. (These will be discussed in Chapter 6.)

THE ACUTE TRAUMATIC NEUROSES

What happens to people subjected to tremendous stress (such as combat) who have reached the breaking point? They may undergo severe anxiety with tremulousness, weeping, depression, and sleeplessness, or they may undergo any one of a number of hysterical conversion reactions (such as hysterical paralysis, deafness, blindness, or amnesia). They may experience recurring panic and terror as they constantly relive the harrowing experience. In the extreme, they may experience an "uncontrolled, catastrophic reaction" which "may vary from wild, impulsive flights to 'freezing' or primitive protective withdrawal, with stupor, catatonia or mutism" (Noyes and Kolb, 1963, p. 453).

Such acute traumatic neuroses, when the disorganization reaches psychotic proportions, are sometimes diagnosed as acute schizophrenic reactions, especially if the clinician is unaware of the overwhelming precipitating stresses. But the important point to remember is that chronic progressive schizophrenic-type disorders are not the result of such acute trauma.

The friends and relatives of individuals who've been diagnosed as undergoing a chronic schizophrenic-type disorder will save themselves a lot of guilt and grief by realizing this. They may remember some terrible incident that occurred between themselves and the suffering individual, but they can be sure such isolated incidents didn't drive anyone "crazy." Just as Rome wasn't built in a day, no chronic schizophrenic-type disorder was caused in a day. Some may object that Rome may well have burnt down in a day. But, to extend the analogy, becoming chronically schizophrenic isn't akin to building a strange new city after the old one has burnt down completely. Rather, it's more like renovating, in a rather unusual way, the old city block by block over a period of many years. (See Chapter 6 for a further discussion of the acute-stress psychotic reaction.)

FEELING UNREAL (DEPERSONALIZATION AND DEREALIZATION)

If you repeat the same word—for example *house*—over and over to yourself, it's a common phenomenon for the word to eventually seem strange, devoid of it's ordinary "feel" and meaning. Similarly, it's not uncommon for all of us to have moments when we seem strange and peculiar to ourselves, or moments when the world seems suddenly strange and peculiar to us. Artists in a sense seek to create this sort of experience, that is, to enable us to see ourselves or the world with new eyes ("The important thing/is to pull yourself up by your own hair/to turn yourself inside out/and see the whole world with fresh eyes." —Weiss, 1965, p. 27)* Anxiety (feeling tense, nervous, jumpy, on edge, etc.) and depression may alter in subtle ways your sense of yourself and consequently promote such "unreal" experiences. You may feel you're a stranger or a robot going mechanically through the motions of life. Such experiences are termed *depersonalization* experiences. Alternatively, you may feel as though the world is unreal, for example, that it's made out of cardboard or that it seems as insubstantial as a cloud or that it seems no more than an image projected on a screen. Such experiences are termed *derealization* experiences.

Depersonalization and derealization occur infrequently in all of us. If you're prone to depression or anxiety, they may occur considerably more frequently. They're usually quite transitory (a few minutes), but in some people, often people with chronic depressed states, such uncanny experiences may last for hours.

The important thing to remember is that such feelings have nothing to do with "going crazy" or with the diagnosis of a schizophrenic-type disorder. (If they did, a lot more artists and philosophers, who are prone to cultivate such feelings, would have to be considered mad than current estimates lead us to believe.) This is not to say that someone undergoing a schizophrenic-type disorder may not have similar anxieties and experiences, but the occurrence of such experiences has nothing to do with, or should have nothing to do with, the diagnosis of a schizophrenic-type syndrome.[1]

*From Peter Weiss, *The Persecution and Assassination of Jean-Paul Marat as Performed by the Inmates of the Asylum of Charenton under the Direction of the Marquis de Sade* (New York: Atheneum Publishers, 1965); reprinted with permission of Atheneum Publishers and Calder and Boyars, London.

THE MANIC STATE

The popular image of the "maniac" wildly running about, believing he's king of the world, or the savior, his mind filled with all sorts of absurd, elaborate schemes on how to become pope, president, or a billionaire, is the image of someone undergoing a maniac episode of manic-depressive-type illness, and not someone with a schizophrenic-type disorder. In the throes of such a disorder, you feel almost boundless energy. A thousand ideas race through your mind. You can scarcely sit still. There is so much to be done. Your mood goes from excited to frantic. You talk a mile a minute. Money means nothing to you. You spend it with wild abandon. You can accomplish anything. You feel utterly exalted. One gentleman I knew told me he took all his savings out of the bank, about five thousand dollars, took a plane to Paris, and in the course of one week managed to spend every cent of it. Did he regret it? Not for one minute. "It was worth every penny."

A manic-type illness is quite different from a schizophrenic-type disorder in many ways. It tends to recur in episodes, and between episodes the person is relatively unimpaired. Many successful individuals undergo periodic manic episodes. As a matter of fact, hypomanic individuals, that is, individuals who constantly seem in a state of high spirits, are quite valued in society; their enthusiasm and vigor and good spirits act as a tonic on us all. They're the kind of people you enjoy being around. It's only when, in individuals prone to manic episodes, these moderate high spirits become elevated ever higher and higher that difficulties ensue. As you become more and more exhilarated, you lose touch with reality. Your judgment becomes completely unhinged. You become frankly delusional. And as often as not, when you find the world isn't going along with your grandiose schemes, you begin to feel at first irritated, then angry, then, at times, utterly enraged.

In the extreme, with your racing, sometimes incoherent thoughts, your fantastic schemes and plans, your delusions of grandeur ("I'm the greatest") or of persecution ("I'm the greatest—that's why everyone's plotting against me"), your occasional hallucinations, and at times your apparent complete disorganization and confusion, it may seem to some clinicians as though you're undergoing an acute schizophrenic reaction. In this extreme state, which is not that common, it's sometimes difficult to distinguish a schizophrenic from a manic reaction, but usually, if you know the way the person was during the initial stages of the developing condition and if you know about prior adjustment and any prior history of similar episodes, there shouldn't be that much difficulty in determining whether a manic episode is the correct diagnosis.

For our understanding of what "going crazy" in a schizophrenic sort of way is about, there are two aspects of the manic reaction that should be emphasized. First of all, in the initial stages of the manic reaction, you often feel quite good and you transmit these good spirits to those about you (moods are quite contagious). People undergoing schizophrenic-type reactions in general don't feel good at all. If there's humor, it's gallows humor. You don't want to join in with their laughter. You feel uncomfortable, not good. Secondly, the manic individual is literally filled with life. His or her mind overflows with plans and schemes. This is the very opposite of what happens during a schizophrenic-type disorder. Life doesn't seem challenging but rather overwhelming. You're more interested in surviving during a schizophrenic-type disorder than in conquering. You feel yourself being cast adrift on some alien sea. Chaos seems to be closing in from all sides. You find yourself losing the capacity to organize or plan anything. You feel more and more paralyzed. You find yourself retreating and not advancing.

The final point I would make is that there are many who've been diagnosed schizophrenic when the correct diagnosis is a manic reaction. As noted, many clinicians are still very imprecise in their use of diagnostic labels. If you're deluded or hallucinating, or talking in ragtime, then they'll call you schizophrenic, or schizoaffective (see the next chapter). Since manic-depressive illness is a fairly well-defined entity, with a typical course and specific modes of treatment, such misdiagnosed people are being done a great disservice.

THE PSYCHOTIC DEPRESSED STATE

We all have days when we're feeling low, when we'd just as soon not go to work, when we don't feel like being around anyone, when we don't even feel like getting out of bed. We're not always aware why we're feeling that way. We just know we are. Our mood is depressed, and though we may keep telling ourselves, "Look, this is ridiculous, there's no reason why I should have been feeling so great yesterday and so rotten today," we can't will ourselves out of our low spirits. Fortunately, for most of us these periods are relatively transitory. For others they may persist for weeks or months (or years). Such individuals should be diagnosed as undergoing a neurotic depressive reaction. Others may find themselves plunged suddenly into the depths of a severe depression. Everything appears bleak and glum and hopeless. You may feel extremely restless and agitated. You may pace the floor and fret all hours of the day and night. Alternatively, saying the least word or making the least movement may seem to require such a monumental effort that you instead remain silent, motionless. Such reactions may occur subsequent to an overwhelming loss, but as often as not they may seem to occur "out of the blue," in some individuals only once, in others repeatedly during the course of their lifetime. If it occurs only once, it's called a psychotic depressive reaction; if repeatedly, manic-depressive illness, depressive-type.

Why is this rather distinctive way of feeling sometimes confused with a schizophrenic-type disorder? The main reason is that when you're feeling depressed enough, it begins to affect your thinking; consequently you begin sounding pretty "crazy." You begin to feel so utterly hopeless, like the most helpless, worthless, useless person that ever lived. You brood over how terrible you are. All your sins of the past come back to haunt you and are magnified into major crimes. You feel so utterly vile. It may seem like your entire body is rotting away. In short, you simply don't make sense anymore. You blame yourself for the most ridiculous trivialities. You elaborate all sorts of delusions. If in addition you appear quite agitated and perhaps, all appearances to the contrary, are even denying that you feel depressed, as occasionally happens, then there are a good many clinicians who would call you schizophrenic. But being deluded and talking "crazy," as indicated above, don't necessarily indicate a schizophrenic-type disorder. Careful attention to the development of the current episode and to the individual's past history should enable a clinician to decide whether someone's primary problem is depression or not.

There can be no doubt that there are many individuals, especially in the United States, who are going around with the diagnosis of schizophrenia when in fact they are suffering from a primary mood disorder (manic-depressive illness). Since we know a great deal more about the cause, course, implications, and treatment of depressive-type illnesses than we do about that conglomerate of disorders called schizophrenia, such individuals are being done a tremendous disservice by being incorrectly diagnosed.[2]

THE GREATER AND LESSER CRIMINALS
(PSYCHOPATHIC CHARACTER
DISORDERS)

Anything which requires a great deal of planning or leadership is usually beyond the capacity of someone undergoing a schizophrenic-type reaction. If you manage to accomplish anything, it's in spite of this disorganizing process, not because of it. One great myth that needs to be laid resolutely to rest is that the great villains of history were "crazy." You only need to read the biographies of the Nazi war criminals. Most were utterly ordinary men. They had their monstrous prejudices. They had their political and racial paranoias, but they also had their intelligence, their rationality, their belief in themselves and in their common ideals. You look into their lives expecting to find crazed monsters or, at the very least, "sick" minds, but in fact you encounter what Arendt has called "the banality of evil." The Neros, the Cesare Borgias, the Hitlers of history could not have survived one year in power if they had been undergoing a schizophrenic-type process. The process would have led to such disorganization, to such insensitivity to the intentions of others, to such distorted judgments of the realistic situation that they would soon have been exploited and disposed of by those around them. So to anyone who has had any experience with individuals undergoing a schizophrenic-type reaction it is quite absurd, for example, to hear Hitler referred to as a "madman." Such labels, categorizing evil as the product of a diseased mind, serve only to protect us from having to face the very unsettling reality that such men were not insane at all, but men very like ourselves. Evil is not something to be cured by a psychiatrist.[3]

Well, what about the lesser criminals? The Lee Harvey Oswalds and the Richard Specks, the assassins and mass murderers? The fact remains that anything requiring elaborate planning is usually beyond the capacity of someone undergoing a schizophrenic-type reaction. There are many individuals who are paranoid to a greater or lesser degree (see section below), and there is good evidence for a tendency to paranoia among criminals. But the vast majority of crimes aren't committed by psychotic individuals, and the vast majority of psychotic individuals aren't violent at all. If one is prone to violence to begin with, then a disorganizing process like schizophrenia, and especially paranoid schizophrenia, may exacerbate those tendencies, but if you are a calm, meek soul, such a process will result in a disorganized lamb and not a disorganized lion. A violent individual—and there are a great many such individuals in our society—who becomes schizophrenic will be both violent and schizophrenic. The important point to remember, however, is that the violence and the schizophrenia are quite independent of each other.[4]

THE BORDERLINE CONDITION

There are a large number of individuals who to the normal observer seem to be walking around in a quite disturbed state of mind but who don't seem "crazy." When you deal with them, unless you know better, you find yourself thinking there is something slightly peculiar about them, something very fragile and vulnerable. They always seem on the verge of "falling apart," but in fact they rarely do so. They have learned to deal with the pain and fury they feel in a very individual and extraordinary way that leaves most of us somewhat baffled. Every day, they solemnly assure us, is the worst day of their life, and yet, day after day, year after year, they manage the essential tasks of life reasonably well. Since they suffer so much despite the often efficiently composed aspect they present to the world, they often find themselves seeking professional help. For decades these "borderline" individuals have baffled clinicians, and the labels used to describe them have proliferated so that every decade and every region of the country seems to have its preferred one. They have been called "latent schizophrenics," "pseudoneurotic schizophrenics," "schizoaffective schizophrenics," "primitive oral hysterics," and so on. I don't think the labels refer to any specific disease, but rather refer to that other great group of people, the "near-crazy," who remain to be classified once we've labeled the "clearly crazy." But it's an important distinction, for these individuals have a rather stable personality structure, and they don't tend over the years to become schizophrenic. They are helped in different ways from someone undergoing a schizophrenic-type reaction (for example, the major tranquilizer drugs such as Thorazine will often make them feel worse).

I've devoted a later chapter to a more detailed discussion of this borderline condition. It's quite important to treat the subject in some detail because an enormous number of such individuals are erroneously diagnosed as schizophrenic somewhere along the way. Further, in my experience, they are the individuals who are most prone to diagnose themselves as schizophrenic. They are also, given the terrible suffering they endure, the most susceptible to the pronouncements of those who've found the latest miracle cure for schizophrenia, whether it be primal scream, "Rolfing," an altered diet, or whatever.

PARANOIA, PARANOID THINKING, THE PARANOID PERSONALITY, AND THE PARANOID SCHIZOPHRENIC

Let's face it. We're all paranoid. The sentiment that "everyone is out for themselves" sums up the basis of some of our daily paranoia. And we were a lot worse when we were children. The forests aren't filled now with nearly as many ghosts, demons, and witches as we thought they were when we were growing up. If something bad happens to us, it's the most natural thing in the world for us to think it happened because somebody wanted it to happen to us. If we don't succeed, it's because somebody wanted us to fail. All of this is good, healthy paranoid thinking. After all, the pedestrian who believes too highly in his fellow citizens' respect for stop signs will soon be an injured pedestrian. A certain amount of caution, scepticism, and paranoia keeps one lively and healthy. Our highly competitive society tends to favor the paranoid approach, and as often as not, the more paranoid you are, the more successful.

The important thing, however, to take away from this discussion is not that paranoia is to be esteemed and encouraged but rather, like it or not, it's one very normal way of adjusting to a world that at times is very harsh. We may describe someone who's constantly suspicious of his fellowmen, who feels he always has to be on guard, and who's always on the lookout for clues to possible bad intentions as a paranoid personality. But this label *paranoid* is really quite misleading. Most such people are not abnormal, and they certainly don't have a mental illness.

Paranoid thinking can, of course, go to extremes. There are some who have become so enamored of their pet suspicions that no amount of reality will change their views. I imagine there's some old-timer somewhere who clings unshakably to the conviction that we were truly invaded by Martians as announced in Orson Welles's 1938 broadcast. It simply explained too many things (for example, why he was fired from his job on the same day, why his wife suddenly disappeared, etc.). Such paranoid delusions can become quite complex; in intricacy of structure and ingenious blending of fact with fantasy, they can rival some of the most artfully conceived productions of the human imagination. Such individuals, despite their eccentricity, often function well enough. They may be quite intelligent and reasonable when dealing with areas that aren't affected by their delusional system. In fact, they may be so secretive about their delusions that you'll never even know they have any.

In the psychiatric literature, such individuals, with their isolated delusional systems, would be classified as suffering from "paranoia." They are not considered to have a schizophrenic-type syndrome since this would imply a rather general disorganization of their ability to function.

As mentioned earlier, manic individuals may become quite paranoid, with elaborate delusions of persecution. Depressed individuals may also become quite paranoid. There is one variety of severe depressive reaction characterized primarily by agitation and hostility and not depression per se. Individuals with such a syndrome may feel they are hated, that others want to get rid of them, imprison them, poison them, and so on. They don't look depressed but instead may seem extremely irascible, belligerent, fearful, or agitated. Needless to say, many of these people are mistakenly diagnosed as being schizophrenic.

The final and most extreme degree of paranoid thinking occurs in paranoid schizophrenia. The important thing to remember here is that, simply put, the schizophrenia, or disorganization, is primary and the paranoia secondary. *Paranoid thinking by itself is not to be taken as indicative of schizophrenia.*

HALLUCINATIONS

"If you're having hallucinations, that means you're really crazy"—of course, it doesn't mean any such thing. For example, many people have vivid hallucinations when they're falling asleep or when they're waking up (hypnogogic and hynopompic hallucinations). Or sometimes simply wanting or fearing something desperately enough will bring vivid images before your eyes—for example, the man in the desert seeing the mirage oasis, or the overnight guest in the haunted house seeing the prescribed ghost. Similarly, someone experiencing a great deal of anxiety may have the strangest visual experiences. A young lady hospitalized for anxiety and depression announced one day that a blue rabbit kept appearing to her. The blue rabbit came by one day, and the next day, his mission accomplished— making the staff very attentive to the young lady—he left.

Those individuals alluded to earlier with their solitary hallucinations of a voice whispering "thud," should have been discharged, after the appropriate investigations, with the diagnosis of hysterical hallucinations, or "hallucinations of unknown origin," but certainly not with the diagnosis of schizophrenia. I can't take issue with the hospitals' keeping Rosenhan's pseudopatients for an average of nineteen days. That would be a reasonable time to observe the patient and to carry out the necessary investigations. (What actually happened during those nineteen days in the hospital is another question.) But to call such individuals "schizo-phrenic" and to discharge them with the diagnosis of "schizophrenia in remission" is really inexcusable.

Hallucinations may occur under many circumstances. They may of course occur when you're feverish and delirious—for example, in alcoholic delirium tremens—or when you've taken certain drugs such as LSD or very heavy doses of marijuana, or under conditions of sensory deprivation—for example, lying motionless in a totally dark and soundless room. They may occur when you're in a rela-tively clear state of consciousness—that is, when you don't feel confused or disoriented—in four conditions of primary concern: (1) in depressive states, (2) in hysterical states, (3) in a condition called alcoholic hallucinosis, and (4) in the schizophrenic-type reactions. A diagnosis of schizophrenic psychosis of unknown origin should only be given after the other possibilities have been ruled out and *only* if there is additional evidence for the presence of schizophrenic-type disorganization and incapacitation.

Finally, the point should be made that while some people undergoing schizophrenic-type reactions do hallucinate, a great many don't. The kind of elaborate fantasy world in which individuals undergoing schizophrenic-type reactions are supposed to live, teeming with wild delusions and bizarre hallucinations, simply doesn't exist for most. The accounts of "craziness" that capture the public imagination are the more sensational and extreme experiences of very atypical individuals. The history of most schizophrenic-type reactions wouldn't make sensational reading at all. There would be pain, suffering, and frustration at every turn, anger, dread, and confusion, without one sensational delusion or hallucination to speak of.

LSD, MARIJUANA INTOXICATION, AND SIMILAR STATES

It's part of the history of psychiatry that the appearance on the scene of LSD and related hallucinogens raised great hopes for the discovery of the key to schizophrenia. It was reasoned that LSD produced a schizophrenialike psychosis. Therefore, it would simply be a matter of developing appropriate medications to counteract the specific actions of LSD to discover the "cure" for schizophrenia. Unfortunately, the LSD psychosis differs from most acute schizophrenic-type reactions in many ways. An occasional acute schizophrenic-type reaction may resemble an LSD reaction, but in general they're quite distinguishable. For example, an acute LSD psychosis is usually dominated by tremendous distraction and a great many perceptual changes. Things seem to change their shape, to twist and turn; colors scream out;

edges, angles, and lines stand out in mesmerizing patterns. Everything cries out for attention. In the extreme, you may become totally disoriented. You may lose all contact with current reality and be lost among fragmented perceptions, thoughts, and memories. The milder LSD reactions don't resemble schizophrenic reactions at all; the individual is in too much control. The severer reactions as described above, the "bad trips," present a picture that only rarely resembles an acute schizophrenic-type reaction. Such dramatic perceptual changes, such a flood of distracting fragmented images, aren't typical of schizophrenic reactions at all.

Sometimes an acute LSD bad trip is cited for having precipitated a schizophrenic-type disorder. Most clinicians have encountered people who have had bad trips and have ended up having to be treated for a persistent schizophrenic-type psychotic reaction. But it's not known whether they would not have had a schizophrenic-type reaction anyway, that is, whether the LSD simply gave them that extra push in the direction of psychosis. We don't know if LSD can precipitate a persistent schizophrenic-type psychotic state in a presumably normal individual. This isn't to say it can't. I repeat, we simply don't know.

With regard to repeated LSD use, the matter is somewhat different. All of the evidence isn't in yet, but a good many clinicians suspect that repeated LSD use—for example, over a hundred trips—can do bad things to your mind. It may produce something very like a chronic schizophrenic-type disorder. While it's clear some people may take a great many "trips" without affecting their capacities to think and function efficiently, it also appears there are others who can't. Of course, we can't say with certainty that such individuals weren't highly prone to schizophrenic-type reactions anyhow, or that they weren't already undergoing schizophrenic-type reactions at the time they began using hallucinogens. Certainly great caution needs to be exercised in drawing any conclusions. Nonetheless, the clinical impression of many observers is that the repeated use of hallucinogens can significantly impair some people's ability to function efficiently. In some, it may lead to a syndrome very similar to that of chronic schizophrenia.

You should also be advised that the above comments apply to all hallucinogens and particularly to the repeated heavy use of marijuana. In India, where the use of various forms of marijuana is common, there have been frequent instances of so-called cannabis psychoses. I have treated two young men whose psychoses developed simultaneously with the daily use of very high doses of marijuana. However, it can't be stated definitely that the marijuana was the cause of the reactions. Even if it were, abuse (very high doses) doesn't necessarily incriminate reasonable use. The same may be said of any drug, including aspirin.

In sum, the usual state produced by hallucinogens, the mild-to-moderate good trip, bears almost no resemblance to an acute schizophrenic-type reaction. An occasional severe bad trip may be confused with an atypical schizophrenic-type reaction. Caution in the repeated use of hallucinogens is certainly indicated. Individuals who have had a schizophrenic-type disorder or who may seem especially prone to such a disorganized state should probably avoid the use of hallucinogens entirely.[5]

ARTISTS, PHILOSOPHERS, MYSTICS, ADOLESCENTS, AND INTROVERTS

There's an old and honorable tradition among men that "he who doesn't think, feel, and live like I do must be crazy." There's also a tendency among those who don't think, feel, and live like they imagine most people do to wonder if they're not crazy. I've listed five groups of people who may be especially prone to such wonderings. When they look into the psychiatric textbooks or popular discourses on mental health, they don't find much ground for reassurance, but rather they're left feeling, at best, severely neurotic, at worst schizophrenic.

A whole book could be written about psychiatrists' misconceptions of themselves—how they believe they're promoting the realization of an individual's full potential, or freedom, or self-actualization, the complete, balanced, authentic and fulfilling life. All this is fine. But in practice, too much deviance from the norm tends to be considered pathological and in need of balancing.

So what happens when those monuments to the unbalanced life—artists, philosophers, mystics, adolescents, and introverts—read about themselves in the psychiatric literature? They discover they're in need of some balancing, perhaps even of some tranquilizers.

If any therapists are reading this and happen to feel outraged by my suggestion that they tend to consider such people unbalanced, I suggest they take a moment to consider their thoughts when they contemplated, for example, a streetcorner Hare Krishna group. Inadequate personalities? Borderline schizophrenics? Latent schizophrenics? Simple schizophrenics? I may be doing the average therapist a great injustice, but I fear the average therapist is doing the average Hare Krishna or other such deviant-group member an even greater injustice. In any case, psychiatric illness is one thing and joining an ashram is something entirely different.

It's a common precept in psychiatry textbooks that, especially in younger people, schizophrenia tends to manifest itself in excessive preoccupations with metaphysics, with God and Truth and the Meaning of Life. They'll sit around for hours trying to figure out the riddles of the universe. Why existence? Why me? They will become acutely self-conscious. Peculiar things seem to happen. They perhaps have mystical experiences, revelations. They will discover strange meanings written in a blade of grass and so on. But what's not emphasized often enough is that adolescence is a time of wonder. Most of us have stopped asking questions because we have found serviceable enough answers or because we have given up hoping to find any. But adolescents know nothing of such settled worldly wisdom. They are carried off into the wildest speculations. The important point to emphasize here is that while such preoccupations may tend to occur in young adults with schizophrenic-type disorders, this is because such preoccupations tend to occur in young adults. It's like saying—and it has been said many times—that one characteristic of schizophrenia in adolescents is a preoccupation with sexual identity. To put it bluntly, concern with the meaning of life in adults or adolescents indicates the persistence of wonder and not the presence of schizophrenia.

In practice, therapists have a difficult time knowing how to deal with mystical experiences. They may be explained by so many psychopathological paradigms, from neurotic wish fulfillment to schizophrenic projective distortion, that in an already emotionally disturbed person it will be most difficult to set religious experiences aside and not consider them to be part of the psychopathology. It is of course absurd to think that psychiatrists have any greater claim to religious understanding than anyone else. What I think is undeniable is that many individuals have profound religious or mystical experiences that sound utterly baffling and "crazy" when translated into words. Similarly, many individuals have parapsychological sorts of experiences such as clairvoyance, telepathy, or precognition, which also sound baffling and "crazy." So far as their ability to deal maturely and effectively with the world is concerned, such individuals often may be exemplars of "normality."

Similar comments could be made concerning the kinds

of experiences described by poets and other artists. In reading some of the psychiatric literature they will discover that their peculiar ways of thinking and of sizing up the world, their wild flights of fancy, their passions and despairs and exhilarations, are all being cataloged under various psychopathological labels. If they read any descriptions of schizophrenia, they may begin to wonder whether their peculiar inability to live calmly and see things in the normal, conventional way isn't due to a touch of schizophrenia. They should be reassured that, with high probability, it's not due to a touch of any schizophrenia or psychosis of unknown origin. While some creative artists have had schizophrenic-type episodes, their best work was almost always done before or after such episodes. Productive insights and creativity are the very antithesis of the kind of disorganization and paralysis engendered by most schizophrenic-type disorders.

Finally, there's that formidable group of individuals known not quite affectionately as introverts. According to the once-popular song lyrics, "People like people who like people"—at which point all the introverts in the world ran out to get their Tums, Alka-Seltzer, Excedrin, or whatever. It's true, however. People do like people who like people. The loner has never been a very popular species. In recent decades, as more and more pressure is brought to bear for everyone to relate and to belong, the loner is actually becoming a bit of an endangered species. In the psychiatric literature they find themselves being labeled "schizoid." If they read the somewhat uncritical, impressionistic literature of a decade ago, they learn that they're especially prone to develop schizophrenia. Recent retrospective studies have cast some doubt upon this speculation. In any case, it's clear that the vast majority of introverts or schizoid individuals don't go on to develop schizophrenic-type disorders. As with paranoia, introversion is one approach to life that should be considered within the range of normal. We are not dealing with a mental disorder, let alone an illness, let alone "latent" or "borderline" schizophrenia. We are dealing with an alternate life-style, unendearing as it may be to those who believe in togetherness.

SUMMARY

Schizophrenia should not be confused with:

1. Hysterical dissociative reactions (split personalities and multiple personalities, amnesic states, and hysterical conversion psychoses).

2. Anxious depressive reactions, with depersonalization and derealization.

3. Acute stress reactions (traumatic neuroses and psychoses).

4. Manic reactions.

5. Psychotic depressive reactions.

6. Psychopathic or antisocial character disorders.

7. The borderline condition.

8. An LSD or other hallucinogen-induced psychotic reaction.

9. Paranoid states such as occur in the paranoid character or in paranoia.

10. Hallucinated states such as occur in severe depression, mania, hysterical reactions, alcoholism, delirious states, and under other special circumstances such as sensory deprivation.

11. Mystical or parapsychological experiences.

12. Introverted or eccentric life-styles.

13. Seeing the world in unique, unusual, inventive, imaginative ways.

4

Types
of Schizophrenic
Disorders

THE CLASSICAL TERMINOLOGY

You may be familiar with such terms as *catatonic, hebephrenic,*
or *paranoid*. These terms derive from a classification, dating
from the turn of the century, of the types of schizophrenic
reactions. It was then thought that the disease entity
schizophrenia had various subtypes or ways of manifesting
itself, in the same way that the "flu" may manifest itself with
predominantly upper-respiratory symptoms or bronchial
symptoms or musculoskeletal symptoms. *Catatonic* referred
to individuals who sat and stared, showing little spontaneous movement (or who, alternatively, would break out into

wild, uncontrolled movement); *hebephrenic* referred to individuals who were silly, giggly, and very disorganized; *paranoid*, of course, referred to individuals who had delusions of grandeur or persecution. These "types" are still listed in the official diagnostic manual. In addition, the following types were listed in the second edition of the *Diagnostic Manual:*

> *Schizophrenia, simple type:* This psychosis is characterized chiefly by a slow and insidious reduction of external attachments and interests and by apathy and indifference leading to impoverishment of interpersonal relations, mental deterioration, and adjustment on a lower level of functioning.
>
> *Schizophrenia, latent type:* This category is for patients having clear symptoms of schizophrenia but no history of a psychotic schizophrenic episode.
>
> *Acute schizophrenia:* This condition is distinguished by the acute onset of schizophrenic symptoms often associated with confusion, perplexity, ideas of reference, emotional turmoil, dream-like dissociation, and excitement, depression, fear. . . . In many cases the patient recovers within weeks, but sometimes his disorganization becomes progressive.
>
> *Schizophrenia, schizo-affective type:* This category is for patients showing a mixture of schizophrenic symptoms and pronounced elation or depression.
>
> *Schizophrenia, chronic undifferentiated type:* This category is for patients who show mixed schizophrenic symptoms and who present definite schizophrenic thought, affect, and behavior not classifiable under the other types of schizophrenia.
>
> *Schizophrenia, other (and unspecified) types:* This category is for any type of schizophrenia not previously described. (American Psychiatric Association, 1968, p. 33–35)*

What you should be aware of with respect to the above categories is the following:

*From *The Diagnostic and Statistical Manual of Mental Disorders*, American Psychiatric Association, second edition, 1968. Reprinted with permission of the American Psychiatric Association.

1. They are no more descriptive of specific disease entities than would be a classification of people into extroverts and introverts, or into liberals, moderates, and conservatives. Liberalism or conservatism are certainly distinctive states of mind. So are the varieties of psychoses. But so far as we can tell, one's political opinions don't seem to represent any specific disease. (This contrasts apparently with the views of some Soviet psychiatrists who reportedly speak, for example, of "reform-seeking schizophrenia," i.e., a schizophrenic reaction in which one of the prime symptoms is an uncontrollable desire to reform society.) The virus which causes certain kinds of radical political thinking has yet to be isolated.

2. If an individual has multiple psychotic episodes, he or she will often shift from one variety—for example, catatonic—to another, such as paranoid. (The young liberals become the middle-aged conservatives.)[1]

3. This classification was based on looking at individuals with "end-stage" schizophrenia, that is, individuals who had been in the back wards of state hospitals for decades. There is reason today to believe that their permanent and devastatingly severe "psychotic" state was more a product of decades of isolation on a hospital back ward than of any "illness" per se. The classically described hebephrenic and catatonic syndromes are rare today. Most individuals are diagnosed as having either an "acute schizophrenic episode," "paranoid schizophrenia," or "chronic undifferentiated schizophrenia". To extend our analogy, the classical distinctive varieties of schizophrenia are equivalent to such extreme political labels as *anarchist* or *fascist*. Most people simply don't fall within these extreme categories. Just as by imprisoning people there's a good chance you'll considerably radicalize their political views, so by chronically hospitalizing some people with schizophrenic-type reactions you can drive them to the extremes of chronic catatonia or hebephrenia.

4. With the relatively enlightened approach to hospitalization and community treatment of recent decades, severe deteriorated states of mind have been largely prevented. Instead of the classical varieties, what you see is an enormous

variety of ways of being disorganized. You can certainly make classifications of different types of schizophrenias, just as you can make classifications of different types of personalities. With most psychoses you're probably not doing more than making an indirect personality classification, saying X's way of "going crazy" is such and such, just as X's way of dressing is such and such. There are, however, some newer ways of looking at classification which do seem to be practically helpful (see the next section).

5. The classification "schizophrenia, simple type" is fraught with problems. The third edition of the diagnostic manual has removed this category, along with that of "schizophrenia, latent type," from the Schizophrenic Disorder classification. Such syndromes are now officially classified as *Schizotypal Personality Disorders.* Such syndromes may also fit the criteria for Asocial Personality Disorder or for the Borderline Personality Disorder. It was of course theoretically possible, and in some instances seems likely, that someone may have a much milder, nonpsychotic variant of one of the disorders in the group "psychoses of unknown origin." But it's obvious that the vague definition of simple schizophrenia as a "nonpsychotic and insidious mental illness" opened the door to all kinds of misuse and, in some instances, abuse of the term *schizophrenia,* which can carry the legal implication that the individual is mentally incompetent to manage his affairs and, as Szasz and others have persistently pointed out, can lead to the unjustified deprivation of legal rights and personal freedom. The term *latent schizophrenia* can obviously lead to the same abuses.

The situation, at least so far as I see it, and as the authors of the new *Diagnostic Manual* apparently have seen it, is that today we are so monumentally confused in our uses of the terms *simple* and *latent schizophrenia* we are probably better off not using them at all. When we come across someone whom we finally agree fits the definition of simple schizophrenia we usually are not at all sure what's going on. We're not sure the person has the same sort of illness or disorder as the one that produces acute psychotic nervous breakdowns. We're not sure the individual has any illness at all. We simply don't know. We're puzzled. The diagnosis "simple schizophrenia" gives us the comforting illusion we know something we don't. It can also destroy the individuals so diagnosed, both in terms of their self-concept and how they are treated by others. The speculative scientific gain seems scarcely to outweigh the damage which may be done, and, as Manfred Bleuler and others have emphasized, the term *schizophrenia* should be reserved for individuals who have a severe, though often transient, psychotic disorder (of unknown origin, as I would add). It's all right for scientists to have their speculations, but they shouldn't be presented to society in general as facts, or as established illnesses or diseases.

6. Regarding schizoaffective type illness, there is very good evidence currently that this variety of psychosis of unknown origin is really a variant of manic-depressive illness. Individuals classified as schizoaffective show many of the symptoms of depression (feeling miserable, hopeless, empty; crying easily; etc.) or of mania (racing thoughts, excited manic mood, irritable hyperactive behavior, etc.). Recent studies have shown that the course of this disorder often resembles that of manic-depressive illness, with good remissions and occasional relapses, the relapses often being not schizoaffective but typically manic or depressive. Also, studies have shown that the relatives of those affected tend to have a slightly increased incidence of manic-depressive illness and *not* of schizophrenic-type illnesses. Finally, such individuals tend to respond better to the various types of antidepressant medications than do those with the other varieties of psychoses of unknown origin.[2] (Schizoaffective disorders have traditionally been considered to be a variant of "schizophrenia." Based on considerations such as those listed above, the formulators of the third edition of the Official Diagnostic Manual have removed schizoaffective disorders from the category of schizophrenic—or schizophreniform—disorders and classified them separately.)

7. Finally it should be noted that the category "Acute Schizophrenia" has been deleted. An acute psychosis lasting less than one week is now classified as a Brief Psychotic Reaction. A schizophrenic-type psychotic disorder lasting more

than one week and less than six months is called a schizophreniform disorder. A schizophrenic-type disorder lasting
more than six months must now, according to the diagnostic
manual, be classified under one of the following Schizophrenic Disorder sub-types:

    a. Disorganized (Hebephrenic)
    b. Catatonic
    c. Paranoid
    d. Undifferentiated
    e. Residual

ACUTE VERSUS CHRONIC SCHIZOPHRENIA

One of the few classifications of the psychoses of unknown
origin which appears to be practically helpful is that distin-
guishing individuals with acute psychotic episodes from
those whose psychotic-type thinking has persisted for
months or years. The reason why this distinction is most
helpful is because *only a small percentage of the individuals with
an acute psychotic episode ("acute schizophrenia") will go on to develop a chronically disorganized or psychotic syndrome* (see Chapter 5).

    Many clinicians have come to the conclusion that it's un-
justified, and monumentally confusing, to label all acute
psychotic episodes "schizophrenic" when in fact only a certain percentage will go on to develop anything like the
chronic severe psychotic illness which was originally defined, by Kraeplin and Bleuler, as schizophrenia. We don't
know whether chronic schizophrenia, the psychoses of unknown origin, represents one or many varieties of disorders.
It seems somewhat ludicrous to perpetrate the illusion that
the acute psychoses of unknown origin, *most of which will not*

even develop into a chronic psychosis (schizophrenia), represent one hypothetical disorder (schizophrenia). This would be akin to labeling every political conservative a fascist. (This unfortunately is a type of thinking not unknown to us in the political arena; one characterizes a group by its most extreme representative, thus justifying, presumably, the violence of one's own attacks against it.)

In Europe, clinicians for decades have distinguished the acute psychotic episode from "schizophrenia." They saw quite clearly that many individuals with an acute psychotic nervous breakdown recovered in a short time and did quite well subsequently. They reserved the use of the word *schizophrenia* for chronic, severely disorganizing disorders of unknown origin. Those other individuals—and they were the majority—who didn't appear to have a chronic schizophrenic-type condition before the onset of their psychotic episode were referred to as having an acute reactive psychosis, or, in Scandinavian countries, a "schizophreniform" (a schizophrenic*like* as opposed to schizophrenic) psychosis.[3]

In the literature on schizophrenia there has been a great proliferation of labels essentially pointing to the same distinction. The official definitions of the "brief psychotic reaction" and "schizophreniform disorder" given above correspond to this "acute psychosis of unknown origin," with the additional (arbitrary) qualification in this instance that it can last no longer than six months. As the episode is acute, this means the person at one point was relatively unpsychotic and that his psychotic state developed over a course of weeks or months (six months in research studies is often used as the somewhat arbitrary cutoff point between acute and chronic symptoms). Such psychotic episodes are often termed *reactive* (presumably in reaction to some current stresses) as opposed to *process* (presumably referring to a slowly developing process of illness). Also, as the acute psychotic episodes as a group, for the reasons discussed above, will tend to have a better outcome than the chronic psychotic states (it should be noted that this is a matter of definition), the former have been referred to as *good-prognosis schizophrenia* and the latter as *poor-prognosis schizophrenia*. If you read through the recent literature and recent attempts to classify the schizophrenic psychoses of unknown origin, you will come across variants of this basic distinction time and time again.

One influential investigator has proposed specific criteria for a "research diagnosis of schizophrenia" as follows:

a. A chronic illness *lasting at least 6 months* before index hospital evaluation without return to premorbid level of psychosocial adjustment.

b. Absence of affective symptoms sufficient to qualify for diagnosis of primary affective disorder.

c. At least one of the following:

1. Delusions or hallucinations in a clear sensorium

2. Lack of logical or understandable verbal communication

d. At least two of the following:

1. Single

2. Poor premorbid social or work history

3. Absence of alcoholism or drug abuse within one year of onset of psychosis

4. Onset before 40 years of age

5. Blunted affect[4] (Feighner et al., 1972, p. 59).

It will be noted that schizophrenia is here considered a chronic illness (lasting more than the arbitrary six months). It should also be noted that the diagnosis is made by excluding manic-depressive-type illnesses, once again pointing to the fact that schizophrenia is a psychosis diagnosed by exclusion. (Manic-depressive illnesses, for example, have specific criteria; they are not diagnosed by "excluding schizophrenia.") Further, under criterion c the specific criteria for a psychotic-type disorder are about the same, in summary form, as those I noted earlier (i.e., very peculiar or disorganized thinking). Finally, under criterion d some of the variables associated with a poorer outcome, or a chronic illness, have been listed. (These will be discussed in the next chapter.)[5]

Two other prominent investigators have put the matter even more succinctly with their definition of schizophrenia as "a severe cryptogenic, potentially psychotic disorder with a poor prognosis, a tendency to relapse and permanent emotional and social deficit" (Klein and Davis, 1969, p. 42). This definition includes simple schizophrenia, the supposed nonpsychotic disorder, but, it will be noted, it essentially excludes most individuals with an acute schizophrenic episode. The label *schizophrenia* is reserved for chronically disordered individuals with "permanent emotional and social deficit."

Numerous other investigators have distinguished between a slowly progressive psychosis often developing from a young age and a psychosis which appears relatively suddenly in individuals who previously had done well. Though they may place both types under the rubric *schizophrenia,* they recognize that they are dealing with very different situations: (1) the acute schizophrenic reaction, in which the individual has a very good chance of recovering and (2) a chronic schizophrenic disorder, in which the individual is going to need a tremendous amount of help to recover and to learn the skills in life that have never been learned.[6]

In this chapter I've summarized what over the decades has been a most confusing situation. Clinicians have puzzled and pondered, trying to figure out how individuals with "schizophrenia," a severe, chronic, presumably progressive illness, could in many instances completely recover. From the 1920s on psychiatrists took the approach of saying that those varieties which recovered really weren't schizophrenia at all, but another type of disorder, "benign stupor," "homosexual panic," "hysterical twilight states," "oneiro-phrenia," "cycloid psychoses," "adolescent turmoil," "schizoaffective psychoses," and so on.[7] In the past decade some careful studies, plus a good dose of humility with re-spect to the limits of our knowledge, have helped to clarify the situation considerably. The psychoses of unknown origin have essentially been broken down into two separate categories: the "chronic psychoses" (called by most inves-tigators "schizophrenia," or "process schizophrenia," or "nuclear schizophrenia") and the "acute psychoses" (which may or may not develop into a chronic psychosis). Figure 3 indicates the current situation.

The area of overlap indicates that most individuals with chronic psychoses will have acute psychotic episodes and that some acute psychotic episodes will lead to chronic psychosis, though many will not. Once again, it should be noted that both groups refer to psychoses of unknown origin and may be referring to one disorder or many types of disor-ders, some of which may be medical illnesses, others not.

Concerning the group of individuals having an acute psychosis of unknown origin (an American hospital would diagnose them as having an "acute schizophrenic reaction" or, according to the Official Diagnostic Manual, most would be diagnosed as having a schizophreniform disorder, with the remainder diagnosed as having a brief psychotic reac-tion, a schizoaffective disorder, or an atypical psychosis),

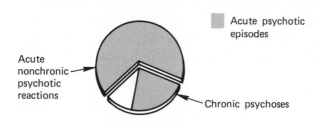

Acute psychotic episodes

Acute nonchronic psychotic reactions

Chronic psychoses

FIGURE 3

there is evidence to indicate we are dealing with a great variety of different conditions with a variety of causes (see Chapter 6). Concerning the groups of individuals with a chronic schizophrenic-type disorder, there is some evidence, primarily genetic (see Chapter 10) to indicate we *may* be dealing with one disorder. However, right now, given the state of the science, this is a hypothesis, or an implication from certain findings, and not an agreed-upon fact.

SUMMARY

1. The classical descriptions of schizophrenia, with its hebephrenic, catatonic, and paranoid subtypes, were really describing deteriorated conditions brought on more by social isolation and neglect than any mental disorder per se.

2. The most frequent types seen today are acute and chronic "undifferentiated" states and paranoid disorganized states.

3. An acute "psychotic nervous breakdown" in an individual who had been doing fairly well up to that time (i.e., who was not grossly maladjusted, inadequate, bizarre, etc.) is a *very different* entity from a psychotic episode in a chronically disordered individual.

4. We would be much better off, and the affected individuals immeasurably better off, if we stopped using the label *schizophrenia* to describe the great number of individuals who have simply had an acute psychotic episode.

5

Recovery from the Schizophrenic-Type Disorders

RECOVERY IN A GENERAL POPULATION OF INDIVIDUALS DIAGNOSED AS "SCHIZOPHRENIC"

It is crucial that the myth that schizophrenia is an "incurable illness" be laid to rest. We have already discussed the use of *schizophrenia* as a label to describe a variety of disorders or psychoses of unknown origin. We have distinguished between an acute psychotic episode and a chronic psychotic disorder and have emphasized the fact that we don't know if we are dealing with one illness, many illnesses, or no illness at all, with a "disorder of learning" or a "problem of living," and so on. Now we must look at the "incurable" aspect of the popular misconception concerning this group of disorders. Consider the table on page 85, which lists recent studies of groups of individuals diagnosed as schizophrenic. *It is clear that at least two out of every three individuals* **hospitalized** *with a diagnosis of schizophrenia do well.* I admit that by listing ten studies (I could have listed many more—these were among the best), I've committed a bit of statistical overkill. But some prejudices die hard.

Most individuals, under current conditions of treatment, may be expected to recover from their acute psychotic "nervous breakdown" within four to eight weeks.

A further point which needs to be made is that most of the studies cited in the table consider all kinds of "schizophrenia" and group the individuals with a sudden acute psychotic episode together with individuals having an exacerbation of a chronic disorder. Thus, these statistics tell us about general outcome without telling us about any specific subgroups that may be expected to do better or worse. An analogous situation would be looking at the "outcome of pneumonia" and finding, for example, that 10 percent failed to recover. However, a closer look would indicate that almost all previously healthy adults recovered and that almost everyone who failed to recover was chronically ill or severely debilitated prior to developing pneumonia. As will be discussed more fully in the next section, most of the individuals who had a poor outcome after their hospitalization for "schizophrenia" were individuals who were very poorly adjusted before their hospitalization—thus demonstrating, among other things, that an acute psychotic episode does not cure chronic maladjustment.

Another point is that the studies in the table are representative of recent well-planned and well-executed follow-up studies. They were not chosen to represent good results.

It should also be noted that in all these studies the indi-

Good Outcome in Hospitalized "Schizophrenics"

Investigator	Place/Date	Percentage*	
Arnold	(Austria, 1963)	72%	(full social remission)
Vaillant	(Boston, 1964)	41	(social remission)
Brown, et al.	(England, 1966)	56	(social recovery)
Stephens	(Baltimore, 1970)	74	(improved)
Bleuler	(Switzerland, 1971)	70	(good outcome)
Niskanen and Achte	(Finland, 1972)	68	(recovered or working)
Gross and Huber	(W. Germany, 1973)	53	(socially healed)
Hawk, et al.	(Maryland, 1975)	60	(good outcome)
Bland and Parker	(Canada, 1976)	67	(no deficit — 58% periodic, mild — 9%
Cottman and Mezey	(England, 1976)	83	(social recovery)
	Average:	64%	

*follow-up an average of five to ten years later

viduals received treatment of one type or another. All of the individuals were hospitalized for a period of time. Most received drugs, some group therapy and individual therapy. Many would have had some types of treatment during the follow-up years such as drugs or psychotherapy. So the results should not be taken to represent the natural course of the psychoses of unknown origin, but rather the course with treatment. (Whether the treatment in fact made any difference is a question which will be dealt with in later chapters.)

There are a great number of parameters which vary from study to study—for example, the precise definition of *schizophrenia;* the method of making the diagnosis (chart review, interview, etc.); the proportion of individuals with acute schizophrenic-type reactions, or first "breaks," or first admissions; the total number of subjects; the types of treatment; the definitions of *recovery;* and the method of follow-up. All of these factors, and many others, will contribute to the variability of the final percentage of individuals reported recovered from schizophrenic-type disorders (ranging from 41 to 83 percent in our table).

Finally, I will repeat: Many individuals whom psychiatrists, or others, call schizophrenic do quite well and return to the level of functioning they had before the psychotic nervous breakdown. *They did not have anything remotely resembling a chronic insidious "mental illness" leading to progressive incapacitation or "permanent craziness,"* though that is what many people, including many supposedly well-informed psychiatrists and therapists, think of when they talk about schizophrenia. The fact is that most individuals whom we call schizophrenic on the basis of an acute psychotic episode recover from the acute psychotic episode. Many psychiatrists then diagnose them as having "schizophrenia in remission." This implies the individual still "has" schizophrenia, only now, luckily, it's in remission. In the same way, one would speak of remissions in patients with arthritis or leukemia. The Rosenhan study of pseudopatients cited earlier had much to say about this use, or misuse, of diagnostic labels. To say that most individuals who have recovered from an acute psychotic episode have "schizophrenia in remission" makes about as much sense as to say someone who has recovered from the mumps has "mumps in remission" or, even more to the point, that someone who has grown up has "childhood in remission."

WHO DOES WELL?

A tremendous amount of research has been carried out over the years in an effort to differentiate those who may be expected to do well from those who may be expected to do poorly.[1] However, the main result can be summarized as follows:

Those individuals who were doing well before the acute psychotic nervous breakdown in most instances do well afterward;

those who were doing poorly before the acute psychotic episode do poorly afterward.

The above statement may seem obvious. However, for decades it didn't seem obvious at all to most psychiatrists. Schizophrenia was considered a severe, progressive, and, by and large, incurable mental illness. Anyone who had had an acute schizophrenic-type psychotic episode was considered to "have" schizophrenia. Psychoanalytic theory taught that such individuals were "untreatable" by analysis, and for decades psychoanalysis completely dominated American psychiatry.

Individuals with "schizophrenia" were relegated to the custodial system of state or private mental hospitals, and the expectation was that over the years the individual would become more and more "schizophrenic." Only a few courageous psychiatrists and analysts were willing to devote their efforts to the psychotherapy of the "untreatable." Their contributions to the humanization of psychiatric care—specifically, to the care of those diagnosed as schizophrenic—have been immeasurable.

Today, it's quite clear that if you did relatively well before an acute-schizophrenic-type psychotic episode, you'll probably do well afterward. You don't need to fear increasingly frequent recurrences leading ultimately to "incurable insanity." That's pure myth. In most instances you're reacting to certain unique stresses (for example, living away from home for the first time) which have occurred at a time of particular vulnerability in your life. The combination of circumstances leading to such overwhelming stresses often is quite unlikely to recur (see the following chapter for a further discussion of the stress psychoses).

In general, we would be much better off talking about psychoses of unknown origin, or schizophrenic-type disorders, occurring in either relatively well-adjusted people or in poorly adjusted people. For example, in one study carried out by Vaillant (1974a), 73 percent of the relatively well-adjusted individuals hospitalized for a schizophrenic-type disorder were found to be doing well one to fifteen years later, whereas only 14 percent of the poorly adjusted did well. In another study, by Stephens (1970), 96 percent of the relatively well-adjusted were considered improved (61 percent) or recovered (35 percent) on follow-up five to nine years later, whereas only 46 percent of the poorly adjusted were considered improved (39 percent) or recovered (7 percent).[2]

In addition to a relatively good adjustment prior to the psychotic nervous breakdown, some other factors which in most studies have been associated with good outcome include the following:

1. *The presence of confusion during the psychotic episode.* When an individual seems delirious—for example, is confused about the time or place, or seems "totally out of it"—this, paradoxical as it may seem, is a good sign. It means being disorganized is totally bewildering. (Someone who has learned to "live with" the disorganization may not seem so bewildered—a bad sign.)

2. *The presence of precipitating factors.* This means there are clear-cut stresses going on in the person's life which could account for the presence of an extremely disturbed state of mind (for example, the loss of a job).

3. *An acute onset* (less than six months). Someone who has become progressively more odd year by year, and consequently has learned to "live with the craziness," isn't going to do as well as someone who "breaks down" over a relatively brief period of time. In my experience it often takes someone as long to unlearn being "crazy" as it did to become crazy in the first place. Therefore, a brief onset, a brief resolution; a long, drawn-out onset, a long, drawn-out resolution.

4. *The presence of depression.* Someone who's upset, very discouraged, depressed, and so on during the acute-schizophrenic-type episode is more likely to do better than someone

who flatly accepts being disorganized (and manifests "flattened affect").

5. *The absence of schizophrenic-type psychoses or the presence of manic-depressive-type psychoses in relatives.*

There are numerous other factors which in one study or another have pointed to a favorable outcome. The best way to summarize them all is to say that, in general, they indicate one of two things—either (1) the individual was relatively well adjusted prior to the episode or (2) the individual probably didn't have a schizophrenic-type psychosis but most probably a variant of manic-depressive illness.

Thus "precipitating stresses," "acute onset," and other such factors—for example, "good premorbid work record," "personality not schizoid," "married," and "no low IQ"—all indicate the individual was probably doing fairly well prior to the psychotic episode. On the other hand, such factors as the presence of depression, the absence of schizophrenic-type disorders, and the presence of manic-depressive-type disorders in the family, along with other factors—for example, "concern with dying," "pressure of speech," "hyperactivity," and "manic mood"—all point to a variant of manic-depressive illness (though many such individuals would be diagnosed as "schizophrenic, schizoaffective type" in the United States, or, according to the revised diagnostic classification, as suffering from a schizoaffective disorder).

The fact someone had a schizophrenic-type disorder (or psychosis of unknown origin) only tells you that he or she reacted to certain stresses (which may include biochemical ones) by becoming, for unknown or incompletely understood reasons, tremendously disorganized. It doesn't tell you whether such stresses will recur in the person's life. As our POWs in Korea and Vietnam discovered, a certain specific combination of stresses will "break" almost anyone. But unless the stresses remain severe and prolonged—as was the case, for example, with some of the inmates of the Nazi concentration camps—most of us don't stay "broken."[3]

WHO DOES POORLY?

The question as to who tends to do poorly has already been answered in the prior sections. By and large it is the person who had done poorly for years before developing a schizophrenic-type disorder. *But this is not to say that all such individuals will do poorly.* First, the studies cited above indicate that a third to a half will do well. (Stephens reviewed thirty-one studies and concluded that about 40 percent of "process schizophrenics" who would be predicted to do poorly in fact were improved on five-year follow-up.)

Manfred Bleuler in summarizing his experience, has written: "On the average the psychosis shows no change for the worse after a duration of five years." He goes on to write:

> **1.** The most severe forms of schizophrenia can be prevented by appropriate therapy. I refer to the psychoses which start early in life with an acute episode followed without improvement by a lifelong chronic condition. This form of psychosis which used to be frequent at the beginning of the century is less common now.
>
> **2.** All schizophrenic conditions can at least be improved and alleviated by therapy.
>
> **3.** With the help of therapy, episodic courses with good intermissions are becoming more frequent and chronic psychoses with constant hospitalization rarer. (M. Bleuler, 1970, pp. 212, 214)*

With respect to the above statements, it should first of all be noted that Bleuler is referring to his own personal ex-

*Reprinted from *Behavioral Science,* Vol. 15, No. 3, 1970, by permission of James G. Miller, M.D., Ph. D., and the author.

perience. Studies by others, however, fully support his statements. Second, you should be aware that when Bleuler refers to *schizophrenia*, by his definition he has already excluded most of the acute psychoses of unknown origin, that is, individuals whom American psychiatrists would tend to diagnose as schizophrenic and who regularly do *well* subsequently. He is using the narrow definition of *schizophrenia* and thus referring to a group of individuals already preselected in the direction of poor outcome.[4]

> *When we attempt the task of predicting which patient will do well or poorly, we must look at what else the individual has besides schizophrenia. It is not the illness that predicts the prognosis, it is the total human being who predicts the prognosis. If someone is bright, beautiful, talented, rich, educated, part of a society that appreciates him, and comes from a family and an environment that offers much support, then he has a good prognosis for life. If the same individual also has schizophrenia, then he has a good prognosis for living with his schizophrenia. . . . People who have a better prognosis for life are individuals who have more coping assets which lead to increased flexibility and increased adaptational capacities. People who have a poor prognosis for life lack these capacities. If they also have schizophrenia, their prognosis for living with schizophrenia parallels their prognosis for life."* (Mendel), 1976, pp. 68–69)*

SUMMARY

1.   On the average, two-thirds of those individuals hospitalized with a diagnosis of schizophrenia will do relatively well subsequently.

2.   Most individuals who were doing well prior to the acute psychotic episode will continue to do well afterward. They shouldn't be considered to have a "mental illness in remission" any more than they should be considered to have "mumps in remission" or "childhood in remission." To call

*Reprinted by permission of the author and Jossey-Bass, Inc.

such individuals "schizophrenic" is an inexcusable misuse of language.

3. The individuals who do poorly following a schizo-phrenic-type reaction are mostly individuals who were doing quite poorly before the psychotic reaction.

4. A good percentage—roughly 40 percent—of individuals with a "poor prognosis" will do relatively well despite undergoing a psychosis of unknown origin.

5. Many individuals are diagnosed as "schizophrenic" today who most probably are undergoing a variety of manic-depressive-type illness.

THE SCHIZOPHRENIC-TYPE DISORDERS IN EVERYDAY LIFE

6

The Acute Schizophrenic-Type Disorders

CLASSIFICATION

As discussed in Chapter 2, anyone who, over a short period of time, becomes extremely disorganized and who doesn't have either manic-depressive illness or an organic-type illness is diagnosed as "acutely schizophrenic." It has been pointed out that this is essentially a leftover or residual category. It may be that all the individuals in this category are suffering from one specific type of illness or disorder "schizophrenia" which manifests itself in many ways and which may or may not recur or become chronic. It may also be that it refers to many different types of disorders. My own opinion is that the latter is the case. I have adopted the following way of looking at and attempting to understand the acute schizophrenic-type psychotic disorders.

First of all, any of us may become psychotically disorganized if the stress is great enough. Thus very mature, well-adjusted people may become severely disorganized if stressed at some particularly vulnerable points in their emotional armor. For example, despite meticulous screening for psychological stability, the stresses of their work frequently lead to emotional "breakdowns" among intelligence agency operatives. This apparently is considered par for the course and not at all grounds for dismissal from the agency. (Consider, for example, the British intelligence agents who knew Coventry was to be annihilated by German bombers. Many had families billeted in the area. Yet they could say nothing for fear German intelligence would discover the British had broken their top-secret code. How would your emotional stability stand up under such "psychological stress"? Think about it for a·moment. The city was, as the Germans put it, "Coventryized," i.e., bombed to ruins, and many died.)[1]

Second, some of us are more mature than others; that is, some of us can deal with the harsher, more painful aspects of reality better than others. Or, put differently, some of us have more adaptive defenses than others. We can laugh off an insult, sublimate our aggressions, repress or forget old fears, and so on, while others become obsessed with their failings, withdraw from the harshness of life, give in to their despairs, and dream of better, less cruel worlds.

Third, some individuals probably do have biochemical processes going on which tend to disorder their experience of themselves and the world. Whether they become psychotic depends on how well defended or mature they are. In the same way, whether the "flu" will slow you down or lay you up for a week depends on how much resistance (or often, how much interest in not being laid up for a week) you have.

Thus there are at least three factors which should be considered in anyone who has gone "crazy" in a schizophrenic-type way:

1. Degree of current stress
2. Maturity level
3. Possible underlying biochemical disorder

If your best friend, or the president of the United States, has had a "nervous breakdown" of the psychotically disorganized schizophrenic type, then you should always keep the following possibilities in mind:

1. Even the strongest can crack under sufficient psychological stress (a commonplace among our contemporary breed of police interrogators).

2. Even the strongest can crack under sufficient biochemical insult (for example, various hallucinogens such as LSD).

3. The weaker your resistance or psychological defenses, the less the psychologic stress or biochemical insult required to precipitate a disorganized episode.

4. The fact that most of us haven't undergone the horrors of an acute psychotic episode doesn't mean we're stronger, more stable, or more mature than someone who has. In many instances, it merely means we're luckier (there haven't been any "Coventrys" in our lives).

5. Lacking more complete knowledge, we should consider someone who has had a schizophrenic-type nervous breakdown no different from someone who has broken and "confessed" under torture. The person may be easily confused and excessively vulnerable—or a hero or heroine of surpassing intelligence, integrity, and moral courage. From the fact alone that someone has had a schizophrenic-type nervous breakdown we can't conclude very much at all about the person.

6. To put the label *schizophrenic* on someone, as though it told us something about his or her ability to handle stress, or

capacity for reasonable thought, or strength of personality, or character, or "moral fiber," is simply reprehensible. This is akin to saying that those who succumbed in the concentration camps did so because they had "weak characters" or "failed to resist." (This pernicious line of argument has in fact been advanced by some.)

THE STRESS PSYCHOSES

Grinker has written the following of the acute psychoses which occurred under the stress of World War II combat:

> These men often looked like the most regressed schizo-phrenics on the back wards of our still existent "snake pits." They were soiled, gibbering, drooling, frightened, animal-like creatures who usually showed concomitant physiological regression. Some crawled on all fours or stood bent over in simian posture. Others were rigid and tremulous like a par-kinsonian. These temporary regressions were most dramatic, because while imitating schizophrenia, they were completely reversible with appropriate therapy. . . . Basically there was little to differentiate the most severe effects from the schizo-phrenic reactions seen in civilian life. (Grinker, 1969, p. 4)

There is an extensive literature on the acute disorganized states which appear to be brought on by situational stresses:[2] Such nervous breakdowns can have all the features of "typi-cal schizophrenia." People may become incredibly paranoid or disorganized. They may have the most flamboyant delu-sions or hallucinations. But eventually they get over their disorganized state.

If you know such people well enough, it's usually not difficult to tell why they had a "nervous breakdown." It's usually apparent they were caught in some sort of intolerable situation with seemingly no way out. Some examples of acute stress psychoses which have earned distinctive labels are:

1. The Ganser syndrome, a kind of unconsciously motivated "craziness" which occurs in individuals facing severe criminal penalties ("not guilty on grounds of insanity" being the obvious gain).

2. Combat psychosis, as described above by Grinker.

3. Nervous exhaustion—for example, from an impossibly demanding work load.

4. Homosexual panic, from the unbearable presence, to some, of homosexual impulses.

5. Postpartum psychosis, occurring in women emotionally unprepared for the reality of motherhood (some of the postpartum psychoses are probably of biochemical origin).

6. Hysterical psychoses—three varieties:

a. *Transient psychoses occurring in borderline personalities.* There are many people who feel vulnerable and insecure and deal in poorly chosen inadequate ways with some, or many, of the problems of living. With most, there is no question of "schizophrenia." However, they will decompensate, or "crack," under certain intolerable stresses just as the rest of us will. The period of psychotic disorganization is often very short-lived, with or without medication (a day to a week, typically). Such transient psychoses are called hysterical because some clinicians have termed borderline personalities "primitive oral hysterics" (the wonders of psychiatric jargon!).

b. *Culturally determined psychotic states.* There are some societies where certain individuals are expected to go crazy in very specific ways. When the proper time comes, the appropriate members of such societies go "crazy" (or "amok," a word which derives from one such society) in the prescribed way.

c. *Psychotic conversion reactions.* Some neurotic individuals who are prone to hysterical reactions such as hysterical fits, blindness, or paralysis may end up unconsciously mimicking craziness in order to obtain certain so-called secondary gains (the above mentioned Ganser syndrome is a variant of this disorder).[3]

The important thing to remember is that none of the above acute-stress schizophrenic-type reactions, whether occurring in the strong and mature or the exceptionally vulnerable and immature, has anything to do with a progressive psychotic illness or chronic schizophrenia. A powerful-enough flood will carry along the sturdiest of oaks with the saplings, and a strong-enough stress will carry off the strong along with the exceptionally vulnerable.

THE EARLY STAGES OF THE SCHIZOPHRENIC-TYPE STRESS REACTION

Do such reactions come out of the blue, or do they build up over a period of time? Can their development be recognized and prevented? Before reading on, stop and try to answer these questions. Give your misconceptions free rein.

The answer to the question is that such reactive psychoses, as they are sometimes termed in the literature, do *not* come on out of the blue. They build up over a period of at least days, most often over a period of weeks. So don't worry about waking up tomorrow morning "raving mad." In almost all instances, any process of "psychotic" disorganization is a very gradual one.[4]

The answer to the second question is that the process *can* be recognized, and, if recognized, it can almost always be reversed before there is any "craziness" or psychotically disorganized thinking at all. (Laing and the "antipsychiatrists" maintain that under the appropriate conditions, becoming psychotic may be a positive experience and that such a process should not be prevented. Having a heart attack may also be a positive experience in that it may transform your outlook and reorder your values; but there should be less devastating ways to attain such positive ends. So far as I'm concerned, heart attacks and acute psychotic episodes are to be prevented if possible.)

Several authors, most notably Conrad (1958), Bowers (1974), and Donlon and Blacker (1973), have made invaluable but unfortunately little-known contributions to our understanding of the way schizophrenic-type psychotic disorders develop.[5] The following is a composite of their observations.

The first stage—generalized anxiety, or *something's wrong.* We're all familiar with this state. We feel anxious, on edge, keyed up. We feel something's wrong; we may or may not know what. We deal with our anxieties the way we always did (overeating, television, compulsive socializing, withdrawing into ourselves, etc.), but the old ways don't seem to work. We find that we're trapped in our ever-increasing anxieties and apprehensions. The important thing is: our old ways of dealing with stress, or the anxiety we're feeling, *don't seem to be working anymore.* The anxiety simply keeps building and building.

The second stage—an altered sense of self, or *"strange things are happening."* The old ways aren't working. So inside, there's a desperate search, more or less hit-or-miss, for new ways. We keep trying, consciously or unconsciously, to find a way out. We keep restructuring, contorting our experience, thoughts, and perceptions, hoping we'll hit upon the solution. We entertain hypotheses we'd never let ourselves entertain before. Maybe my wife is involved with someone else. Maybe someone really is plotting against me. Maybe there is some special message in the song the radio's playing. Maybe there really is some special significance in the way the sky looks today. Maybe there is in fact something about me that everyone's noticing. Maybe all this is really only a bad dream . . . and so on and on, searching for a solution, for a way out. The world seems to be subtly transformed. It may seem alien or strange. It may seem frightening or filled with all kinds of special significances. Clinicians have described such world-transforming experiences as *primary delusional experiences* (Schneider, 1959), or *apophanous experiences* (Conrad, 1958) or *loss of vital contact* (Minkowski, 1953) or *destructuring of conventional reality* (Bowers, 1974).

Meanwhile, in the throes of such perplexing experiences, the anxiety keeps building. We can't concentrate. There are too many thoughts, or our mind keeps going blank on us. We can't sleep. We don't dare let ourselves sleep. We may be up three or four nights in a row, exhausted but wired up, shot through with what seem like electric currents. We're trapped, frightened, desperate. Some kind of survival seems to hang in the balance. Panic, fear, dread—we're trapped. There's *got* to be a way out. *But there is no way out!*

The third stage—psychosis, or *"cracking up."* Finally we're overwhelmed. We can't fight anymore. We let our thoughts have their own way; consequently, they may not even seem like our own thoughts anymore. Yes, we say in our exhaustion, the Communists have caused it all. Yes, the way the clouds are arranged does mean I'll die tonight. We feel alternatively horrified and stupified as, utterly overwhelmed, we watch madness unroll before our eyes. Or as Yeats has written,

> *Things fall apart; the centre cannot hold; Mere anarchy is loosed upon the world*—Yeats, *The Second Coming**

That's a general description of what it's like. Every individual, however, reacts in his or her own unique way. If you

*From .W. B. Yeats, "The Second Coming," from *Collected Poems of William Butler Yeats* (Copyright 1924 by Macmillan Publishing Co., Inc., renewed 1952 by Bertha Georgie Yeats. Reprinted with permission).

dealt with upsetting situations in the past by withdrawing from people, in the psychotic extreme you may become catatonic, saying, in effect, "You don't exist, none of you exist." If you dealt with such situations by passing the buck and blaming others, in the psychotic extreme you may become acutely paranoid, saying in effect, "It's all your fault, not mine." If you dealt with such situations by trying to laugh them off, pretending they didn't matter, then in the psychotic extreme you may become hebephrenic, saying in effect, "It's all a joke. Who cares about anything?"

However, as I said in an earlier chapter, there are as many ways to "crack up," or as many types of acute schizophrenic disorders, as there are types of people. We've relied for decades on a handful of simplistic categories (catatonic, hebephrenic, etc.) to describe the almost limitless varieties of psychotic ways people react to overwhelming stresses. Beyond certain very general characteristics, there are no typical acute schizophrenic-type disorders. Cities are characterized by a great many people living together, acute schizophrenic disorders by a great many conflicting thoughts, feelings, perceptions, and desires all going on together. Beyond that, as with cities, the differences are every bit as important as the similarities.

THE HYPOTHETICAL BIOCHEMICALLY CAUSED ACUTE SCHIZOPHRENIC-TYPE DISORDERS

Having separated out the types of psychotic disorders which seem to be attributable to clear-cut stresses, we're left with a large residual category of psychoses of unknown origin. The working hypothesis of many researchers is that these psychoses are due to imbalances in the central nervous system's chemical transmitter substances. There is no reason to believe that such a hypothetical disorder can lead only to "chronic schizophrenia." Such an imbalance may occur once and never occur again, like measles; or recur several times with no difficulty between recurrences, like the flu; or it may be chronic, like diabetes. When it does occur it may vary from a very mild imbalance to a very severe one, and, like any one of the mentioned diseases, it may strike the healthy as well as the not-so-healthy.

All of the above-mentioned possible variables (episodic versus chronic, mild versus severe, healthy versus not-so-healthy) make for a very confusing picture when attempting to understand what precisely is going on in a given individual. It makes it very difficult to predict whether such an apparently non–stress-related disorder will recur. The problems faced by someone with a chronic schizophrenic-type disorder, with all of its ups and downs, will be discussed in the next chapter. Here I will limit myself to some points particularly worth remembering with respect to the schizophrenic-type psychotic reactions occurring in the absence of obvious precipitating stresses.

1. This residual category of apparently non–stress-related acute schizophrenic-type disorders may include many different types of disorders, different biochemical imbalances, possible viruses, autoimmune diseases, and so on. At present we don't know if we're looking for one cure or many different types of cures.

2. We also don't know if there is any reality to this hypothetical category. Some psychiatrists would maintain that all acute schizophrenic-type disorders are due to stress. A well-trained analyst can always discover tremendous unconscious stresses and conflicts to explain almost anything. Further, it should not be forgotten that stress itself can lead to major biochemical

alterations (for example, in steroid and epinephrine—or "adrenaline"—levels.)

3. Many acute schizophrenic-type reactions, especially those with good prognosis, are currently being reclassified by many researchers as variants of manic-depressive illness. It is being found that even if the individual has any number of classic schizophrenic-type symptoms, there are other symptoms which, if present, make the diagnosis of manic-depressive-type illness more appropriate—for example, if someone tends to move around a lot (hyperactivity), talk a lot (pressure of speech), and be very touchy emotionally (labile mood), or if someone seems to be really quite depressed and perplexed by his or her state of mind,—then no matter how "crazy" they are in other ways, it turns out that (a) they tend to have manic-depressive-type illnesses, if any, running in their family; (b) they tend to be helped by the medications effective in manic-depressive illness (antidepressants and Lithium), and (c) they tend to get over their disorganized state relatively quickly and to do relatively well subsequently.[6]

4. Some individuals who have had an acute psychotic break get over it, for no evident reason and are never bothered again. We don't know why they had it. We don't know why it never happens again. We simply don't know.

5. But even in situations such as the above, the disorganized state doesn't arise out of the blue. Such individuals go through stages similar to the stages outlined above. They feel an increasing sense of things not being right when, to all appearances, everything in their lives may be going well. They begin to have unusual thoughts and experiences. They find it more and more difficult to concentrate. They can't sleep. They don't know why they can't concentrate, or sleep, or why they feel so scared. Then, after several days or weeks of such experiences, they become psychotically disorganized.

6. Here, as with the stress-related psychoses, it's important to recognize the early stages, because most acute psychotic

states can be prevented with appropriate "crisis intervention."

WHAT HELPS

Medication. The major tranquilizers are often helpful in relieving the acute panic and disorganization (see Chapter 15).
Other medications, such as the minor tranquilizers, antidepressants, over-the-counter sedatives, "nerve pills," and
sleeping pills are usually of little if any benefit. In some instances they may actually be harmful and increase or prolong
the period of disorganization.

Elimination of Precipitating Stresses. Often the stresses are obvious enough, and often there is a great deal that can be
done to extricate the person from the intolerable situation. In
some instances, a hospital may provide the appropriate refuge from an unbearable reality (see Chapter 16).

Support. Individuals undergoing acute psychotic reactions
usually feel dreadfully isolated and alone no matter how
many people there may be around them. They're like people
panic-stricken in a theater after a fire has broken out. It
doesn't help to join in the general sense of panic (as many
relatives and friends often do). How would you deal with a
panic-stricken person in a theater? Think a moment. The
usual rule is: stay calm yourself. The second rule would be:
be firm when necessary.
     If someone undergoing an acute schizophrenic-type
psychotic reaction can see you're not getting caught up in the
emotional frenzy yourself, that you're staying calm and acting in a reasonable and firm manner, then he or she will tend
to calm down and act more reasonably. To a significant extent emotions are contagious. If you sit in a room with a lot of

angry people, you tend to get angry. If you sit in a room with a lot of depressed people, you tend to get depressed. If you sit in a room with a calm, composed group of people, you tend to feel calm and composed yourself. Of course, it's enormously difficult sometimes to remain calm and composed while someone else is becoming more and more disorganized before your eyes, to "keep your head while all about are losing theirs." Panic and disorganization are also quite contagious, especially if you've been in close contact with someone day in and day out for weeks, or months, during the development of the acute psychotic state. This is why an outsider—for example a therapist or counselor—can often be more helpful than someone emotionally involved.

Most people in the throes of an acutely disorganized state very much appreciate your being there, provided you're not ranting and raving and becoming emotionally unbalanced yourself. There are some, however, who seem to be saying, "Get lost; leave me alone." Be assured the reason they want you to leave them alone is because they are frightened and afraid you will hurt them or disturb them even more. No matter how much they withdraw (into acute catatonic-type states) or push you away (with all kinds of paranoid delusions), inside they need and want someone they can trust. If they didn't have such a howling need, they wouldn't react in such extreme ways. People who don't really need or care about other people react to the rest of humanity not with fear or paranoia, but with contempt, or, at best, indifference. Existentialist psychiatrists, including to some extent Laing, have recognized this need for someone undergoing a psychotic reaction to have someone else there to accompany them through their dreadful nightmare journey. But you have to be there in a calm, considerate, understanding, and firmly sensible manner if you're going to be of any help at all.

Good Advice. There is usually no lack of good advice from everyone. Proper advice can often abort or calm down a "break" that is underway; improper "good advice" merely speeds it on its way. As a person becomes progressively more disorganized everyone and his mother come up with more and more good advice. All of which runs like water off the proverbial duck's back. The good advice may in fact be good advice, but the important thing is the setting in which it is given and the way it is given. If, for example, a psychotic young man hears the good advice coming from his overbearing parents, he's not likely to listen. If it comes from someone else who says in essence, "See, I told you so—if you'd done what I told you to do, you wouldn't be in this mess," he's also not likely to listen.

Good advice is often very bitter medicine. If you want people to take it, you've got to convince them you're trustworthy, understanding, sympathetic, sensible, and, above all, that you're on their side. You must convince them that you're there primarily to help them and not yourself or someone else such as parents, spouse, or employer.

Further, you shouldn't expect anyone in the throes of an acutely disorganized psychotic state to follow your good advice. They may or they may not. You shouldn't become hysterical if they don't. You should continue to deal with the situation in a reasonable but firm manner. Often the best advice is to insist that the psychotic individual seek appropriate professional help. If the person is too deluded, too disorganized, or otherwise too incapacitated to seek help, then family or friends or whoever should act in a firm manner to insure that the person does receive treatment.

The more extreme civil libertarians such as Szasz argue vehemently that no one, psychotic or not, should be treated or "helped" against his or her will.[7] A bright young businessman developed an acute paranoid psychosis. He was placed on major tranquilizer medication and his psychosis cleared completely within several weeks. About six months later he stopped taking his medication, refused all treatment, became moderately paranoid, stopped working, threw his wife out, and sequestered himself in his house. At the time (I was a first-year resident in psychiatry) I was under the spell of the civil libertarians' rhetoric and failed to have him involuntarily committed to a hospital to receive the treatment which would have cleared up his psychotic state within a couple of weeks. His wife called me several months later. He was still paranoid. He was without work. He had gone to court to obtain custody of the children, struck one of the court officers, went to jail; now he was out, sequestered in his room. She was proceeding with the final divorce. He was not paranoid enough so that anyone else would take the responsibility of committing him for treatment. Nonetheless, both his family and I knew he was in a completely altered state of mind, as different from his usual state as night from day. His career was wrecked; his marriage was wrecked; he had a criminal record; his life was going down the drain of chronic paranoia—all for the lack of a week or two of appropriate treatment.

Magnificent rhetoric and exalted, unassailably pure and noble ideals are one thing; having a wrecked life on your conscience is something else. I suppose we can all become morally hard and pure enough, or consistently consistent, as the moral philosopher Kolakowski would put it, so that we can let young men and women who want to jump off bridges, jump off bridges; or old men who just want to lie down in the snow and die, lie down in the snow and die; or children who want to walk out in front of trucks, walk out in front of trucks; or a deluded businessman who believes he's the son of Jesus Christ and the next vice-president of the United States, as the man described above believed, go on being deluded. But my morals aren't that diamond-hard and pure, and hopefully yours aren't either.[8] Psychotically disorganized persons desperately need help, and if you don't insure that they receive help, who on earth will help them?

Prevention. Prevention is obviously the best cure. I've already discussed the early stages of an acute psychotic decompensation. If help is sought during the early stages, the entire disorganizing process is usually easily reversed.

AFTER THE ACUTE EPISODE

The main problem for people who have successfully gotten over an acute schizophrenic-type episode is that they have been diagnosed as having had an acute schizophrenic-type episode. They then run the very considerable risk of becoming the victims of our very considerable prejudices. If they thought they had big problems before, now they *really* have some. Listen, would you buy a used car from this schizophrenic? Would you elect this schizophrenic to the legislature? Would you trust your child's education to this schizophrenic? Would you marry this schizophrenic? I could go on and on. Given our prejudices and misconceptions, which would be merely ludicrous if they weren't so monstrous, the best that people who have had an acute schizophrenic-type reaction can do is simply not tell you they had one, or tell you they were suffering from "nervous strain" or "emotional exhaustion" brought on by overwork or a personal crisis. In most instances this way of phrasing things comes considerably closer to the truth than does the label *schizophrenic disorder*. (According to the revised nomenclature most such individuals *should* be diagnosed as undergoing a brief psychotic reaction or a schizophrenic disorder—or in some instances, a schizoaffective disorder or an atypical psychosis.)

SUMMARY

1. From the fact that someone has had an acute schizophrenic-type disorder we can't conclude that such a person is necessarily weaker or less stable than someone who hasn't undergone such a reaction.

2. Acute schizophrenic-type disorders may be precipitated by severe stress. They typically occur when someone feels trapped with no way out of a psychologically unbearable situation.

3. Acute psychotic "nervous breakdowns" or schizophrenic-type disorders do not come out of the blue. There is usually a period of increasing agitation and apprehension, followed by a period of uncanny experiences, before psychotic disorganization occurs.

4. There are some acute schizophrenic-type disorders which don't appear to be precipitated by severe stress. The cause or causes of such disorders are not known at present.

5. Many of the acute schizophrenic-type disorders which (*a*) are not clearly stress-related, and (*b*) appear to have a good prognosis, are currently being reclassified as variants of manic-depressive illness.

6. The elimination of the precipitating stresses, along with appropriate support and medication, often quickly reverses the state of acute disorganization.

7. In dealing with someone in a state of acute disorganization the basic rules are (*a*) stay calm yourself, (*b*) be reasonable, and (*c*) be firm when necessary.

8. It's reprehensible *not* to help someone if they're too psychotic or too confused to ask for the help they clearly need. Respect for an individual's "right to be crazy" is one thing; it's quite something else to permit clearly disturbed individuals to—physically or mentally—destroy themselves because they're too disorganized, or too deluded, or too terrified to notice or care.

9. People's often very subtle prejudices constitute one of the main problems encountered by many following recovery from an acute schizophrenic-type disorder.

7

The Chronic Schizophrenic-Type Disorders

You only have to walk down this street once with your eyes open. . . . So much helplessness, so much dread, so much misery. . . . How could nature generate so much indifference towards its most helpless, its most pitiable of creatures. This boundless capacity to engender suffering. This boundless genius for generating and propagating misery. Right now, right here, in this street, this actual affliction of thousands of individuals. Uncomprehendingly, helplessly we have to watch. . . . (Bernhard, 1971, p. 20—my translation)*

Indeed, as Bernhard writes, nature does seem to have a boundless genius for generating indifference toward its most

*From Thomas Bernhard, *Gehen*, 1971, p. 20. Reprinted in English translation with permission of Suhrkamp Verlag.

helpless of creatures, for engendering suffering and for propagating misery, and individuals with chronic schizophrenic-type disorders have received more than their fair share of indifference (*our* indifference), suffering and misery. However, we don't have to stand by watching uncomprehendingly and helplessly. There is much that we can do to overcome our indifference, to gain some understanding, and to be of some help.

WHERE HAVE THE "MADMEN" GONE?

One of the most surprising and disconcerting experiences of my life was to work on a chronic mental ward as a medical student. Where were all the raving madmen I had read about in books and seen in movies? Where the people smearing feces on the walls and running around believing they were Martians, God, Napoleon, Satan, or Godzilla? Where the threats, the wild curses, the clenched fists, the eyes filled with mayhem and murderous rage? Where, where, oh where was the craziness?

Well it was there, but not in any way I'd been led to imagine. It was there as fear and despair. It was there as thoughts that kept wandering off, or that wouldn't come. It was there as feelings that came out the opposite of how they were supposed to (laughter out of terror, smiles out of pain, anger out of love, indifference out of despair). Yes, and it was there in a few as delusions ("I'm in hell," "I'm being followed everywhere," "I'm being controlled by radar") and hallucinations ("The voices keep telling me to keep quiet, not to move"). But most of all it was there as a desert silence, a look of defeat, a sense of someone utterly lost in a world that didn't care. These were the "madmen"—frightened, frustrated human beings who were grateful to have someone to talk to; who, when given the chance, spoke reasonably, though perhaps mournfully, or bitterly, about how empty, how painful they found their lives. So this was madness, an immeasurable sadness, an immeasurable being hurt until you couldn't go on trying, feeling, thinking anymore. Frightened, quiet, lonely people, bruised, staggering, reeling from their devastating encounters with life and man's insensitivity to man. A strange kind of madness, something basically not so bizarre or odd or difficult to understand at all.

About a year later, however, I found the "madmen." I'd gone to interview patients at an old state hospital out in the country. They had many buildings. One was for the severely brain-damaged who had survived into adulthood. The sight was heart-rending. But here they were, bizarrely grimacing and gesturing, driveling, grunting, babbling crazily. Here they were, the "madmen" who populated such films as *The Snake Pit* and *Marat/Sade*. Well, enough of that. There are tragedies of fate the human mind can't bear to contemplate for too long.

Another building was a very special one. It was for the chronic mental patients "left over" from the early decades of the century. Almost everyone there had been there for thirty years, many for much longer. They were considered beyond all hope and thus had their own building (this was over a decade ago—hopefully since then there have been some changes). Here madness indeed looked like it looked in the old movies (or the textbooks of psychiatry). This was "end-stage, burnt-out" schizophrenia. Actually, as I came very quickly to realize, it was end-stage, burnt-out institutional abandonment and social neglect. The condition of those howlingly desolate souls had little to do with a chronic schizophrenic "illness" but a lot to do with how our society had come to regard and treat them (get them off the streets, put them away).

SOME REMARKS ON THE ORIGINS OF OUR "CRAZINESS"

We don't refer to someone with a cold as "the cold," or someone with an ulcer as "the ulcer," or someone with cancer as "the cancer." But we feel perfectly comfortable referring to someone with a schizophrenic-type disorder as "the schizophrenic." We are trying to be "scientific," but in fact we are being obscene. It only takes a moment's reflection to think of the sorts of disorders we end up using as epithets to characterize the entire person, as though from our point of view the only thing important about the person anymore is the disorder itself. We speak of "lepers" and "syphilitics." But we don't speak of "malariacs" (individuals with malaria) or "goutics" (individuals with gout). We end up referring to someone by their "disease" when there's something corrupt, degrading, and threatening in our mind about the disease. We even grant people with the plague the relative honor of being called "plague victims." This at least, like "disaster victim," evokes a certain sort of pity. But in the past, lepers (the devil's work) and syphilitics (moral degenerates) were considered dangerously corrupt. We couldn't let ourselves relate to them as if they were human beings deserving of compassion and love, else we might get too involved and become corrupted and diseased ourselves. In a similar manner, we can't let ourselves get too involved with the "enemy" we're bombing, else we'll stop bombing them. If we're going to survive, we have to think of all these enemies as nonpersons, as things with labels, as "Huns," "Gooks," "Dinks," or "lepers," "syphilitics," "lunatics," "schizophrenics," so that we can go on despising, persecuting, maiming, or bombing them as the case may be, with relatively untroubled consciences. So now let's consider a young man with a chronic schizophrenic-type disorder, or a typical "schizophrenic," as some might call him.

A SCHIZOPHRENIC YOUNG MAN

The first time it happened I thought I was a secret agent. I was receiving commands from the TV set. . . . One day I took the piano apart, three little ugly screws got lost. The devil will help you, I thought. I bowed and found them. . . . Now I think people get offended if I bow. They think I'm worshipping the devil. I know it's ridiculous. I feel like the devil's controlling my hands. Then I move to a more rational realization. I'd like to change my whole self. I'd like to be beautiful. Have everyone want me, like me. My mother used to tell me, "You're ugly." I thought my mother was the devil. Even in the beginning Eve gave the apple to Adam. Watch out for women, they're evil.

Several months later:

I keep blanking out. I can't concentrate. People have to repeat things. I feel like I don't have a memory. I feel like people know what I think. I'm afraid to go to school, afraid I won't be able to understand. I can't talk to anyone; my whole family is illiterate. I went out with this girl. She called me her "big ape." Her parents said I was an idiot, a bum who wouldn't amount to anything. I decided to become a fantastic pianist. . . . I think of suicide. I'm no good at all. I feel panicky. I can't talk to people. I can't look people in the eye. I'm afraid my face will show what I'm thinking. I'm not getting any better. I'm insecure about my looks, my vocabulary, people looking at me. I feel like I can't think anymore. I feel lousy, like a vegetable.

Two years later:

I'm paranoid. I feel like people are watching me all the time. I keep looking around to see if they're really looking. But I guess I have to fight it. Nobody really knows what I'm thinking. . . . I feel horrible. I'm so preoccupied with myself. . . . I'm unbearably preoccupied with r's. I'm afraid to say a word if it has an r in it. People with speech impediments have trouble saying r's. . . . I've got a real difficulty keeping up relationships. I'm afraid to look people in the eye. I saw *The Exorcist* last night. I went home; my hair stood on end. I felt like the devil was there in the darkness. . . .

The above are excerpts from some meetings I had with a young man in his early twenties. He talked about being ugly though he was quite good-looking. He talked about being inarticulate, though he was quite articulate. He talked about being the devil, though he was one of the more decent people on this earth. He thought of himself as ugly and deformed in every way. For example, he felt his mouth, which looked perfectly normal, was twisted into the shape of an ape's mouth ("you big ape"). He was so preoccupied with r's because he felt an inability to pronounce them correctly was a sign of mental retardation—and he thought he was mentally retarded. Whenever he would get into a stressful situation, he would become more and more preoccupied with his "ugliness." Eventually he would become delusional, believing alternatively either that he was the devil or that others were the devil giving him the "evil eye." Whenever he stopped taking his medication, even minor stresses would tip the balance toward delusional preoccupations. Two years later he was dealing with many of the same problems (a horrible self-image, self-defeating behavior, fear of other people, and so on). Four years later he was still struggling.

CONCERNING THE CAUSES OF CHRONIC SCHIZOPHRENIC-TYPE DISORDERS

The above is merely one example of the sort of lives which earn the label *chronic schizophrenia*. But what is going on with this young man? Why can't he, as we say, "get it all together"? We can think of several extreme possibilities.

First, he simply wasn't born with the kind of "emotional equipment" most of us have. We might say there are constitutional limits to the emotional development he can attain (just as there are limits to his height, etc.). He is condemned to using less mature (or more childish) modes of dealing with stressful situations.

Second, he was born with the right emotional equipment, but grew up "all wrong." He learned to hate himself and distrust everyone else through a series of devastating life experiences.

Third, he was born with the emotional equipment, and grew up in a loving, considerate environment with many positive experiences, but at some point, either when he was a child or later, prior to his first psychotic break, a disorder arose which made it increasingly difficult for him, despite his best efforts, to think and feel in an organized, realistic manner.

These are some of the possibilities. Of course, there are any number of various combinations among these three possibilities alone (for example, a mild deficit in "emotional equipment," a mild biochemical disorder, and a moderately disturbed upbringing) which may eventually lead to a severely disorganized life (chronic schizophrenia). I met with the young man over several years, and I must say I still don't have a good idea as to what the "fundamental cause" of his difficulties may be. But when I read the literature I tend to feel rather stupid because there are so many authorities who claim to know what the basic problem is.

For example, I'm told the primary problem with this "typical schizophrenic" is clearly faulty learning from his "schizophrenogenic family." (Didn't he call his mother the devil?) Or I'm told the primary problem with this "typical schizophrenic" is clearly faulty emotional equipment, a developmental arrest at the oral-narcissistic infantile stage which can't be explained entirely by how he was treated as an infant. Or I am told the primary problem is clearly biochemical, since in so many other ways he did relatively well until suddenly at age twenty he became overtly psychotic. His problem is clearly vitamin deficiency, or magnesium deficiency, or an allergy to his own brain cells.

But for the life of me I don't know who's right. I don't know how they know they're right. I feel abysmally stupid. I must have been missing something obvious in my dealings with the young man. But the truth, as you should be well aware by now, is that I wasn't missing anything obvious. Apart from speculations and hypotheses, we simply don't know for sure why someone like this young man is the way he is.

In general, we don't know, but this is not to say we can't to some extent understand what he's going through, nor that we can't be of significant help and comfort to him. Whatever the cause or causes of his state of mind, we can always help him deal with his fears and anxieties in a less self-defeating manner. We can always help him get on with his life in a more efficient way. We can always, at the very least, get to know him well enough so that when he tells us that he feels like the Devil (or a "big ape" or "mentally retarded") we understand that he's not really talking "crazy" at all, but telling us, in his own way, how awful he feels about himself.

The term *chronic schizophrenic-type disorder*, when it is used as equivalent to *chronic psychotic disorder*, is grossly misleading. There are very, very few "chronic schizophrenics" who are truly out of touch with obvious realities (though this does occur frequently in acute schizophrenic-type disorders). Once you get past their facade or defense of peculiar behavior, or once you understand the "code" of their sometimes quite eccentric language (which serves to keep you at a safe distance as effectively as if they'd decided to communicate only in Swahili), you find people who are quite in touch with the obvious realities—often very painful and humiliating realities—of their actual situation.

Though we speak of "chronic schizophrenia" (or the "chronic psychoses of unknown origin"), in fact, such individuals, with current approaches to community care, are rarely truly psychotic. The "psychosis" or obviously deluded or chaotic thinking usually only occurs during an acute decompensation.

Of course, there are, as I have said, a very very few individuals who are truly "chronically psychotic." But the vast majority of people with chronic schizophrenic-type disorders are not. The label *schizophrenia*, however, seduces us into considering all this vast multiplicity of "chronically failing and eccentric" people to be "crazy," "mad," "psychotic," or "schizophrenic." You find yourself no longer looking at the vast differences between all these people. You stop trying to understand why all these vast differences exist. You concentrate all your energies on discovering the "similarities," the "schizophrenia," the "thread of madness," the "root cause." Eventually, if you are an assiduous enough generalizer, you will discover some "basic cause" and write a book about it. All of which is very interesting, but not much help at all to the chronically disturbed individual who doesn't happen to fit your particular definition of "craziness" and who doesn't happen to respond to your proposed cure.

A NONPSYCHIATRIC VIEW OF THE "TYPICAL CHRONIC SCHIZOPHRENIC"

Anyone whose judgment hasn't been blinded by the label *schizophrenic* would probably agree that there isn't any "typical chronic schizophrenic." If we look carefully at the types of individuals who are diagnosed as "schizophrenic," we see every variety of individual and a tremendous diversity of life-styles. By psychiatry's definition, they are usually failing in some important way, but beyond that, there is all the diversity in the world.

> What is meant by the term "schizophrenia"? Unfortunately there is no consensus on this point. Frequently, the diagnosis is accorded to anyone who shows serious behavioral disturbances or marked impropriety of behavior or who expresses his thoughts in language and words that have no shared meaning. (Weiner, 1975, pp. 866–67)

However, there was a time when there were many "typical chronic schizophrenics." They were produced by chronic "back-ward" institutionalization. A classification system widely used in Germany and partially reflected in our catatonic-hebephrenic-paranoid classification was explicitly based on deteriorated, "end-stage" schizophrenia.[1] Because many of these unfortunate victims of our ignorance and neglect are still around, we persist in describing "chronic schizophrenia" in terms of their pathetic state.

Psychiatrists, because they are so preoccupied with normality and freeing humanity from all of its maladjusted symptomatology, tend to look upon the tremendous diversity among human beings with a somewhat jaded eye. They end up defining a large proportion of the population mentally disturbed and in need of treatment. A director of the National Institute of Mental Health has said: "Between 15 and 20 percent of the population have diagnosable mental disturbances and is in need of care" (B. Brown, 1977, p. 16).

Most of these people the general public wouldn't consider to be "sick" at all. They wouldn't even consider them to be particularly odd, but rather they'd consider them to be people dealing, like the rest of us, with their own unique problems in their own unique ways. Many whom psychiatrists call "chronic schizophrenic" aren't viewed by their acquaintances to be "mentally ill," let alone psychotic, at all. A certain number are viewed as "characters" or "colorful eccen-trics" with strange or peculiar or idiosyncratic or unique life-styles. Others are viewed as simply "unlucky," "down-and-out" people who've had a lot of "bad deals" in life. Others are viewed as careless, or irresponsible, or unambi-tious, "easy-come, easy-go" types. Still others are viewed as inadequate, bumbling, awkward, easily embarrassed, easily flustered "losers" (the Casper Milquetoasts of this world). There are of course a number of individuals whom both psychiatrists and the general public would view as obviously "a bit cracked" or "crazy" or "schizophrenic." But in many instances the average man-in-the-street's tolerance for "craz-iness" seems to be much greater than the average mental health worker's.[2]

The best the general public can do under such circum-stances is to recognize that psychiatry is at best a very impre-cise science, especially when it comes to dealing with "schizophrenia." If very eccentric, even semidelusional people manage to succeed in life (certain political and reli-gious cult leaders should come to mind), they're hardly ever diagnosed as schizophrenic. If they were to have been un-lucky enough to have failed, they would almost certainly have been diagnosed either schizophrenic or borderline schizophrenic.

Except for those individuals who are obviously "crazy" (e.g., "I own South America, you know," or "I gave birth to my two hundred and ninety-eighth child yesterday"), the general public is better off forgetting about "chronic schizophrenia" and "schizo-phrenics." Let the psychiatrists and other mental health work-ers shuffle their labels about for their own theoretical and speculative purposes. For your own part, just concentrate on being fully human and humane in your interactions with your fellow human beings, no matter how failed or pained or peculiar their lives may be.

CONCERNING HOPELESS OR
IRREVERSIBLE INSANITY

Bleuler in his 1911 monograph defining the "group of schizophrenias" noted that even the most severely deteriorated individuals with chronic schizophrenic-type disorders seemed capable for brief periods of acting and talking in a completely normal fashion. What could that mean? Think about it.

When I was a medical student I visited a state hospital outside Baltimore which had set aside one of its buildings for the severely disorganized and presumably irredeemable victims of decades (thirty, forty, and even fifty years) of "snake-pit" back-ward mental hospitalization. I noticed one woman in her fifties who, unlike most of the others, appeared genuinely to have gone beyond the pale of all sanity, a pathetic, bizarre creature, a still-living wreck and ruin of human grace, reason, and dignity. The psychiatrist told me she had been like that—precisely like that—for years; as "mad as a hatter," for over twenty years, as I recall. Then several years ago a most astounding thing happened. She went in for thyroid surgery, and following the operation for several days *she was normal.* He couldn't believe it. He read back again through her old records. Nothing like this had ever happened before. Then, after only a few days, she sank back again into her regressed, crazed state. Subsequently, I heard numerous other reports of the most "hopelessly insane" suddenly, for hours or days or weeks, becoming "sane" again, usually in response to some overwhelming crisis that demanded their presence of mind for survival (e.g., a fire in the building, or a medical emergency). Once again, you should ask yourself: What could that mean? What does that tell me about "hopeless" or "irreversible" or "chronic" schizophrenia?

In past years, many seemed content to write off the

chronically disorganized as "irreversibly schizophrenic." But if individuals with chronic schizophrenic-type disorders could recognize what was "normal" as well as the next man, then *no matter how "schizophrenic" they seemed*, they still would have the potential to think and act "normally." For example, after investigating their ability to recognize the finest nuances of "normal" associations in our language, I satisfied myself that even among the most "deteriorated" back-ward "schizophrenics" the ability to recognize what was normal was preserved.[3] The "normal" and the "abnormal" existed side by side. It was, to use an analogy, not a matter of losing one's ability to see but rather of being compelled, for whatever reasons, to keep one's eyes shut. Most individuals with a chronic schizophrenic-type disorder hadn't lost the ability to "see" (i.e., to distinguish "crazy" from normal thinking and behavior), but for some reason or another, they had been compelled "not to see" (i.e., to experience the world in a "crazy," eccentric fashion and consequently to think and feel and act in a "crazy, eccentric fashion).

However, at another level, most such individuals are quite aware that they are thinking or feeling or acting in a "crazy" fashion.

Finally, the very fact that "emptying the back wards" and providing the chronically isolated with personal attention, encouragement, and a socially stimulating environment has proven of such benefit should be indication enough that there is no "end-stage, burnt-out schizophrenia." To borrow another metaphor (from the existentialist psychiatrist Binswanger),[4] they are people who know perfectly well how to walk (that is, what being "sane" means), but who have wandered off and lost their way in life (become chronically schizophrenic). They are hopelessly and irreversibly lost or "schizophrenic" only in the sense that they can't find their way back by themselves. They do need some help—our help.

In sum: *In the absence of demonstrable organic causes, it is unwarranted to think of anyone as "irreversibly" disorganized or "crazy." Since to date schizophrenia refers to disorders of unknown cause, it is never warranted to think of anyone with a schizophrenic-type disorder, no matter of how long standing, as "irreversibly" or hopelessly "schizophrenic."*

How disorganized someone with a chronic schizophrenic-type disorder becomes depends a great deal on you. You don't help people who've lost their way by forgetting about them (i.e., storing them away in the back wards of hospitals).

HOW TO DEAL WITH "OBVIOUS CRAZINESS"

Every now and then we all run into someone who's "obviously crazy." How do you react?

With fear? There's no more reason to be afraid of someone who's "obviously crazy" than of anyone else. Don't worry about the "craziness." If the person looks mean or evil (according to your definitions), then watch out. If the person doesn't, then there's no more reason to be afraid of him or her than there would be to be afraid of any other "nonviolent-looking" person. As a matter of fact, what you can almost always count on is that such people are infinitely more afraid of you than you might be afraid of them. If someone is "chronically crazy," the craziness often serves as a last-resort defense against *being hurt by you.* You must remember that such people are terribly hurt by the most trivial matters—a brusque remark, a condescending glance, or whatever. You don't have to worry about them hurting you. Instead, your main concern should be to avoid hurting them. This means you have to make an effort to be especially kind and considerate and understanding.

Well, how do you react? Humor them in their "craziness"? You may, of course. But I don't advise it. You see, most of the time, "in the back of their mind," such people know they are talking or acting "crazy." They partly believe their wild ideas, while another part of them knows the ideas are all nonsense. You're not expected to go along with the "craziness" yourself. If you do, then you're very likely to be written off as a hypocrite, or as someone who's ridiculing them, or, at the very least, as someone who doesn't respect them and refuses to carry out a serious, honest, and non-condescending conversation with them.

Well, how do you react? Most of the time you need only be a sympathetic listener. When such people see that you're *really* listening and that you are *really* sympathetic, then you'll make the remarkable discovery that there's less and less "craziness" and more and more normal everyday conversation.

If you assume the person understands quite well what you're saying and is perfectly capable of carrying out a normal conversation, you'll discover that most of the time the person will stop "being crazy" and carry out a normal conversation. You should *always* keep in mind that such people are usually capable of being relatively reasonable and of recognizing quite well the craziness in their "craziness."

For several years I was puzzled by the fact that such "schizophrenic" individuals seemed to carry out relatively reasonable conversations with me. I kept thinking I was overlooking something. Finally it became clear that the reason they were relatively organized with me and so woefully disorganized with others was that I didn't consider them to be "crazy" at all when I was talking to them. There was a part of them which didn't believe their delusions any more than I did. Once it was clear I understood what they were going through and that I cared, they could risk letting the reasonable but very very vulnerable part of themselves come to the fore. (In the same way, many of us have "social selves" which are often quite different from the very protected and very vulnerable "private selves" we only let our family and intimate friends know.)

In sum: *For many "chronic schizophrenics," their "chronic schizophrenia" (or "craziness") is a defense against you. If you can manage to be sincere and honest and respectful and sympathetic and understanding (a tall order!), then they don't need (or aren't forced) to be "crazy" anymore.*

If you expect such people to act "crazy," they will usually oblige you.

If you don't expect them to act "crazy," as often as not, they won't act "crazy".

This is not to say that the problem is all ours and not theirs. Their problem is that they are excessively vulnerable (for whatever reasons). Because they are so excessively vulnerable, they can be exquisitely demanding upon our understanding and concern and tolerance. We often find ourselves getting frustrated, furious, fed up with them, while they spiral progressively deeper into futility and "craziness." They very much need help. And they should be urged to seek it. Their "craziness" in a certain sense protects them from the rest of us, but it also cuts them off from themselves and from any chance of improving the wretched state of affairs of their lives.

WHAT HELPS

The chronically disorganized will often have periods when they become even more disorganized (an "acute exacerbation"). The most common causes of such acute exacerbations seem to be related to increasing difficulties in their lives (precipitating stresses) or, if they are taking major tranquilizer medication, to decreasing or stopping the medication. However, there are many times when such exacerbations simply seem to "just happen," thus living up to their reputation as "psychoses of unknown origin." Our discussion of what helps the acutely disorganized individual in Chapter 6 applies equally here. Appropriate interventions to relieve the stressful situation (e.g., providing an alternative living or work situation, financial assistance, family counseling, day hospital care) and appropriate adjustments in medication are often quite helpful in cutting short such episodes and eliminating the necessity of hospitalization. Of course, prevention is the best cure. For some people maintenance major tranquilizer medication appears to be helpful in preventing such episodes (probably by decreasing their emotional over-reactions to stressful situations). In addition, the early stages of psychotic decompensation are usually easily recognized. They are similar to those described in Chapter 6 and have been elegantly described by Donlon and Blacker (1973). Their paper should be consulted by anyone interested in prevention, since relatively simple measures often suffice at an early stage to prevent the development of a floridly disorganized or psychotic state.

Apart from relieving or preventing acute psychotic exacerbations, what else can we do to help the chronically disorganized? Our first concern should be: What kind of help do they want? People we call "chronic schizophrenics" have spent many years adjusting their whole existence to a certain style of life (reclusive, or eccentric, or "crazy," etc.). There is a man in my neighborhood who spends the entire day walking the streets whistling "Yankee Doodle." He stops occasionally to launch into a whacky monologue on the current world situation, which inevitably spreads some genuine good humor among his listeners. He then walks on, whistling "Yankee Doodle." He's been doing this for years. He's a thoroughly pixilated chap who seems relatively satisfied with his unique way of relating to his fellow man. I've no doubt that behind that somewhat cynical smile of his there's a full house of heartbreak and loneliness. But he's found a way of dealing with it—his way. We need to respect that. We can reach out to him, try to get behind the facade, offer all kinds of help if we care to, but he's the one who has to decide whether he wants anything to do with us or not. [5]

Many such individuals do not want our help if they see we are intent on changing them. They want us to *accept* them, not *change* them. Once they see we accept them, that they are not pariahs (remember the litany: "lepers," "syphilitics," "schizophrenics"), outcasts of society who must constantly be on guard to protect themselves from being hurt by us, then they may possibly agree to change (that is, give up some of the craziness that keeps them at a safe distance from us). The trick, which should be no trick at all, is to get our pixilated whistler of "Yankee Doodle" to believe again in humanity, and as often as not, that comes down to believing again in one or two human beings. Then such people might be tempted to go from, as they see it, "the purgatory of loneliness into the hell of togetherness" (Bernhard, 1973, p. 162). They just might dare to join the human "race" again. They just might agree to go through all those monumental pains of learning to be mature, well-adjusted, adaptable adults (if you think that's easy, think of what you went through yourself).

Because such people tend to push you off in one way or another, it's a very difficult task to stick with them, month in and month out, year in and year out, until they're finally convinced that you, as a representative of humanity, are indeed a decent, trustworthy, compassionate person, and, above all, that you genuinely respect them. Then they *may* finally dare to make some changes. But to get past such a person's "defenses," his or her attempts to push you off, you have to have the tenacity of a bulldog. Few average citizens have that tenacity—hence the value of therapists and counselors, of groups, foster homes, communal work shops, and so on where there are people who will hang on like bulldogs, partly because it's their job, partly (and primarily one would hope) because they genuinely care.

SOME CONCLUDING QUALIFICATIONS

It should be stated that many chronically disorganized people, even if they wholeheartedly want our help, can be helped only so far. They can be helped to a more fulfilling, dignified, independent life, but they're unlikely to be transformed into fashion plates of "normality." Medication in particular has come under heavy attack for not "curing" chronic schizophrenia. But because certain interventions (medication, psychotherapy) don't cure, that doesn't mean they may not be helpful. Insulin doesn't "cure" diabetes, but it helps some people lead better, more stable, less frightening lives. The same may be said of medication, psychotherapy, and various community support programs. There are some studies which have shown that the "long-term outcome" for many chronically "odd" or disorganized people today is not so much different from that of thirty or forty years ago. Many still remain unemployed, or marginally employed, or at low-level jobs; many remain dependent upon their families for support; and so on.

One response to such results would be: so what? Many of these people labeled "schizophrenic" do not want high-power employment. They do not want to work hard for success. They do not want to live for the same values you and I may want to live for. They do not want to get caught up in the same spiraling ambitions. But what they do want is peace of mind, freedom from harassment, genuine friendship, and respect. The most important measure of "outcome" should be whether their lives have more dignity than they did twenty or thirty years ago, not how much they may be able or willing to conform to our competitive ideals. In many respects their lives do have more dignity today than they did twenty or thirty years ago. The difference between being stored on a back ward as a piece of human wreckage and living a semiindependent existence in an enlightened community is immeasurable.

What helps? *Your concern, your tolerance, and, above all, your respect help.* If you don't remember anything else from this chapter, remember that.

SUMMARY

1.   There is no "typical chronic schizophrenia." The "typical chronic schizophrenic" was a product of chronic backward institutionalization.

2.   Today, *chronic schizophrenia* is a label often used indiscriminately to refer to the "less successful eccentrics" in our society.

3.   The chronic disorganization of some of these individuals may be due to a genetic predisposition, a variety of as-yet-undiscovered biochemical disorders, various types of disturbed upbringing, or any number of other possibilities.

4.   With most such individuals we simply don't know why they've come to adopt such a peculiar way of behaving and thinking. We can speculate and theorize. But we don't know.

5.   Though we speak of "chronic schizophrenia," most such individuals are not "chronically psychotic" at all.

6.   It is never warranted to think of anyone with a schizophrenic-type disorder, no matter of how long standing, as "irreversibly" or "hopelessly" schizophrenic.

7. Most chronically disorganized people who are acting in an obviously "crazy" way are perfectly aware they are acting in an obviously "crazy" way.

8. For many "chronic schizophrenics," their chronic schizophrenia, or "craziness" is a defense against you. If you can manage to be sincere and honest and respectful and sympathetic and understanding, (a tall order!), then they don't need, or aren't forced, to be "schizophrenic" anymore.

9. There is no reason to be more afraid of someone "obviously crazy" than of anyone else. They are more afraid of you than you are of them.

10. "Humoring" someone in their "craziness" is a sign of smugness and disrespect.

11. If you assume the "obviously crazy" person understands what you're saying and is capable of carrying out a normal conversation, you'll discover that most of the time the person will stop "being crazy" and carry on a normal conversation.

12. Many chronically disorganized individuals are miserable and want help. Others have managed to adjust to their eccentric life-styles. They may not want to change. Our first concern should always be: what kind of help do they want?

13. Many chronically disorganized individuals need to have their faith in humanity—and themselves—restored before they will even dare to begin to change. Counselors, groups, foster homes, and communal workshops are often helpful in providing supportive environments where such faith can be restored.

14. Medication is often helpful in enabling such individuals to lead independent, self-respecting lives.

15. Except for those individuals who are severely disorganized and unable to care for themselves, the general public is better off forgetting about the labels *chronic schizophrenia* and *schizophrenics*. Such labels, with all their attendant prejudices, have already done enough damage. We and, above all, the chronically eccentric individual can do quite well without them.

16. Above all, what helps is your concern, your tolerance, and your respect.

8

The Borderline Condition

SOME DEFINITIONS

The Austrian novelist Thomas Bernhard has described the essence of the borderline condition with the following words:

> Instruments of decline, creatures of agony, everything declares itself to us and we understand nothing. We populate a trauma, we're terrified, we have a right to be terrified, in the background we already see, even though obscurely: the giants of dread. Whatever we think is an *after*thought, whatever we feel is chaotic, whatever we are, is unclear. We don't

need to be ashamed, but we *are* nothing, and deserve nothing, but chaos." (Bernhard, 1970, pp. 7–8—translation by P. O'Brien and S. Wilkins).*

Trauma, agony, terror, dread, chaos: these are some of the hallmarks of the "borderline" state of mind. Turning from less literary to more clinical perspectives, Kernberg has described the place occupied by the "borderline disorders" within the realms of psychopathology as follows:

> There exists an important group of psychopathological constellations which have in common a rather specific and remarkably stable form of pathological ego structure. The ego pathology differs from that found in the neuroses and the less severe characterological illnesses on the one hand, and the psychoses on the other. These patients must be considered to occupy the borderline area between neurosis and psychosis. (Kernberg, 1967, p. 641)

Gunderson and Singer have reviewed the extensive, and often contradictory, literature on the "borderline syndrome," and formulated the following "operational criteria" for the diagnosis of borderline disorders:

> Six features that provide a rational means for diagnosing borderline patients during an initial interview: the presence of intense affect, usually depressive or hostile; a history of impulsive behavior; a certain social adaptiveness; brief psychotic experiences; loose thinking in unstructured situations; and relationships that vacillate between transient superficiality and intense dependency. (Gunderson and Singer, 1975, p. 1)

Brophy has summed up the current status of the "so-called borderline diagnosis" as follows:

*From Thomas Bernhard, "Rede" (a speech), in Annelise Botond, *Uber Thomas Bernhard*, 1970, pp. 7–8. Reprinted in English translation with permission of Suhrkamp Verlag.

The so-called borderline diagnosis . . . is being used more frequently as the classic psychiatric syndromes appear less prevalent. There is no unanimity of opinion on what constitutes the diagnosis, although most clinicians see it as a stable pathologic personality organization with variable presenting symptoms. In some cases there may be transient psychotic episodes, particularly under stress, whereas in others the initial picture is predominantly neurotic with marked anxiety, phobias, etc. (Brophy, in Krupp and Chatton, eds., 1976, p. 618)

SOME QUESTIONS AND ANSWERS

What do Sören Kierkegaard, Adolf Hitler, Marilyn Monroe, and Ludwig van Beethoven all have in common? Or Fyodor Dostoyevsky, Ludwig Wittgenstein, Lawrence of Arabia, and Marcel Proust? Or any number of other famous, or infamous, people, with their tortured, empty, or chaotic personal lives? What do they all have in common?

The answer is they would all be diagnosed by some psychiatrists as having borderline personality disorders.

What do you call someone who is not disturbed enough to be called schizophrenic, but is too disturbed to simply be called neurotic?

The answer is a "latent schizophrenic" or a "pseudoneurotic schizophrenic" or simply a "borderline."

If "schizophrenia" is a residual category describing all those people who are severely disorganized or out of touch with obvious realities for unknown reasons, then what about all those people who are not quite out of touch with obvious realities, who are not quite "schizophrenic"—what do we call them?

The answer is "borderline."[1]

We've seen that people use the term *schizophrenia* in

many different ways, some employing a very narrow definition. Is there a similar variation in the use of the term *borderline?*

Absolutely. There is probably even *more* variation.
Some authors have cast their net so wide as to include drug
addicts, sociopaths, hysterics, along with egotists and existentialists; others limit it to a very specific constellation of
personality traits.[2]

Are we justified in saying borderline personalities have
a mild form of "schizophrenia"?

Absolutely not. We don't even know if schizophrenics
have "schizophrenia" (i.e., a specific illness). Furthermore,
we don't know whether the borderline-type disorders have
anything to do with the schizophrenic-type disorders.

Well, couldn't they?

Certainly. It's theoretically possible that some "not-
quite schizophrenic" people may have a mild form of some
variety of a schizophrenic-type disorder. For example, one
study has suggested that a few individuals with borderline
personality disorders (called in the study "schizophrenic
spectrum disorders") may have relatives with schizophrenic-type disorders.[3]

Well, don't borderlines go on to develop "schizophrenia" eventually?

Decidedly not. Several studies have shown that they
don't go on to develop schizophrenia at all, but stay "borderline."[4]

But the very fact that they don't always think reasonably, that they give in to irrational impulses so frequently,
that they see the world as such a bleak, miserable place, that
they feel so wretched and empty and meaningless—all that
must mean there's something seriously wrong with them.

Of course there are many things seriously wrong with
them. There are also many things seriously wrong with the
world.

Why do we need to discuss these "borderline" people anyway?

The answer is because they are the ones most often misdiagnosed as "schizophrenic." It's not only the psychiatrists that misdiagnose them as schizophrenic. They are very prone to misdiagnose themselves as schizophrenic. Under stress, a minority of them may occasionally have very brief psychotic episodes. Many of them have some of the symptoms that the textbooks tell them are signs of "schizophrenia." Consequently they end up thinking of themselves as "mentally ill" and "schizophrenic."

So what if they do?

Well, what if you thought of yourself as "schizophrenic"? Is that helpful in any way?

But aren't the same things helpful for someone with a "borderline personality disorder" as for someone with a schizophrenic-type disorder?

Definitely not. For example, the major tranquilizer medications don't seem to be especially helpful. In fact, many "borderlines" will actually feel worse and in even less control if they take them. Furthermore, a whole different set of issues are involved concerning the value of hospitalization and concerning the types of therapy which are most helpful.

Do you think we should get rid of the term *borderline?*

Absolutely not. As with the term *schizophrenic-type disorder*, it's a useful term for clinicians or researchers to describe certain sorts of problems.[5] In recent years the definition has become more precise,[6] and the writings of several authors, most notably Kernberg, Kohut, and Masterson, have contributed greatly to our understanding of the difficulties encountered by certain types of borderline personalities. But everyone should be clear, most of all the "borderline" individuals themselves, that they don't go on to become "schizophrenic." They merely go on being miserable, outraged, desperate, despondent, or furious, as the case may be.

THE BORDERLINE CONDITION

The world described in so much of twentieth-century fiction is the world of the borderline. Things happen. One is pushed and shoved this way and that, victimized, enslaved in a world that lacks any ultimate meaning. It seems, as Shakespeare wrote, "a tale told by an idiot, full of sound and fury, signifying nothing." It is the world of the existentialist antiheroes, of the wasteland and the hollow men. We meet the ubiquitous borderline in the plays of Beckett, Ionesco, and Albee, in the novels of Kafka, Proust, Fitzgerald, Sartre, Camus, Durrell, and Bernhard, in the films of Bergman, Resnais, Antonioni, Fellini, and Altman, and in the works of numerous other chroniclers of the "absurd" or of the emptiness and futility of life. We see people who go through the motions of living, doing what they're expected to do, trying to care about what they're supposed to care about, while inside there's a howling void, inside everything seems, in the final analysis, stupid, or cruel, or senseless, or utterly absurd. They spend their lives searching for ideals which always fail them (waiting for Godot). They vacillate between fantastic hopes and frustrated furies. They dedicate themselves to fanatical obsessions, somehow hoping to fill up the emptiness with manufactured meanings. But even if successful, they can never be loved enough; they can never triumph enough. Their longings are insatiable, their emptiness infinite. Some may become presidents, dictators, millionaires, scholars, artists, scientists, actors. The world may envy them, while inside they feel every success turned to ashes. They are forever driven, forever seeking, and seemingly never finding.

> [I am] the representative of my inner emptiness, an emptiness that replaces everything else and is not even very great. (Kafka, 1965, p. 323)

Frankl has described such a condition as an "existential

neurosis," Odier as a "neurosis of abandonment," but currently most are content to use the term *borderline*.

Well then, what do we make of all these desperate,
driven, distraught people, people not out of touch with reality, neither deluded nor disorganized in a "schizophrenic"
sense of the term, yet put together in such a way that reality
can never give them enough? What do we make of these
people with their rage, their selfishness, their hollowness,
their seemingly insuperable loneliness (Grinker's definition
of the characteristics of the borderline condition)? What do
we make of these people, whom so many philosophers, and
sociologists, and psychologists, and artists tell us are the
very archtypes of contemporary man, the living testaments
to everything that is wrong with our world? How do we cure
such an "illness"? How do we cure these multitudes upon
multitudes of people storming down the sidewalks and
storming into our lives and occasionally, only occasionally,
storming into the therapist's office, with their fervor and
their fury, their despairs and their obsessions? How do we
calm them down? How do we help them balance the good
against the evil, the kindness against the cruelty, the love
against the indifference, the fullness against the emptiness,
the sense against the senselessness? How do we help them
to give up their impossible dreams? How do we help them to
accept their own limitations and, above all, to accept your
limitations? How do we help them to forgive and forget, to
compromise and be satisfied with so much less than they
demand?

SOME CONCLUDING REMARKS

As may have been deduced from the tenor of my rhetoric
(and my failure to give answers to the above questions), I
have my problems with the ever-more-popular (in clinical

circles) concept of the "borderline syndrome." Those critics who have leveled their big guns at psychiatry for attempting to legislate by fiat the "normal" nature of man by calling strangeness or marked deviance "schizophrenic" would have been more on target if they had aimed their guns at the diagnosis "borderline personality disorder."

Most of the critics argue from one form or another of the premise that since the world is insane (murder, exploitation, oppression, etc.), then it's insane to be sane (i.e., normally adjusted to the collective insanity). Only the insane (the psychotics, the "schizophrenics") are really, in a deeper sense, sane, since they cannot accept an insane reality. Thus the schizophrenic is glorified as the unwitting prophet of sanity. You need only recall the films *Marat/Sade* or *King of Hearts* or *One Flew over the Cuckoo's Nest* to see the popular distillation of this premise. However, such a premise is mistaken and based on an ignorance of what schizophrenic-type disorders are really about, an ignorance this book aims to dispel. Schizophrenic-type disorders are primarily characterized by disorganization, panic, paralysis. To be blunt and oversimplify, they are no more alternative adjustments to an insane reality than breaking your leg is.

If the critics really understood the psychiatric jargon, they would understand that our contemporary world is not properly described as "insane" or "schizophrenic" at all. It has its form of organization, its efficiency, its "rationality," and its progress and development, together with its rage, its selfishness, its hollowness, its seemingly insuperable alienating processes (Grinker again on the borderline syndrome), and its senseless obsessions. In short, to use psychiatric labels *correctly*, the world is not mad, insane, or even "schizophrenic," but "borderline." And to paraphrase Adorno (1972, p. 78), in adjusting to the borderline whole, the cured patient becomes, not schizophrenic, but borderline.

Psychiatrists are already responding to their critics and cutting down greatly on their use of the label *schizophrenic*. But what is occurring, almost imperceptibly—behind the scenes, as it were—is a greatly increased use of the label *borderline personality disorder*. It becomes apparent when one sees more and more articles in the literature devoted to "borderline personality disorders" and when one hears, for example, analysts complaining that fewer and fewer "neurotics" are coming in for treatment and more and more "borderlines."

Despite the efforts of some to carefully delimit the label to a group of very disturbed but not schizophrenically disordered individuals, you should recognize that in general the label *borderline* is another wastebasket term used to describe an enormous agglomeration of unusual character types.

The points you should especially remember are the following:

1. These character types have, in general, nothing to do with "schizophrenia."

2. Many of our greatest men and women would fit some current definitions of the "borderline syndrome."

3. What some clinicians may consider to be a "borderline" existence, others (including Camus, Sartre, Heidegger, Wittgenstein, Kierkegaard, Nietzsche, Kafka, Bernhard, Kaufman, and Jaspers) may consider to be a truer, "more authentic" existence.

4. Most of us, if our lives are too painful, too empty, or too defeating (self-defeating, as is usually the case), can always benefit from some help from another human being, whether that other human being be a skilled therapist or a sympathetic friend. There are "more authentic" lives and there are egregiously self-defeating lives, and the two should not be confused.

SUMMARY

1. The *borderline personality* is a term used to describe people whose difficulties seem to lie somewhere between the neurotic-type and schizophrenic-type disorders.

2. As used by many, the "borderline syndrome," like the "schizophrenic syndrome," is a wastebasket or residual category used to describe those people whose lives (especially their "inner" lives) are disturbed or deviant enough so as to seem "almost schizophrenic."

3. Others have used the term *borderline* in a narrower sense to describe a group of angry, self-centered, impulse-ridden, impossibly demanding people plagued with a deep abiding sense of emptiness and alienation.

4. Some individuals described as borderline personalities may have fleeting acute psychotic episodes brought on by stress. However, individuals with borderline-type personalities do not go on to develop chronic schizophrenic-type disorders.

5. Clinicians who use the term *schizophrenia* loosely will diagnose many borderline personalities as "schizophrenic."

6. Many individuals with borderline personalities will diagnose themselves as schizophrenic. (There may be as many "borderlines" as individuals with schizophrenic-type disorders in Schizophrenics Anonymous).

7. Many types of borderline personalities are "abnormal" primarily in the sense that they don't think and feel like the "average man-in-the-street." What some (e.g., psychiatrists) consider a disorder or illness, others (some philosophers, sociologists, artists, etc.) may consider a more authentic or honest existence. ("You can't think decently if you don't want to hurt yourself"—Wittgenstein, quoted in Malcolm, 1958, p. 40).

8. Many of mankind's finest achievements have been brought about by borderline personalities (e.g., Beethoven). Many of mankind's most monstrous crimes have been perpetrated by borderline personalities (e.g., Hitler).

9. However, most individuals with borderline-type personalities are neither geniuses nor monsters, neither existential heroes, nor martyrs to truth, nor victims of magnificent obsessions. Rather, they are the quixotic heroes of their own distortions, martyrs to their own self-defeating behavior, and the victims of their own insatiable longings.

THE
CAUSES
OF THE
SCHIZOPHRENIC-TYPE
DISORDERS

9

An Approach
to the
Developmental
Theories
of Schizophrenia

The literature devoted to explaining why someone with a schizophrenic-type disorder ended up with a schizophrenic-type disorder is enormous. There are numerous reviews of the psychodynamic theories of schizophrenia which devote a page or two to each school of thought. I have found such reviews singularly uninformative (as singularly uninformative as those two-page summaries of relativity theory, or Buddhism, or Freud). I am not going to perpetrate another such review here. In order to gain a proper understanding of what is being hypothesized and why, it is necessary to read the theorists themselves. There is no adequate substitute for this (in the same way, for example, a plot summary of *Hamlet* is no substitute for reading the play itself). Instead, what I would like to provide you with here is a general orientation toward all such theories and an approach toward evaluating them should you care to read further.[1]

CONCERNING PSYCHODYNAMIC EXPLANATIONS

You should be aware that human behavior and personality development (like human history in general) is explainable by an infinite number of constructs (or systems of explanation). I can see or understand your behavior from any number of perspectives—from a Jungian, or a Freudian, or a behaviorist, or a Marxist perspective, for example. Within certain limitations, each system may be an equally valid explanation of why you ended up doing something.

The second point to keep in mind is that the explanation you end up believing ends up changing you. You see yourself from a different perspective; you reinterpret yourself. By your changed behavior you're the living proof that the explanation was "right." Consider the parallel example of a religious conversion. Once you accept one among an infinite possible number of religious systems, it changes you and "explains everything." Though there are significant differences, it will make what I'm saying easier to understand by thinking of someone's psychological theory—of man or of schizophrenia—as somewhat similar to a religious belief system.[2]

A third point is that much of current psychodynamic explanation rests on the remarkable ability of the human mind to think dialectically. The philosopher Hegel legitimatized it (though it goes back as far as the sophists), Marx and Freud perfected it, and ever since then we have gone wild with it, mesmerized and half-blinded by our own brilliance. It's dialectical thought which turns, as easily as flipping a coin, one thing into its opposite. A good dialectician can make freedom look like slavery (Marcuse), war look like "pacification" (State Department jargon), or "crazy," disorganized behavior look "sane" (Laing).[3]

A psychologist who is a good enough dialectician can, after the fact, explain all of your behavior by his theory. A good explanation, of course, is not completely arbitrary, but you should be aware that when we're talking about an explanation of how or why someone came to act or think in a particular way (e.g., became "schizophrenic"), we're talking about any number of possible explanations, any one of which may prove more or less useful in helping the person to view and understand himself or herself *in a new way,* and thus enable or inspire the individual to *make changes,* hopefully for the better. The fact that the explanation (or the religious belief system) is accepted and that it has enabled the individual to change is then accepted as proof that the explanation is "true" (or that the religious belief system is the "true" religion).

AN APPROACH TO THE DEVELOPMENTAL THEORIES OF SCHIZOPHRENIA

You should be aware of one glaring fact concerning all the developmental theories of schizophrenia:

They are based on the reports of adults with schizophrenic-type reactions remembering their childhood.

Think about that for a moment. And remember what I said above about "true" explanations. A few theories (most notably Laing's and Lidz's) are based on intensive observations of the interactions in the families of individuals who have already developed a schizophrenic-type disorder. Their impressions about hypothetical childhood family interactions have thus a somewhat more objective basis than impressions based on the individual's report alone. But basically the point made above stands. A corollary to the above point would be that since we are dealing primarily with historical reconstructions and historical explanations, *any developmental theory of schizophrenia which is dialectical enough will be able to explain, after the fact, why a given adult developed a schizophrenic-type disorder.*

Some of the theories which are "dialectical enough" to explain the development of schizophrenia include Freudian theory, Jungian theory, Kleinian theory, existential theories (Binswanger, Sartre), double-bind theories (Bateson, Haley, Laing), Pavlovian theory (popular in the Soviet Union, not here), social-learning theories (Sullivan, Lidz), and various sociopolitical theories (Szasz, Foucault, the later Laing).

Currently there is little basis for deciding among all these various theories. Only by carefully following the development of individuals who eventually manifest schizophrenic-type disorders will we be able to sort out some of these theories. In the past decade several prospective studies have been undertaken of "high-risk" individuals (for example, individuals both of whose parents have had a chronic schizophrenic-type disorder), and the information they provide over the next decades should prove most valuable.[4]

AN EXAMPLE:
THE SCHIZOPHRENOGENIC MOTHER

Arieti in the first edition of his classic text on schizophrenia leaned heavily on the concept of the "schizophrenogenic" mother, contending that almost every individual with a schizophrenic-type disorder had a mother who treated him in a seriously disturbed way, thus generating the disorder. His patients told him about how terrible their mothers were when they were growing up, and apparently whatever contacts Arieti had with the patients' mothers confirmed this hypothesis. In the second edition of his text he essentially recants, saying he finds that "only 25% of the mothers of schizophrenics fit the image of the schizophrenogenic mother" (Arieti, 1974, p. 81). He now considers the patients' stories of their terrible mothers to be in most instances distortions and falsifications. Sharpening his dialectical edge, he now recognizes the very real possibility that the disorganized child may have produced the disorganized mother, and not vice versa.[5]

But how is one to decide? What was the actual situation? The best way to know is to have been there yourself to observe and not to have to depend on retrospective reports. This is what the prospective studies on high-risk children attempt to do.

I should emphasize that I'm not at all discounting the value of the observations or theoretical perspectives of so many dedicated clinicians and researchers. I am only saying that, limited as they have been thus far to historical reconstructions of the childhoods of individuals who later develop a "psychosis of unknown origin," any number of historical (developmental) explanations of the events leading to a schizophrenic-type disorder are possible. Like astronomy before Galileo invented the telescope, we haven't had the kind of observations needed to decide which of several competing theories (the earth is the center of the universe, the sun is, etc.) best fits the facts.

And even after we have a much better, more direct knowledge of the actual childhoods of individuals who develop schizophrenic-type disorders, there will still remain any number of alternative ways of interpreting the events, each of which will have its own limited validity.

Further, in reading about anyone's developmental theory of schizophrenia, it should be recognized that clinicians have a tendency to treat only those patients who fit their theories (the other ones often aren't accepted into therapy, or drop out) and to base their theories more on their successes than their inevitable failures. Thus their explanations may very well be "correct," but they may only apply to a very select subgroup of individuals with schizophrenic-type disorders.

For all we know, various opposing explanations of how "schizophrenia" develops may not be "opposing" at all. They may simply be describing different subgroups within the overall group of "psychoses of unknown origin."

Thus some individuals with a schizophrenic-type disorder may have been left with a severe defect in reality sense ("ego") as a result of disastrous conditions during their first year of life (Freudian or Kleinian theories); while others may have started out perfectly well and over the course of their childhood learned to think and feel in a "schizophrenic" way for a number of different reasons—because of double-binds (Bateson) or other disordered parental communication patterns (Lidz, Wynne), and so on.

You see what a dilemma we're in. As I've said repeatedly, we don't know if "schizophrenia" is one disorder, or many disorders produced in many different ways, including many different developmental ways. *We don't know if we should be looking for one theory or many theories.* Then again, we don't know for any given individual which theories among an infinite possible number of theories (or explanations) fit his or her actual childhood best. Finally, even if we are able to observe the actual childhood (through prospective studies), we still have a lot of equally valid theories, or explanations, or perspectives to choose from.

I imagine you're feeling fairly fed up with my qualifications by now and are wishing I would just tell you about "schizophrenogenic mothers" and "double-binds" and "fixations at the oral stage" and "regressions to paleologic thinking" and "pseudomutualities" and "bad breasts" and all the rest. But you can read about all that elsewhere. It's much more important that you know what you're doing when you're reading anyone's particular theory of schizophrenia. Once you begin reading in the literature you'll encounter so many different claims and theories and explanations that you'll probably turn away from it all in disgust, feeling like you've just stumbled into some medieval debate on the relative workings of the four humors. Or else you'll accept lock, stock, and barrel the author who has the winningest style (for most, Laing and Szasz win hands down) or whose ideas most conform to your own misconceptions. One of the ways to save yourself from some of these fates is to keep the skeptical yet very realistic approach I've outlined above continually in mind. Thus when someone tells you, for example, that "schizophrenia is caused by the conditions of political repression in our society," you'll know how to put such information in its proper perspective.

THE BRIEFEST OF OVERVIEWS: THE THEORIES

Infamous Infancies. Basing themselves in part on the importance placed by Freudian theory on "good-enough mothering" (Winicott) during infancy (the "oral" phase) for establishing a stable sense of self and of the world, and finding support in studies by Spitz and Bowlby and others concerning the disastrous results of maternal deprivation during infancy, many theorists have assumed that individuals with chronic schizophrenic-type disorders must have had disastrous experiences (all "bad breast," to use Kleinian terminology) during their infancy. The theorists differ in how they conceptualize this disastrous experience—for example, whether it's due to relatively subtle or relatively gross "pathological mothering." Most of the psychoanalytically oriented theorists ascribe to one form or another of this hypothesis. They differ in how much emphasis they give to the uninhibited reign of primitive passions (libidinal drives or "id") versus a defective sense of self and the world (the dominance of primary-process thinking or weak "ego boundaries").[6]

Ferocious Families. The disastrous infancy theories see the individual as pretty much set on his or her "schizophrenic" course by the first year of life. Subsequent experiences only help to minimize the damage. Other theorists see subsequent experiences as all-important. Since the family is the dominating force throughout childhood and adolescence, they see the family as determining whether someone later develops a schizophrenic-type disorder. Instead of emphasizing some basic defect (of ego, or sense of self, or reality testing, etc.) within the individual, they emphasize basic defects in the family structure. They tend to see the family as "sick" or deviant. The individual with a schizophrenic-type disorder is merely the family "scapegoat" or the "labeled sick person." The theorists differ in how they see the family determining the individual's "schizophrenic adjustment." Some, for example, emphasize that the "schizophrenia" is not really irrational or "crazy" at all. It's one of the few possible ways of dealing with impossible demands (e.g., "double-binds"). Others hypothesize that the individual with a schizophrenic-type disorder has learned to think and communicate in a "crazy" way as a result of the "crazy" ways his parents communicate. There are numerous other variations, some attributing a more active role, others a more passive role, to the "sick" family member; some emphasizing the reasonableness of the individual's adjustment to the situation, others stressing the individual's increasing helplessness and "regression to childlike magical solutions."[7]

Cruel Worlds. Some theorists, while recognizing the importance of mothering during infancy and of the entire family experience during childhood, view the problem of "schizophrenia" from an even broader perspective. In simplest terms, they see the "sick individual" to be a reflection of a sick society. Modern society creates disordered families (viz. the rising divorce rate) and consequently disordered individuals—individuals who, even if they survive their upbringing, still have to go out into a "sick world." Once again the individual can be viewed as actively making an appropriate "adjustment" to a crazy world or as passively being "driven crazy" by it.[8]

SOME FINAL POINTS

First, it should be remembered that all of the above theories are just that—theories.

Second, most of the currently popular theories do *not* view the parents as "mentally ill" or "schizophrenic," and certainly not as evil or sadistic or intentionally perverse or negligent. The "guilty" parents are generally viewed as good-intentioned but inadvertently "on the wrong track." The theories are talking about very subtle types of interactions (e.g., types of physical contact during the first months of life, or types of communication patterns during later childhood), which, until quite recently, *even psychologists had failed to recognize.* (How then were the parents supposed to have recognized them?)

Third, most recent developmental theories have let genetics and biochemistry in "by the back door." They recognize that some individuals don't develop schizophrenic-type disorders despite the most apparently psychopathological or "schizophrenogenic" environment. Consequently, while reserving the preeminent place for developmental factors, they recognize that some individuals may be constitutionally more disposed to "break down" than others. They also recognize that emotional upheavals may cause biochemical upheavals, and that various biochemical-emotional chain reactions can thus be set in motion.

SUMMARY

1. Developmental theories attempt to explain how experiences during infancy and childhood produce someone who will develop a schizophrenic-type disorder. Most theories are referring to individuals with chronic schizophrenic-type disorders, not someone who may have had an isolated acute "psychotic break."

2. There are numerous different developmental theories. They are all based on historical reconstructions of the childhood of individuals who later develop schizophrenic-type disorders. Just as there are numerous ways of explaining historical events, so there are numerous ways of explaining the development of "schizophrenia," each of which may have its own limited validity.

3. Prospective studies of children at high risk to develop schizophrenic-type disorders are currently underway and should prove helpful in sorting out some of the theories.

4. I've divided the theories into three groups: infamous infancy" theories, "ferocious family" theories, and "cruel world" theories. There is absolutely no substitute to reading the theorists themselves for gaining a proper understanding of what is being hypothesized and why.

5. Despite the talk of improper mothering and "sick families," it should be recognized that few theorists now view the family members of someone who develops a schizophrenic-type disorder as necessarily mentally ill or schizophrenic, and certainly not as evil or sadistic or intentionally perverse or negligent. Parents are generally viewed as good-intentioned but inadvertently "on the wrong track."

6. Many of the developmental theories are probably valid *partial* explanations of why *a limited number* of individuals develop schizophrenic-type disorders.

7. Currently we don't know whether we should be looking for one theory or explanation or many theories. For any given individual we don't know how much of a role genetic or biochemical factors may also be playing in the development of his or her schizophrenic-type disorder.

10

Schizophrenia as an Inherited Disorder

The subjects of the epidemiology and genetics of the psychoses of unknown origin have generated an enormous amount of research during the past fifty years. As soon as you begin to consider the details of all the studies with their myriad differences in methodology, you begin to feel as though you've wandered into something remotely resembling a bog. Numerous reviews are being written all the time summarizing the primary conclusions to be derived from the mass of the literature. Unfortunately, the primary conclusions you're supposed to reach according to one authoritative reviewer are often the very opposite of the ones you're supposed to reach according to some other authoritative reviewer.[1]

In attempting to simplify and clarify the situation, the best I can hope to do in this chapter is to present some of the basic data and to give you some idea of the controversy surrounding it.

Before delving into the data on inheritance, some discussion of the general occurrence of schizophrenic-type psychoses is in order.

HOW FREQUENTLY DO THE PSYCHOSES OF UNKNOWN ORIGIN OCCUR?

The figure most commonly encountered in population studies of the frequency of "psychoses of unknown origin" is a lifetime rate of about 1 percent; that is, one out of every hundred or so people "walking down the street" may be expected to have at some time or another in their lives a psychotic nervous breakdown diagnosed as schizophrenic.

Of course, how one defines *schizophrenia* will determine the number of individuals diagnosed as schizophrenic. The 1-percent figure is derived from studies where a narrow definition of *schizophrenia* was used (corresponding roughly to Manfred Bleuler's given in Chapter 3). If one were to use a looser definition, and thus include all the individuals in Figure 3 (Chapter 4) and not merely the small "chronic schizophrenia" wedge, then the incidence figure would be considerably higher than 1 percent. For example, a recent National Institute of Mental Health report (Research Task Force, 1975) indicated that one out of twenty American children who survive beyond the age of fifteen will develop schizophrenia sometime during their lives.

This statement, as you should be aware by now, is highly misleading and representative of what is wrong with our use of mental illness labels. One out of twenty American children will not develop anything like a chronic schizophrenic-type disorder. They will develop a variety of disorders which American psychiatrists like to call schizophrenia but of which only about 20 percent would be called schizophrenia elsewhere. Nonetheless, 5 percent of us (one out of every twenty) is given a label which in the popular mind is synonymous with such reprehensible terms as *madman, maniac,* and *lunatic.*

The occurrence of individuals diagnosed as schizophrenic varies from population to population. In one review (Rosenthal, 1970) it varied from a low of three per thousand individuals (0.3 percent, Berlin in the 1930s), to a high of three per hundred (3 percent, Geneva, Switzerland, in the 1960s). It has been noted to occur, with varying frequencies, in all societies, from the simplest to the most technologically advanced. Some of the variation is undoubtedly due to different (or for some societies, inappropriate) criteria for diagnosing psychosis of unknown origin. But there also seems to be a genuine variation. The explanations for this variation come hot and heavy in the literature. One investigator summarizes a great array of studies by concluding that schizophrenic-type psychoses occur more frequently in "Westernized technological societies"; another finds an increased incidence in isolated rural areas. Given the current situation, one can interpret one's data to support about almost any conclusion one wants concerning what causes schizophrenia. One can, for example, assume that the small, isolated Japanese or Swedish village, as has been reported, has a high rate because of genetic inbreeding, or because of its relative isolation from the rest of society. You can pick either explanation, or any of several others, depending on what you want your conclusion to be.[2]

POVERTY, SOCIAL CLASS, AND SCHIZOPHRENIA

Many studies have shown an increased proportion of individuals diagnosed as having schizophrenic-type psychoses of unknown origin in the lowest class, or more simply, among the poor. This seems to be the case, at least in our society, and at least in the larger cities. Why it's the case isn't clear. Poor people tend to be hospitalized and labeled "schizophrenic" more frequently than their upper-class peers. Higher-class individuals with chronic maladjustment, including psychoses of unknown origin, tend to drift down to lower-level employment or unemployment. Finally, genetic or environmental factors associated with the stresses of poverty may be playing a role. Currently we can make no more than educated guesses.

You should be very sceptical of any "expert" proclaiming that this kind of society, or this kind of political system, or this kind of social class, or this kind of life-style is the cause of schizophrenia, "craziness," psychosis, "madness," or whatever. Quite simply, most of the data could probably as well be interpreted in line with *your* prejudices, whatever they might be, as with those of the supposed expert. (You need only remind yourself of the current controversies concerning IQ and race to get an idea of what I'm talking about.)[3]

THE BASIC DATA

If someone has a schizophrenic-type disorder, what is the likelihood that another member of the family will be diagnosed as having a similar type of disorder? The following data are based on tables compiled by Rosenthal (1970, pp. 106–26). The given figure is the median percentage; that is, half of the studies reported higher percentages and half lower percentages. The median thus gives a representative middle value.

1. Parents: 4% (studies range from 0.2 to 12%)
2. Siblings (brothers or sisters): 7% (range 3 to 14%)
3. Nonidentical twin: 8% (range 2 to 11%)
4. Identical twin: 33% (range 0 to 69%)
5. Children: 10% (range 7 to 17%)
6. Grandchildren: 3% (range 2 to 6%)
7. Nephews and nieces: 2% (range 1 to 4%)

What should especially be kept in mind in understanding the above data are the following:

1. Most of the above studies are based on looking at someone who has a relatively *severe chronic* form of a schizophrenic psychosis of unknown origin.

2. The more recent studies in general report *much lower* rates than the older studies. (This is probably not a reflection of any changing incidence of the psychoses of unknown origin but rather of more precise design and methodology in the research.)

3. The studies don't say *how much* of the increased incidence of psychotic-type illnesses in family members is due to environment or learning (the hypothesis being that schizophrenic parents may teach their children to be schizophrenic also). Several of the studies on adopted children, however, control for this variable to a certain extent.

4. The studies don't demonstrate that an illness ("schizophrenia") is inherited—as, for example, are mongolism and cleft palate—only that a *predisposition* to a psychotic schizophrenic-type nervous breakdown in *some* individuals *may* be inherited. Why one child of a schizophrenic parent, or

one identical twin, develops, at some point in his or her life, a schizophrenic-type disorder, transient or chronic, and why another doesn't, isn't known. With identical twins, who have precisely the same genes, environment must certainly play a role.

FAMILIES OF INDIVIDUALS WHO HAVE HAD AN ACUTE SCHIZOPHRENIC-TYPE EPISODE

As noted, many of the genetic studies would not even include a good proportion of such relatively well-adjusted individuals with "acute psychotic episodes" in their definition of *schizophrenia.*

Studies which have carefully distinguished schizoaffective type disorders from other schizophrenic-type disorders have tended to find a greater incidence of *manic-depressive-type illness* in the individual's relatives and *not* of schizophrenic-type disorders.

A recent very influential (because of it's extremely careful design) study carried out by a group of American and Danish investigators (Kety, et al., 1968) looked at individuals who had been adopted at a very early age. *Relatively well-adjusted individuals who had had an "acute schizophrenic" psychotic reaction showed no instances of schizophrenic-type disorders in their family members.* On the other hand, individuals with a chronic schizophrenic-type disorder showed an incidence of schizophrenic-type disorders in their family members similar to that detailed in the section above. Since the individuals who developed schizophrenia were raised by, in general, psychologically healthy nonschizophrenic, presumably "nonschizophrenogenic," foster parents, the increased incidence, above an appropriate control group, of the psychoses of unknown origin was almost certainly due, in part at least, to genetic factors.[4]

This study also showed that borderline schizophrenic disorders (the chronically disturbed not-quite-schizophrenic group of disorders discussed in Chapter 8) tended to run in the same families as those showing schizophrenic-type disorders. The conclusion, however, should not be that we are dealing with one disorder, "schizophrenia," and that "borderline schizophrenia" is a milder variant of it, thus justifying our use of the single disease label *schizophrenia* for all such individuals. Suffice it to say here that so far as schizophrenia is concerned, we are probably dealing with many types of disorders, *some* of which may have milder forms.[5]

MENTAL DEFICIENCY AND THE PSYCHOSES OF UNKNOWN ORIGIN

On the issue of the relation of mental deficiency to schizophrenia, I will simply quote Rosenthal's summary statement:

> Psychologists have a long history of trying to establish whether the intelligence levels of schizophrenics are different from those of the population at large. Although the literature is uneven, there is no certain evidence to indicate mental deficiency is more common among schizophrenics than among well-matched controls. (Rosenthal, 1970, p. 177)

There is no clear relationship between susceptibility to a schizophrenic-type "nervous breakdown" and intelligence level.[6] *If someone has had a schizophrenic-type "nervous breakdown," one cannot draw **any** conclusions about that person's intelligence.* It is a favorite pastime of some commentators to collect the names of geniuses who have been schizophrenic. I will spare you the relatively lengthy list.

IS SCHIZOPHRENIA INHERITED?

Most studies to date have shown an increased occurrence of the psychoses of unknown origin in **some** *families. However, approximately 90 percent of the individuals diagnosed as schizophrenic will not have any similarly diagnosed disorder in their families.* [7] Thus some individuals who develop a psychosis of unknown origin or schizophrenic-type disorder may have inherited a specific predisposition to such a disorder. With many others who have had a psychosis of unknown origin, there's no reason to implicate genetic factors.

Some other, more tentative conclusions to be drawn from genetic studies are the following:

The severer, more chronic, and more debilitating the disorder, the more likely one is to find similar disorders among other family members.

The corollary to the above is:

The milder psychoses of unknown origin—the acute or good-prognosis schizophrenic-type disorders—show little if any incidence of similar disorders in family members.

Thus, practically speaking, most individuals with an acute schizophrenic-type "nervous breakdown" don't need to concern themselves with possible genetic factors. The only two groups of individuals that should give some thought to the matter are the following:

1. Those individuals with a severe, disabling, chronic schizophrenic-type disorder. However, studies show that well over 50 percent of such individuals show *no* evidence of similar disorders in their families. For those who do, especially if *several* family members have had a psychosis of unknown origin, serious consideration should be given to possible contributing genetic factors.

2. It probably behooves any individual who has had a psychotic "nervous breakdown" and who has had one or, more importantly, several family members with similar problems to give some consideration to possible genetic factors.

All of the above statements should be interpreted in light of the fact that many experts up to the present day disagree greatly about the role of inheritance in the psychoses of unknown origin. Some will deny it is of any significant importance. They maintain that all the findings can be explained by an unfortunate childhood and situational stresses. Others will go to the opposite extreme and say that inheritance appears to be the most important factor in determining why some people develop schizophrenia. (It should be noted that they are almost always referring to the *severe chronic psychoses*.) Most experts take a moderate, middle-of-the-road stand and feel that inheritance may be important in some individuals and in others not so, or, more commonly, that you can't separate out inheritance and environment that well. We clearly inherit things (Chinese children do not look like English children). And we clearly learn things. We inherit a potential which we either develop by learning or which we leave undeveloped. So, most experts would have it, it's reasonable to presume some individuals may inherit a potential or predisposition to be extraordinary, in either a good or a bad way, and either will learn to develop it—into genius or psychosis or whatever—or will leave it undeveloped.

SUMMARY

1.   Forget all your fiction- and Hollywood-inspired notions of hereditary taints, inherited insanity, and so forth.

2.   Genetic factors can be demonstrated to play a role in only a relatively small number of individuals who have had a schizophrenic-type psychotic "nervous breakdown" (less than 10 percent).

3. Conversely, even in families where schizophrenic-type disorders occur, they occur in general in only a small percentage of the family members (of the order of one out of ten for first-degree relatives).

4. The acute psychotic "nervous breakdowns" occurring in relatively well-adjusted individuals show virtually no tendency to be inherited.

5. Genetic factors may play a role in the disorders of some individuals with a chronic disabling schizophrenic-type disorder (though probably in less than half). There is also a suggestion they may play a role in some "borderline" schizophrenic-type disorders.

6. The role heredity plays, in those instances where it may be implicated, is very subtle and complex. It probably determines a predisposition to certain extraordinary ways of reacting and feeling. Why one person becomes psychotic and another doesn't isn't known at present.

11

Biochemical
Theories

Throughout this book I have been describing schizophrenia, or the schizophrenic-type disorders, as a residual group of psychoses of unknown origin. There are of course many theories about what causes schizophrenia, but no one theory has been generally agreed upon to give the answer. In fact, given the current state of knowledge, for any group of experts supporting one particular theory—for example, that the schizophrenic-type disorders are primarily a result of inheritance or of a biochemical disorder—you will find an equal number of experts holding to precisely the opposite theory—for example that the schizophrenic-type disorders are primarily the result of disturbed communication patterns within the family. In short, we have many theories, but no answer to the question: What causes schizophrenia?

The question itself is a loaded one, akin to "When did you stop beating your wife?" because it presupposes that (1) schizophrenia is one illness, and not a variety of disorders, and (2) this one illness has one primary cause. (What causes the grass to grow—sunshine or water? The answer, of course, is both.) In terms of our current state of knowledge, the diagnosis of schizophrenia, as has already been pointed out, is similar to the diagnosis of "sore throat" and may well be a term describing a variety of disorders, with a variety of very dissimilar causes, just as a sore throat may be caused by shouting too much, or by a viral or bacterial infection, or by an allergy, and so on.

One of the primary areas of investigation throughout the decades has been the search for a biochemical cause of the psychoses of unknown origin.[1] Over the years a multitude of exciting "discoveries" have been made as to the possible cause of schizophrenia. Almost all of these discoveries have amounted to no more than leads which failed to lead anywhere—except in most instances to better-designed, better-controlled studies the next time around. Given the enormous amount of research which has been carried out over the decades on individuals with schizophrenic-type disorders, it's only too easy to see why so many "positive" findings concerning this or that "cause" of schizophrenia have turned up, since about one out of every twenty such experiments will, by chance alone, come up with a "significant correlation," or positive finding, when in fact there is no actual relationship. This is due to the fact that many studies define a significant finding as one which would occur by chance alone only one time out of twenty (called in the literature the "5 percent level of significance"). Thus if twenty studies are made of the relationship between being born before noon and having a schizophrenic-type disorder, one out of twenty will find a "significant correlation." This study will be reported in the literature. The nineteen negative studies usually will not be considered worth reporting.

The way to find out if in fact there is a relationship (between, for example, a particular vitamin deficiency and schizophrenia) is to repeat the same study several times, preferably by several groups of completely independent investigators. Then the probability that the "significant" result occurred by chance alone becomes minimal. Most of the heralded discoveries as to the probable cause of schizo-phrenia, often given sensational press coverage, have died quite unheralded deaths, laid low by other investigators simply repeating the original experiments and finding quite different results.

But then there have been a number of results which have survived the acid test of independent replication. Most of these "positive findings" died a different sort of death. In prior decades, in order to ensure that the subjects were guaranteed "schizophrenics," most studies involved patients from mental hospitals with a diagnosis of chronic schizophrenia. Many of these patients had been hospitalized for ten or twenty years or more. As we have since discovered, living for many years on the back ward of a mental hospital does terrible things to the human being, body, mind, and spirit. Their mental deterioration was the result of years of neglect and isolation, and many of their physical, including biochemical, peculiarities turned out to be a result of the life we condemned them to—that is, institutionalization—and not of any "schizophrenia" per se. For example, vitamin deficiencies may have been found among such patients because of the unappetizing diet they were forced to eat. Certain unusual substances may have been present in their blood or urine simply because, for example, they drank more tea (the "pink spot in schizophrenic's urine") or took certain medications (the "mauve factor"). Their general physiological functioning, with its attendant biochemical and hormonal changes, may have been subtly (or grossly) altered because they were isolated in dreadfully unstimulating environments with little opportunity, let alone incentive, for physical activity. Most of the older organic theories of the cause of schizophrenia have died honorable, or in some instances slightly dishonorable, deaths.[2] This includes most theories involving gross abnormalities in the brain, ranging from tumors or infections to differences in the cellular structure of the brain. *The general consensus of opinion currently is that the brain, or central nervous system, in individuals with schizophrenic-type disorders shows no evident structural abnormality.* There are no evident "missing" or "peculiar" parts.

THE DISORDERED-TRANSMITTER HYPOTHESIS

The leading biochemical hypothesis today—and to date it remains only a hypothesis—is that the reason the central nervous system in such individuals appears to function so peculiarly at times is that there is some interference with the conduction of nervous impulses from one cell to another in certain important areas of the brain.

If I decide I want to move my foot, then a nerve impulse is relayed through a chain of neurons (nerve cells) to the muscles in my leg, causing them to contract. How does the nervous impulse bridge the gap between one nerve cell and the next? The answer which has been meticulously worked out is that the impulse is passed on from one cell to another by means of chemical transmitters. In a series of falling dominoes, the weight of each domino falling causes the next one to fall; in a chain of firing neurons, each neuron releases a spray of chemical molecules which "fall on" the next neuron, causing it in turn to depolarize or fire off its packet of chemical molecules at the next neuron "down the line." Given this mechanism, which has been conclusively demonstrated to be involved in central nervous system functioning, one can imagine all sorts of possibilities for dysfunction. The firing cell may release too few or too many transmitter molecules. The cell on the receiving end may be hypersensitive and, for example, fire when only one molecule touches it, or utterly insensitive, refusing to react no matter how many molecules come banging at its door. Another possibility is that there may be "false molecules" floating around, molecules which impersonate or mimic the molecules which the nerve itself fires. It can easily be imagined what kind of chaos these might cause in this most exquisitely tuned of all systems.

It's currently a hypothesis—or speculation, to put it more bluntly—that some or all of the schizophrenic-type psychoses of unknown origin are caused by a dysfunction of the chemical transmitters. A great deal of vigorous, fascinating, and elegant research is currently being conducted in this area. There are many reasons for the current enthusiasm for such research. It would certainly be a momentous, almost miraculous discovery for suffering humanity if it turned out that, in fact, a specific biochemical disorder—or put more colorfully, one mad molecule—were responsible for schizophrenia and the vast sum of human suffering which that one term encompasses. So even if the chances are very slim, the fact that there is a *possibility* that there is such a simple answer has been enough to inspire a generation of researchers to truly monumental efforts.

Beyond that one overriding consideration, there are numerous reasons to lead one to suspect that biochemical factors *may* play at least *some* part in at least *some* of the schizophrenic-type disorders or psychoses of unknown origin. (You may be getting tired of my qualifications, but it's important *always* to make these qualifications when discussing "schizophrenia," even if it is tiresome. There may be other areas where lazy, oversimplified thinking won't mislead you too much, but not here. You will be led down someone's garden path—the geneticist's, or biochemist's, or Laing's, or Szasz's, etc., unless you constantly keep such qualifications in mind.) Some of the evidence suggesting that biochemical factors may be involved relate to the effects of hallucinogens, amphetamines, and the major tranquilizer drugs.[3]

THE EFFECTS OF HALLUCINOGENS

We're all familiar with the fact that LSD, mescaline, and other such "hallucinogenic" drugs can produce extremely bizarre states of mind, including hallucinations and delusions of every variety. What's particularly interesting about these strange states of mind is that they're qualitatively different from "deliriums." Any number of poisons, intoxicants, or metabolic disorders can produce a delirious state which is usually characterized by extreme confusion and disorientation in addition to hallucinations and delusions. As discussed previously, such organic deliriums present a picture that bears little resemblance to schizophrenic-type disorders, which typically occur in a state of relatively clear consciousness—that is, without any sleepy or "drugged" feeling, without great confusion (for example, you can add 3 + 3 + 3 + 3 and come out with 12), and without significant disorientation (for example you know perfectly well who you are and where you are). Someone under the influence of a moderate dose of LSD or other hallucinogen will typically be in a state of relatively clear consciousness, with minimal confusion or disorientation despite all the amazing things he or she may be experiencing. LSD psychoses were thus felt to bear a much greater resemblance to a schizophrenic-type psychosis than to an organic delirium. It was felt if we could understand the way these drugs produced psychosis, we might be able to understand the way it is produced in individuals with a schizophrenic-type disorder. As discussed in Chapter 3, when it became clear that hallucinogen-produced psychotic states differed in fairly typical ways from the typical schizophrenic-type psychosis, much of the initial enthusiasm for the role the hallucinogens might play in solving the mysteries of the psychoses of unknown origin began to wane. However, there remain certain intriguing facts about these substances.

First of all, the structure, or part of the structure, of many of the hallucinogens mimics the structure of some of the naturally occurring chemical transmitters in the brain—specifically, the structures of serotonin, norepinepherine and dopamine. This indicates that a substance which probably acts by interfering with the chemical transmission mechanism—and not, for example, by "poisoning the cell"—can produce what would conventionally be termed "craziness," and most importantly, not the kind of "craziness" associated with a delirious state of mind, but a "craziness" which bears a strong, though not complete, resemblance to the "craziness" seen in some individuals with a schizophrenic-type psychosis.

Secondly, some of these hallucinogenic substances are effective at astoundingly minute doses. LSD in particular is a drug of almost unparalleled potency, enormous effects being produced by what, biologically speaking, amounts to only a few molecules. This indicates that states of schizophreniclike "craziness" can be produced by minute alterations in chemical transmitters in minute, very specialized centers of the brain. Thus there is the possibility that the totally encompassing, world-shattering, and devastating experience which occurs during so many acute schizophrenic-type psychotic reactions may be due to some dysfunction of the chemical transmitters in a miniscule but vitally important regulatory center of the brain.

There are a number of investigators pursuing the hypothesis that the schizophrenic-type disorders—or at least *some* of the schizophrenic-type disorders—are produced by hallucinogenic substances which the body makes in abnormal quantities. Many different substances have at one time or another been implicated. One of the most controversial was a substance called "adenochrome," which enjoyed a sensational career in the 1950s. It was found to òccur in the blood of individuals with schizophrenic-type disorders and not in normals' blood. It was also found to produce a schizophreniclike state. However, subsequent work by independent investigators failed to confirm either of these findings.[4] One reviewer summed up the situation as follows: "The drug was no more active than tap water. . . . [The breakthrough] was.no more than another demonstration of the extraordinary power of suggestion" (Snyder, 1974, p. 57).

In terms of our current knowledge, what you should bear in mind is: *There is simply no convincing evidence to date that individuals with schizophrenic-type disorders produce any abnormal hallucinogenlike substance.* It is of course possible. My own suspicion is that since hallucinogen-type substances can be produced, even if only in trace amounts, in the human body, it is certainly reasonable to hypothesize that some individuals with a psychosis of unknown origin *may* have their psychosis on this basis. But it would probably be only a relatively small number of individuals, constituting a small fraction of the total number of individuals with schizophrenic-type reactions. Further, as long as researchers continue to look primarily at the total population of "schizophrenics" (based on the hypothesis it's all "one illness") instead of very select subgroups, they are not likely to identify such individuals, since the significance of individual differences tends to get lost in the analysis of group averages. In any case, *to date, no such subgroups have been identified. Anyone who indicates that such subgroups have been definitely identified is simply misinforming you.*

THE AMPHETAMINE ("SPEED") PARANOID PSYCHOSIS

Two of the chemical transmitters in the central nervous system that are thought to be of particular importance in schizophrenic-type psychoses are norepinephrine and dopamine. A chemical substance called amphetamine closely resembles these two transmitters. Amphetamine and other substances closely related to it are the primary ingredients in "pep pills," "wake-up pills," and many diet pills. On the street it's known as "speed." In most people a moderate amount causes a feeling of almost euphoric well-being accompanied by a state of intense alertness. Students cramming for an exam or truck drivers on long hauls may end up taking it to ward off sleep. As one of its side effects is a great decrease in appetite, many overweight individuals will end up taking it (as the primary ingredient in their diet pills). Others simply take it for the "high" it gives. In the past it has been used to treat depression, but the general consensus currently is that its effect on depression is only transient and that it creates many more problems than it relieves. *There are other, more effective ways of treating feelings of depression,* and in only rare instances should amphetamines be used.

What is of primary interest to us here, however, is what happens to individuals who take very high doses of amphetamines, particularly those who take high doses for a prolonged period of time. A certain number of such individuals will develop a psychotic state which most clinicians agree is virtually indistinguishable from certain schizophrenic-type paranoid psychoses, complete with auditory hallucinations and a well-organized delusional system. While such a state typically results from prolonged high use, it has also been shown to result from taking a large amount of amphetamine over several days. Such a psychotic paranoid state is not permanent. When the drug is withdrawn, most individuals will undergo a period of abysmal depression (the "crash"). Eventually they return to their usual state of mind, and all the amphetamine-induced hallucinations and paranoid delusions become merely bad memories.

It's now known that amphetamines affect the central nervous system by increasing the number of norepinephrine and dopamine transmitter molecules impinging on the receptor neuron. This puts the receptor neuron in an abnormally stimulated and irritable state. A stimulus which would normally have no effect (that is, which would cause the release of too few transmitter molecules) will now have an effect. There are certain centers deep within the brain that regulate sleep and wakefulness, and it seems fairly clear that amphetamine keeps a person awake by rendering these centers hypersensitive to the least stimulus, by increasing the amount of norepinephrine in the area. It's not clear why amphetamines produce such a distinctive paranoid psychosis. But the fact is they do, and it's a reasonable hypothesis that some naturally occurring schizophrenic-type psychoses, particularly the paranoid psychoses, may be a result of an abnormally irritable state in the same neurons which the amphetamines affect. Unfortunately, to date we don't know which specific neurons are responsible for the amphetamine psychosis. Further, we don't know whether a naturally occurring dysfunction in those neurons is the cause of any one individual's schizophrenic-type reaction. It remains a hypothesis—a very intriguing hypothesis, but nonetheless a hypothesis. If it turns out there are naturally occurring psychotic states produced by the same means as the amphetamine psychoses, it would probably only account for a limited number of the psychoses of unknown origin (see note 3).

THE MAJOR TRANQUILIZERS AND THE DOPAMINE-NOREPINEPHRINE HYPOTHESIS

As will be discussed in Chapter 14, the major tranquilizers are very effective in reducing psychotic symptoms such as hallucinations, delusions, and extremely disorganized thinking. The question is why they are so effective (when various other types of "tranquilizers," such as the sedative "sleeping pills" or minor tranquilizers Valium and Librium, are so ineffective). Clearly these medications are doing something very special. Since the major tranquilizer, a chemical substance, appeared specifically to reverse many of the psychotic symptoms, this pointed to a biochemical imbalance as the underlying basis for the psychotic symptoms. The hope was that if one could discover precisely which central nervous system transmitters the major tranquilizers such as Thorazine affected, then the chemical imbalance which caused "schizophrenia" would be discovered.

A tremendous amount of research has been conducted in this area in the past decade. The major tranquilizer medications have been shown to have a wide range of effects within the central nervous system. One of the problems has been to sort out the important ones from the unimportant ones. Much of the current research is centered around the fact that the major tranquilizer medications are particularly potent in affecting two of the brain's most important chemical transmitters, dopamine and norepinephrine, that is, the same ones which are primarily affected by the amphetamines and some of the hallucinogens.

The major tranquilizers act as "false transmitters" which keep the genuine transmitter molecules from reaching the receptor neurons. Technically, the "impersonator" false transmitters attach themselves to the receptor site, consequently blocking access of the genuine transmitter molecules (dopamine or norepinephrine) to that site. Thus, some researchers currently hypothesize that "schizophrenia" is caused by an overactivity of certain specific dopamine or norepinephrine centers, or tracts, in the brain. The major tranquilizers hypothetically act by blocking some of this overactivity, thus restoring the system's level of activity to normal. (Further, too much major tranquilizer medication, according to this model, would tend to block all activity in the system, thus producing the zombielike emotionally deadened state seen in some individuals who are taking too much medication.)

It should be understood that this particular biochemical hypothesis, the dopamine-norepinephrine hypothesis, like all other biochemical hypotheses as to the cause of the schizophrenic-type disorders, is currently no more than a speculation. There are a number of other neurotransmitters in the central nervous system, and probably a great many which remain to be identified; any number of them, to a greater or lesser extent, may be involved in the causation of some of the schizophrenic-type disorders. Two of the particular difficulties which the dopamine-norepinephrine hypothesis has run into are (1) in many instances the major tranquilizer medications fail to "cure" the "schizophrenia," that is, whatever the drugs are doing to dopamine and other chemical transmitters in the brain, it appears in many instances they aren't doing enough; (2) even though in some individuals there may be a disorder in the dopamine-norepinephrine transmitters, still this may not be the fundamental disorder at all. For example, an infected tooth may produce a tremendous amount of overactivity in the nerves transmitting pain to the brain. The overactivity can be relieved by a nerve block (for example, with Novocain). But the basic problem is the infected tooth, and the basic solution is to treat the infection. Similarly, the basic problem may not be dopamine hyperactivity but a dysfunction elsewhere.

The dopamine-norepinephrine hypothesis is probably the most favored one currently among those investigating biochemical factors involved in the psychoses of unknown origin. It has not received the popular press coverage enjoyed by other theories, which are often presented as discoveries—for example schizophrenia as a vitamin-dependent disease, or schizophrenia as a result of some specific toxic substance in the blood, or schizophrenia as a result of an allergy (or autoimmunity). Nonetheless, among many researchers, the feeling is that the most promising line of investigation at present involves studying the dopamine-norepinephrine and several other closely related chemical transmitter systems (for example, serotonin) in the brain.[5]

There are, however, numerous other hypotheses and numerous other investigators pursuing other biochemical leads. In the following sections some of the more popular competing hypotheses will be outlined briefly.

SCHIZOPHRENIA AS A VITAMIN-DEPENDENT DISEASE

A number of clinicians feel they have cured many individuals with schizophrenic-type psychoses by altering their vi-

tamin intake. Consequently, they have concluded that vitamin deficiency, or a disorder in the individual's utilization of
vitamins, must be contributing to the production of
"schizophrenia." Many other researchers feel there is no
convincing biochemical evidence to support this claim. (See
Chapter 15 on megavitamin therapy.)

SCHIZOPHRENIA AS AN
AUTOIMMUNE DISEASE

If we have an infection—for example, a "strep" throat—the
body makes proteins called antibodies which neutralize
some of the more toxic productions, called antigens, of the
offending organism. There are certain human diseases,
called autoimmune diseases, in which the body mistakenly
makes antibodies against its own cells, that is, it treats them
as invading "foreign bodies." Rheumatoid arthritis is a familiar example. According to the autoimmune hypothesis,
schizophrenia may be caused by the body mistakenly making antibodies against its own brain cells, or against the brain
cells in certain crucial areas in the brain—for example, those
areas where dopamine-norepinephrine chemical transmission is predominant.

Groups of Soviet and American researchers have been
vigorously pursuing this hypothesis. Such researchers are
involved in, among other things, meticulous studies of certain proteins in the blood called globulins. If the body is making specific antibodies against the brain, then the hope is
they can be discovered as an abnormal or abnormally elevated globulin in the blood. To date, research in this area has
produced equivocal results. The main problem has been that
investigators in one lab appear to have great difficulty rep-
licating the findings of those in another lab. Nonetheless,
tentative findings have often received sensational press

coverage announcing the discovery of various "abnormal proteins" or "brain antibodies" in the blood of "schizophrenics." In past years a substance called tarexin received great publicity.[6] In recent years proteins called alpha-2-globulins have received their fair share of notoriety. The important thing to remember is that currently we are dealing with "hypotheses" and "leads" and not "discoveries." No abnormal protein has been shown to be the cause of even *some* of the psychoses of unknown origin, let alone the cause of "schizophrenia" itself. Further—and this is even more discouraging—no abnormal protein or abnormally elevated globulin has been demonstrated to be associated consistently with the schizophrenic-type disorders (at least, consistently by several groups of independent investigators). Though some stimulating and fascinating findings have been reported, the autoimmune hypothesis remains just that—a hypothesis or speculation. It's not the leading hypothesis currently, but it's certainly a reasonable approach to the problem, and, all extravagant claims aside, one can only hope that the labors of a lot of dedicated scientists will eventually prove of some benefit, in an as yet wholly inscrutable way, to at least some of those individuals with schizophrenic-type disorders.[7]

THE SEROTONIN (INDOLEAMINE) HYPOTHESIS

Serotonin is another one of the chemical transmitters in the brain. There is a certain amount of evidence that a disorder in this system may be involved in some of the schizophrenic-type disorders. LSD is a very specific blocker of serotonin chemical transmission. However, as mentioned above, current enthusiasms lean more toward the dopamine hypothesis.

THE BUFOTENIN-DMT HYPOTHESIS

The bufotenin-DMT hypothesis states that certain hallucinogenic substances (bufotenin and DMT) occur abnormally in some individuals and may cause "schizophrenia." Numerous other hallucinogenic substances, including the already-discussed adenochrome, have been hypothesized to be produced by individuals with schizophrenic-type disorders. The above two are mentioned because they are more likely to be mentioned in current press reports than others. At present, most researchers would agree that the evidence supporting any of these "mad molecule" hypotheses is so slim as to be virtually nonexistent. Something may possibly turn up someday, but all claims and popular press reports to the contrary, nothing has turned up yet.[8]

OTHER HYPOTHESES

Other central nervous system transmitter substances have been hypothesized to be abnormal in the schizophrenic-type reactions—for example, a substance called GABA and the recently discovered pain-killing polypeptide "endomorphins."[9] Some have hypothesized, based on the most tenuous evidence, that some of the schizophrenic-type disorders may be due to a "slow virus" infection. In general, almost any new discovery involving the functioning of the brain ends up, at some time or another, being investigated as a possible cause of "schizophrenia" (slow viruses and endomorphins are two recent examples). As discussed already, if enough investigators carry out experiments, some of those experiments will, by chance alone, turn out to be positively related to "schizophrenia." The "successful" experiments are reported in the press. But you should bear in mind that the true test of any of these biochemical findings is consistent replication by a number of independent investigators. This is a process which takes years to accomplish. Once such consistent replication by a number of independent investigators has confirmed the finding, you will find almost all researchers and scientists accepting it as a "fact." From the fact that there is so much controversy surrounding *all* the biochemical theories of schizophrenia, you may safely conclude that the scientific establishment is still dealing with speculations, leads, and tentative findings. (You may apply the same line of reasoning to the latest miracle diets or cancer cures and save yourself from the trouble and, at times, the tragedy of being victimized by other people's ill-founded enthusiasms.)

SUMMARY

1.   There are many theories as to what causes the schizophrenic-type disorders. They all remain to this day precisely that—theories and speculations.

2.   The "cause of schizophrenia," whether biochemical or otherwise, has not yet been established.

3.   There is at present no convincing evidence of a definite biochemical abnormality in the central nervous system of individuals with schizophrenic-type disorders.

4.   There is suggestive evidence that a biochemical abnormality may be involved in the schizophrenic-type disorders of *some* individuals. This is based primarily on the effects of certain chemicals in producing (LSD, amphetamines) or alleviating (the major tranquilizers) schizophrenic-type psychoses.

5.   One of the leading hypotheses at present is that *some* schizophrenic-type disorders may be caused by a disorder in

certain specific chemical transmitters (dopamine and nore-pinephrine) in important areas of the brain. This, however, is only a promising lead for further research and far from being an established fact.

6. There are numerous competing hypotheses as to the cause of the psychoses of unknown origin. Schizophrenic-type disorders have been hypothesized to be the result of a vitamin-dependent or of an autoimmune disease (tarexin and alpha-2-globulins), or of abnormal hallucinogenic substances produced by the body (adenochrome, bufotenin, DMT). All of these theories are at present speculations which may or may not turn out to be implicated in the schizophrenic-type psychotic disorders in some individuals.

THE
TREATMENT
OF THE
SCHIZOPHRENIC-TYPE
DISORDERS

12

Brain
Surgery

A standard psychiatric textbook, written while brain surgery was still an accepted treatment for certain especially refractory cases of a psychosis of unknown origin or "schizophrenia," described a "not uncommon" result of prefrontal lobotomy as follows:

> The patient's relatives must expect him to show an absence of self-consciousness, a facetiousness, and childlike pleasure in simple things. Sarcastic remarks and undesirable behavior must be overlooked. Not for several months, if ever, should most patients be permitted to assume financial responsibility or to attempt unusual social adjustments. Long and persistent re-educating and rehabilitating efforts should be continued. With the best results, the patient loses his anxiety, be-

comes cheerful and friendly, takes an interest in matters
about himself, and even works regularly but without ambi-
tion. (Noyes and Kolb, 1963, p. 553)

Such a result, to put it bluntly, is, in many instances, almost
as bad as the original disorder—unless your aim in life is to
become an unreflective, sarcastic, ill-mannered, unmoti-
vated, and irresponsible four-year-old. And in some instances, the cure may be much worse than the disease. It
should be emphasized, however, that the above description
applies to the results of frontal lobotomies, lobectomies and
leucotomies (all are procedures which sever all or many of
the connections of the frontal lobes with the rest of the
brain). In order to circumvent many of the unfortunate
side-effects of these operations, numerous modifications
have been made on the original procedures. (Frontal lobotomy itself was first introduced as a treatment for mental disorders in 1935.) One of the most popular current procedures
is known as a "cingulotomy," which severs a small and very
specialized nerve tract running along the inner side of each
of the cerebral hemispheres.

The object of all these surgical procedures is to somehow help the emotionally overwhelmed individual feel less
emotionally overwhelmed by operating on areas in the brain
which serve to increase emotionality. The frontal lobes of the
brain (the area of the brain directly behind the forehead)
serve, among other things, to delicately coordinate what we
are thinking, or planning, with what we are feeling. The feelings (anger, joy, sadness, etc.) appear to be generated elsewhere and communicated through various channels to this
area of our higher awareness. The antipsychotic drugs probably act by putting the "damper" on emotionality in the area,
known as the limbic system, where it appears to be primarily
generated; brain surgery attempts to interrupt the channels
of communication, or nerve tracts, which convey this emotionality to our awareness. The difficulty with all these ap-

proaches is that everything is so utterly interrelated (thoughts, feelings, awareness, desire, and so on) within us that interfering with one area creates consequences in all others—as often as not, unpleasant consequences. The results of brain surgery to date have been fraught with all sorts of untoward consequences—individuals who have seemed worse off, though in a different way, than they were before brain surgery. Even the more refined approaches used today are not free from this considerable risk.

And, of course, any changes by brain surgery are irreversible. An inappropriate use of medications in general carries nowhere near the consequences of inappropriate surgery. A "slip of the scalpel" or, what is more often the case, an unsuspected variation in anatomy, can lead to troublesome, very bad, or simply catastrophic consequences.

Even when brain surgery was one of the few helpful treatments for some severely suffering individuals (i.e., before the advent of the major tranquilizers), it was recommended for use in only the most severely disturbed or suffering individuals who continued in their confusion or agony despite all other attempts to help them. (The actual facts of the use of brain surgery during those years, especially the 1940s, are probably somewhat different, with many individuals being submitted to it who should never have been.)

Most psychiatrists today avoid brain surgery like the plague. And for good reason. There is no good evidence at all that it is more effective than other drastically less radical procedures for helping individuals with schizophrenic-type disorders.

Theoretically there may be a few individuals for whom brain surgery—for example, a cingulotomy—would help where all other approaches have been to no avail. But that is purely theoretical. I haven't come across the situation yet where I even remotely thought that brain surgery might be indicated.

If any individual is told that some form of brain surgery would be the most effective treatment for his or her difficulty, several independent psychiatric opinions should be sought. And by independent, I mean independent—that is, psychiatrists having no connection whatsoever with any of the institutions with which the neurosurgeon and his psychiatric consultants are associated.

I would go into much more detail in this chapter if in fact the practice (and abuse) of psychosurgery were more widespread. The actual situation appears to be quite different, and the use of brain surgery to treat psychiatric disorders appears to be gradually dying out. A recent report estimated that in the United States in the early 1970s about four hundred neurosurgical procedures were performed annually for psychiatric conditions. Further, the rather striking fact was brought out that "two neurosurgeons performed 45% of the procedures reported for 1973." The report concludes: "This study reveals the absence of a factual basis for the highly publicized, highly emotional statements, current during the early 1970's regarding the use of psychosurgery" (Donnelly, 1977, p. 33).

But unfortunately, for those few individuals still submitted to psychosurgery, there is still a need, in the absence of the psychiatric profession's will to monitor its own abuses, for publicized and highly emotional statements regarding the inappropriate use of psychosurgery.

However, there are times when psychosurgery may be considered as a last resort. Very severe obsessive-compulsive neuroses, one of life's most unbearable afflictions, may be relieved by psychosurgery where all other approaches have failed.

But psychosurgery is rarely to be recommended, almost never in the schizophrenic-type disorders. It should never be carried out without the explicit agreement of a panel of independent experts that such a procedure is advisable. It would be a good idea to have a lawyer around also. (For some reason, lawyers on the scene seem somehow to make for wonderfully comprehensive, balanced, meticulous, and humane judgments.)

CONCLUSION

I'll conclude by citing the views of Silvano Arieti, a clinician who has devoted his life to the treatment of schizophrenic-type disorders and has seen the heyday of brain surgery come and go:

> By doing surgery on the patient, we give up all hope. We share the pessimism and hopelessness of the patient. We are ready to make him more docile but less human without any possibility of redemption. . . . It is enough to stay for a few hours in close interpersonal relationship with some of these operated patients in order to realize that they are not normal. Perhaps their abnormality cannot be differentiated or illustrated by the usual psychiatric examination or by the common psychological tests. This proves only the limitations of these tests. Not only is the operated patient in an abnormal state, but his abnormalities are serious. He lacks initiative, originality, foresight, moral judgment. . . . important areas, necessary for the highest processes of symbolism and interpersonal relations, are destroyed for the lifetime of the patient. (Arieti, 1974, pp. 671–72)*

While the newest experimental approaches (e.g., transient ultrasound disruption of neural pathways) claim to obviate

---

*From *Interpretation of Schizophrenia*, second edition, by Silvano Arieti, M.D. © 1974 by Silvano Arieti, © 1955 by Robert Brunner, Basic Books, Inc., Publishers, New York. Reprinted with permission of Basic Books, Inc., Granada Publishing, Ltd., and the author.

the subtle deficits described above by Arieti, there is no compelling evidence that they in fact do. Therefore, so far as I'm concerned, Arieti's conclusions still stand.[1]

SUMMARY

1. There is no good evidence at all that brain surgery is more effective than other less radical procedures for helping individuals with schizophrenic-type disorders.

2. Psychosurgery is rarely to be recommended, almost never in the schizophrenic-type disorders. It should *never* be carried out without the explicit agreement of a panel of *independent* psychiatric consultants that such a procedure is advisable.

3. Anyone considering any psychosurgery for emotional problems (and not primarily neurological ones, such as a seizure disorder) should be well aware of the significant risk of permanent, damaging personality change occurring as a result of psychosurgical procedures.

13

Electroshock Therapy

"Generally, electroconvulsive therapy has been thoroughly discredited in the treatment of schizophrenia." (Mendel, 1976, p. 111)*

The above statement is made by Werner Mendel, a professor of psychiatry at the University of Southern California, in his text on the treatment of schizophrenia—a text which, as he states, is based on the "longitudinal phenomenological observations of hundreds of patients over a quarter of a century." There will be occasion to quote him again in a later chapter. The present chapter on electroshock therapy may be considered an extended footnote to the above statement.

*Reprinted by permission of the author and Jossey-Bass, Inc.

Ensconced within his laboratory, supplied with a complex of machinery apparently sufficient to launch a rocket to the moon, we see the demented scientist, usually a doctor or professor, pulling the switch which will deliver a sizzling electric current to the brain of his innocent victim. This image occurs again and again in science-fiction and horror books, in films, and on television shows. One of the more popular current variants is to portray the evil scientist as a psychiatrist and the victim as some variety of noble undercover agent, reporter, political idealist, or simply an innocent, truth-seeking citizen who is reduced to silence by being hauled off to an institute where shock treatments are administered until the victim's mind is reduced to a state of docile imbecility.

Such images come all too readily to the public's mind, and certain contemporary critics of psychiatry, the anti-psychiatrists including Laing and others, have made full use of these emotionally loaded images of the evil scientist destroying the mind of the innocent victim to mobilize strong, even vehement feelings against the psychiatric establishment.

The fact is, electroshock therapy *has* been greatly abused in this country. Many psychiatrists are unwilling to face this, and in the heat of the current controversy over whether the use of ECT (electroconvulsive therapy) should be severely restricted by the state (e.g., in California), the rationalizations and justifications and semihysterical self-righteous distortions appearing regularly in the press, psychiatric, antipsychiatric, and popular, rival the Watergate hearings in subtlety, sophistry, and inability to face obvious realities. Hopefully this chapter will make the issue somewhat clearer in the public's mind, if not in the minds of my fellow psychiatrists.

The realities concerning electroshock therapy, at least so far as can be ascertained from our current state of knowledge, are fairly simple and straightforward:

1.   *Electroshock therapy is an effective treatment for certain kinds of depression.* However, it is only slightly more effective than

the antidepressant medications. For any five individuals with a severe manic-depressive-type depression, there is probably one person out of the five who would be specifically benefited by electroshock therapy. Two would have gotten better anyway on their own, one would have responded to antidepressant medication, and one would have continued depressed. Most clinicians now consider antidepressant medication the preferred treatment for severe depressions, with ECT reserved for certain special situations.[1]

2. *Electroshock therapy is an effective treatment for schizophrenic-type disorders. However, it is in general no more effective than the major tranquilizer medications.*[2] Before the major tranquilizer medications were discovered in the 1950s, ECT proved to be, throughout the '40s and '50s, one of the few helpful ways of significantly relieving and shortening the sufferings of individuals with schizophrenic-type disorders. But it now appears to offer no advantage over medication. Consequently, in most relatively up-to-date treatment centers it has fallen into disrepute as a treatment for the schizophrenic-type reactions. One proponent of ECT has summarized his review of studies on the effectiveness of ECT versus drug therapy as follows: "A fair conclusion would seem to be that drugs are generally superior to ECT in the treatment of schizophrenia, but ECT has been successful in some cases where drugs have failed" (Greenblatt, 1977, p. 1004). Another way of putting this would be:

If someone is undergoing an acute schizophrenic-type disorder, electroshock therapy should not be the treatment of first choice.

Further, it should probably not even be the treatment of second or third choice, since various other therapy approaches (for example, changing the social situation, or a trial of different major tranquilizer drugs) may well prove helpful.[3]

Greenblatt further states, summarizing a Massachusetts ECT task force committee report: "When ECT is used in schizophrenic patients, more favorable results occur if the illness is of short duration, features major affective elements, has an identified precipitating event, and involves a well-adjusted premorbid personality" (Greenblatt, 1977, p. 1002). As we know from the discussion in Chapter 5, these are precisely the characteristics of the good-prognosis individuals who may be expected to do well anyhow, or who in any case should certainly do quite well with the help of medication. So we find ECT being recommended as most useful where it's needed least.[4]

ECT may be helpful for someone with a chronic schizophrenic-type disorder who has found no relief from other treatment approaches. This, however, is a relatively rare occurrence. Most chronically disorganized individuals who remain so despite various interventions will remain so despite ECT also. Any benefits are usually transient, and to chronically give someone electroshock treatments, up to fifty or a hundred over the years, is scarcely justifiable today given our knowledge—or in some respects, our lack of knowledge—of the effects of a large number of ECT treatments.

From a practical point of view what should be remembered is:

a. It's not necessary to use electroshock therapy to adequately treat an acute schizophrenic-type disorder. If a physician uses it, you may well question what he's doing. It would be *highly* advisable to seek an independent opinion from another well-informed psychiatrist as to whether ECT is in fact the treatment of choice.

b. Very rarely ECT may prove more helpful than other approaches in individuals with *chronic* schizophrenic-type disorders. The emphasis is on the *very rarely*. An independent opinion as to the advisability of ECT should be obtained. Further, the number of times someone receives ECT should be limited (probably to under twenty treatments).

3. *ECT is not a harmless procedure.* ECT was first used as psychiatric treatment in 1937. Electrodes were attached to each side of the head and a relatively large current was passed between them, producing unconsciousness and a convulsive seizure (drugs were also later used to produce seizures). Many refinements in the technique of administering ECT have been made since then, with a very small current— just enough to produce a seizure—being passed through one side of the brain (unilaterally). The individual receives a medication which prevents any muscle spasm, a short-acting anesthetic, and the entire treatment is over in an instant. Afterward the individual often feels light-headed and confused, with no memory of what happened. As currently practiced, the procedure is one which should cause almost no subjective distress. However, there are problems associated with the use of ECT:*(a)* there is considerable evidence that some minimal cellular damage occurs as a result of ECT;[5] *(b)* there are major difficulties with memory for several weeks, or months, after a course (eight to ten treatments) of ECT; *(c)* a certain number of individuals, on the order of 30 to 60 percent, will complain of continuing memory difficulties many months after a course of treatment.[6]

Electroshock treatments used to be given bilaterally, and individuals would often receive as many as fifty to a hundred treatments over the course of several years for recurrent depressions or schizophrenic-type relapses. There seems little doubt that such relatively massive use of ECT produced many problems not seen with current, more conservative approaches. ECT probably helps by altering the balance of chemical transmitters in the brain (see Chapter 11), with any cellular damage being incidental. With current unilateral techniques, any cellular damage which occurs may be negligible, in the sense that the "bruise" will heal, and any long-term memory difficulties minimal. This appears to be the case, but given the state of our current knowledge, and our knowledge of the deleterious effects of ECT as previously administered, the greatest of caution and prudence in the use of ECT is indicated. This unfortunately has not been the case in many quarters.

4. *Electroshock therapy has been greatly abused by psychiatrists.* In the late 1930s it was discovered that some chronically disorganized individuals appeared to be helped by various radical procedures, including insulin coma, convulsions, and brain surgery. A whole generation of psychiatrists spent the next twenty years extensively employing these procedures on "schizophrenics." In their zeal they even began to use them on patients with all types of other disorders, such as severe obsessive-compulsive neuroses, sociopathic characters, and so on. When the medications were developed in the 1950s many of the veteran psychiatrists somehow never gave up their old habits. In addition, insurance companies made their old habits all the more irresistible by paying differentially high fees for administering ECT.[7] A psychiatrist could spend one hour in the morning administering ECT to a series of patients and be payed hundreds of dollars. The result was that any number of psychiatrists became known as "zappers," and the institutions they frequented, usually private psychiatric hospitals, became known as "shock shops." Many of these psychiatrists believed with almost evangelical zeal that ECT was (1) essentially harmless and (2) good for about anything. Almost anyone who walked in the door was started on ECT. I can remember in 1971 listening to one of these wizards telling me how wonderfully effective ECT was for confused or delinquent adolescents, for alcoholics, and for husbands and wives locked in depressing marital conflicts. "It seemed to make their problems so much less important to them." Of course it did. Owing to the short-term memory loss produced by ECT, they were probably having a difficult time remembering what their problems *were*. This gentleman appeared more ignorant than venal. Concerning some others I reserve comment.

Over the years, conscientious psychiatrists knew of such "shock shops," reacted with horror, but, as is conventional, did nothing to curb the rampant abuse. It was left to patients' organizations, legal rights committees, and legislatures to stir psychiatrists from their apathetic tolerance of such abuses. Now there is great controversy. But the shock shops still abound. The psychiatrists who use shock indiscriminantly still roam about unchecked (it would be instructive to check Blue Shield and Medicare billings for ECT), and the inappropriately treated patients still suffer and suffer and suffer.[8]

In sum:

1. *There are only two conditions today in which electroshock therapy should be used: (a) as a treatment for certain types of severe depressions; (b) as a treatment for the rare individual with a schizophrenic-type disorder who remains severely impaired despite other vigorous treatment approaches.*

2. *If it is recommended for any other conditions—for example, a*

disturbed adolescent or chronic depression or alcoholism or sociopathic character disorder—my advice would be to consult another psychiatrist.

3. If someone attempts to impose ECT on anyone without informed consent, a lawyer should be contacted immediately.

MY OWN PREJUDICE

Finally you should be aware of my own prejudice. I have found it necessary to resort to ECT on only one occasion thus far in my own practice. This involved an elderly lady with a severe depression and heart disease. In this instance medication (antidepressants) would probably have constituted more risk than ECT. Beyond the occasional rare instance, I and many other therapists find it possible to help individuals satisfactorily without recourse to ECT.

It should be emphasized, however, that in some situations it is a perfectly reasonable alternative mode of therapy. Further, if it is properly administered and the number of total lifetime treatments are limited, it may not have any more unfortunate side effects than the antidepressant or major tranquilizer medications. And certainly in some instances primarily involving depression and *not* the schizophrenic-type disorders, it would be poor judgment on the physician's part not to recommend ECT.

SUMMARY

1. Electroshock therapy is an effective treatment for certain types of *depressions*. It's only slightly more effective than the antidepressant medications.

2. ECT is an effective treatment for some individuals with schizophrenic-type disorders. In general, it appears to be *less* effective than the major tranquilizer medications.

3. ECT is not the treatment of choice for anyone undergoing an *acute* schizophrenic-type disorder.

4. On rare occasions it may prove helpful in relieving persistent psychotic-type symptoms where other approaches have been tried and failed.

5. The technique of administering ECT has been modified greatly in recent years. There should be little if any discomfort involved and no cause for fear. The Hollywood version of ECT treatment couldn't be more at odds with the nonsensational reality.

6. There is good evidence that ECT as administered in past years produced some brain cell damage. Even as administered today it produces acute memory loss and, in some individuals, complaints of persistent memory difficulty months after the treatment has been terminated.

7. Unilateral ECT is as effective as bilateral and produces considerably fewer complications. If shock therapy is recommended, individuals should ascertain that it is in fact unilateral ECT. Old-time clinicians may persist in their old-time habits.

8. ECT has been greatly abused by some psychiatrists: *(a)* it has been used to treat conditions it shouldn't be used to treat (disruptive adolescents, sociopaths, transient situational disturbances, alcoholism, and so on); *(b)* it has been used to treat other conditions such as chronic disorganized schizophrenic states with gross inappropriateness in the face of better alternative treatments or in the face of obvious ineffectiveness; *(c)* even where initially appropriate, the treatments have often been continued for far too long, with some individuals receiving treatments ranging in the hundreds.

9. Up to now, psychiatry has proven itself incapable of curbing abuses of ECT through its own organizations.

10. Consequently, if ECT is recommended, an alternative, independent opinion should be obtained. There are situations in which ECT is a reasonable alternative approach, and competently trained psychiatrists should recognize these. There are many situations where it's not, and the individual must protect himself against those who would continue to abuse ECT.

11. If the attempt is made to compel someone to undergo ECT without truly informed voluntary consent, legal counsel should be sought.

12. As with the major tranquilizer medications, abuse does not argue against legitimate use.

13. "Generally, electroconvulsive therapy has been thoroughly discredited in the treatment of schizophrenia" (Mendel, 1976, p. 111).

14

Drugs

In some quarters it's quite popular to damn the use of drugs in psychiatry. Drugs are considered modern science's answer to the straitjacket. (They are sometimes referred to as chemical straitjackets.) Psychiatrists are portrayed as rather sinister figures controlling any deviant, rebellious, or undesirable behavior by forcing you to take various mind-controlling drugs. Or alternatively, psychiatrists are pictured as well-intentioned bureaucratic pawns of the state reducing the disruptive and wilder members of society to a harmless, zombielike condition by filling them up, with or without their consent, with a variety of mind-numbing chemicals. The most notorious drugs of all are those used in treating the schizophrenic-type psychoses, the major tranquilizer drugs, or, as they are also known, the anti-psychotic drugs. These drugs are pictured as the psychiatrists' ultimate control weapon, the most uncooperative of patients supposedly being reduced to a passive, will-less, jellyfishlike mass simply by injecting enough Thorazine or similar drugs into them.

The truth, fortunately, is vastly otherwise. [1]

HOW THE MAJOR TRANQUILIZERS MAY BE HELPFUL

In simplest terms, if you are psychotically disorganized, the major tranquilizer drugs help you to feel more organized. They help you to feel *more* like yourself, not *less,* as some critics would have it.

If, in a relatively calm, organized state of mind, you took these medications, you'd initially feel sleepy, then a sort of dull feeling. You'd be able to function, but you wouldn't feel quite like yourself. You perhaps might describe yourself as feeling as though the intensity of your inner feelings were dulled or dampened, as though your emotions were wrapped up in cotton wadding. If you continued to take the medication for several weeks at a relatively low "maintenance" dose, even this subjective effect would begin to abate and you'd start feeling pretty much like your old self again. If, however, you were undergoing an acute disorganizing or psychotic process, after starting the medication, you would immediately begin to feel less overwhelmed, less panic-stricken, less chaotic, and *more like yourself.* (Of course, there are some people undergoing schizophrenic-type psychotic reactions who don't want to get back to themselves. They can't stand themselves. They can't bear taking the medication and being themselves, and they can't bear not being themselves—that is, being in a state of psychotic disorgani-zation. As far as they're concerned, they're caught hopeless-ly between the devil—themselves—and the deep blue sea—psychotic disorganization.)

Far from turning individuals into zombies, the major tranquilizers usually do precisely the reverse. They *increase* the ability of psychotically disorganized individuals to cope—that is, to concentrate, to organize their thoughts, and to control their emotions. They enable those whom a schizophrenic-type reaction may have turned into apparent zombies, who, for example, may sit staring blankly for hours or days on end—to escape from their prison of blocked thoughts and paralyzing fears. They will help someone who is frantic with rage, terror, or despair calm down; but, just as importantly, they will help any number of emotionally paralyzed individuals become more active, involved, and alive. *Instead of imposing a chemical straitjacket, the medication more often than not removes an emotional straitjacket.* None of this seems to be widely appreciated in popular reports.

HOW THE MAJOR TRANQUILIZERS MAY BE ABUSED

The problems arise when the major tranquilizers are abused. And just as there's no doubt that the medications have been tremendously helpful, there's also little doubt that at times they have been terribly abused. The criticism that some hos-pitals "put Thorazine in the drinking water" is, in some in-stances, perhaps not unjustified. All too often psychiatric medications, in inappropriately high doses, seem to be used to "snow" the patient population in general. Inappropriately high doses of the major tranquilizers will in fact tranquilize you to almost any desired degree. Thus if an understaffed hospital doesn't want any trouble from complaining patients, it simply ends up increasing the tranquilizers until the patients cease complaining, that is, until they're too numb inside to even think about complaining. But, as I've pointed out, *in appropriate doses* the major tranquilizers are not even tranquilizing. As others have noted, the use of the term *tranquilizer* is misleading. A more proper term would be *stabilizer*. The medication is abused when it is used to "overstabilize" individuals to the point of emotional paralysis.

A further abuse of the medications occurs when they're given to individuals who shouldn't be taking them in the first place. This practice, though less notorious than overmedication with the major tranquilizers, is probably even more widespread. Careful research has delineated the sorts of situations where major tranquilizer medications are specifically helpful and specifically *more helpful* than other alternative approaches—for example, psychotherapy. But all too often the medication is doled out to obstreperous teenagers, cranky grandfathers, harried insomniac executives, depressed husbands, jittery housewives, and so on.

The inappropriate use of these medications inside the hospitals is probably only the faintest reflection of the inappropriate use of these medications outside the hospitals.

THE TYPES OF PSYCHIATRIC DRUGS

The Classes

Basically there are four classes of drugs used for emotional or psychiatric disorders:

1. The minor tranquilizers (for example, Valium, Librium, Serax, and Tranxene).

2. The antidepressants (for example, Elavil, Tofranil, Sinequan, Aventyl, Vivactyl, and Norpramine).

3. The antimania drug: Lithium.

4. The major tranquilizers (for example, Thorazine, Stelazine, Haldol, Navane, and Prolixin).

Uses

1. The minor tranquilizers are primarily helpful for *anxiety* and *mixed anxiety-depression.*

2. The antidepressants are primarily helpful for the *severer types of depressions,* that is, the presumably biochemically determined depressive illnesses. They are *no more* helpful than the minor tranquilizers for other types of anxiety and depression.

3. The antimania drug Lithium is specifically helpful for *mania* and for preventing recurrences of manic or depressive episodes in individuals with *manic-depressive illness.*

4. The major tranquilizers (antipsychotics or neuroleptics) are specifically helpful for *acute or chronic schizophrenic-type disorders.* They may also be helpful for certain types of manic-depressive reactions (acute mania and agitated depressions). They are *no more* helpful than the minor tranquilizers for anxiety and depression.

Equivalence

In the first section above I have listed in parentheses the trade names of some of the more popularly prescribed representatives of each class of psychiatric drug. When a reviewer sits down and sober-mindedly evaluates all the well-designed double-blind studies, the conclusion is usually reached that, within each class, all of the drugs are approximately equivalent. No one is superior to any of the others in treating any one specific symptom or disorder.

To repeat: *Within each class, all the drugs are approximately equivalent in effectiveness. Specifically, all of the major tranquilizers are equally effective in treating the schizophrenic-type disorders.* It has not yet been demonstrated consistently that any one specific subtype of the schizophrenic disorders—for example, acute or chronic, good-prognosis or poor, catatonic or paranoid—responds any better to one of the major tranquilizers than to any of the others. *The differences between the major tranquilizers are in the extent and severity of side effects, not in their antipsychotic action.*

The primary qualification which needs to be made to the above generalization is that some individuals, for unknown reasons, respond better to one drug than to another. But as said, *averaged over a group of individuals,* no one drug shows consistent superiority.

Clinicians choose a drug based on familiarity with its side effects, or out of habit. As far as effectiveness is concerned, they could choose any of the other representatives of the drug (for example, Thorazine, or Stelazine, or Prolixin).

THE MAJOR TRANQUILIZERS

There are several different subclasses of major tranquilizers which have different side effects, but in terms of treating the schizophreniclike reactions they are all equivalently effective. The table on this page is a list of the most commonly used major tranquilizers.

Trade name	Generic name	Approximately equivalent to 100 milligrams of chlorpromazine
Haldol	(haloperidol)	2.5 mg
Mellaril	(thioridazine)	100 mg
Navane	(thiothixene)	5 mg
Prolixin	(fluphenazine)	2 mg
Stelazine	(trifluoperazine)	5 mg
Thorazine	(chlorpromazine)	100 mg
Trilafon	(perphenazine)	10 mg

There are numerous other major tranquilizers, and each year a whole group of new ones are introduced to the market. So far none has proven any more effective than Thorazine, though many have less troublesome side effects. It should also be mentioned that the major tranquilizers are sometimes referred to as phenothiazines because Thorazine, the first discovered, and many of the others belong to this chemical class. There are others such as Haldol and Navane which aren't phenothiazines. Their pharmacological effects, however, are similar.

THE USUAL SIDE EFFECTS

The minor side effects experienced by almost everyone when initially taking the major tranquilizers are *drowsiness* and a *dry mouth*. The drowsiness disappears over the course of several days, the dry mouth usually after several weeks. Additional typical mild side effects include a few moments of dizziness when standing up suddenly (postural hypotension) and some difficulty reading very small print. Some of the major tranquilizers, such as Thorazine and Mellaril, cause more of the above side effects than others (for example, Haldol or Prolixin).

Another group of common side effects relates to *movement disorders.* The occurrence of these side effects is related to the type of major tranquilizer—for example, they occur much less frequently with Thorazine than with Haldol—and to the dose of medication taken. These side effects include the following:

1. *The "cramp"*—a severe "tugging" or outright spasm of, in most instances, the muscles of the head and neck, causing,

for example, wry neck or a knotted-up tongue. Though frightening, this side effect is completely reversed within minutes by an appropriate antispasm medication such as Cogentin, Artane, or Benadryl. If this side effect doesn't occur within the first weeks of therapy, it's not likely to occur at all.

2. *The "motor"*—an extremely restless feeling. For example, you feel forced to keep pacing the room or to fidget constantly when you're sitting down.

3. *The "stiff man"*—a feeling of stiffening up, so that your face shows little expression and your movements are markedly reduced; for example, you shuffle your feet and you don't swing your arms when you walk.

Depending on the medication and the dose, any of the above movement disorders may occur in from 10 percent (on low doses of Thorazine) to almost 100 percent (on high doses of Haldol or Prolixin) of individuals. Such reactions are completely reversed either by adding an antidote (for example, Cogentin) or by stopping the medication. There is *no lasting or serious nervous system disorder involved*. The important thing is to recognize the reactions when they occur and not to confuse, for example, "the motor" with increasing anxiety, or "the stiff man" with increasing depression or catatonia.

UNUSUAL SIDE EFFECTS

The major tranquilizers are very potent medications with potentially very serious side effects. Fortunately, these side effects are relatively rare. *But the major tranquilizers should never be "popped" like an aspirin (or even a Valium). They must **always** be taken under expert supervision.*

There are a number of unusual but very troublesome

side effects which may occur with these medications. They include all sorts of allergic skin rashes, hypersensitivity to the sun with easy burning, decrease in sexual drive, weight gain, and various bowel and menstrual irregularities.

Among the serious side effects which may occur are the following:

1. *Agranulocytosis*—the temporary suppression of the production of leukocytes (the white blood cells which defend the body against infection). This is *extremely rare*, but when it occurs it is *extremely serious*. One of the signs is a severe sore throat (often accompanied by high fever), and this should be reported immediately to a physician for further evaluation.

2. *Hepatitis*—a type of liver inflammation. This is also rare and appears to be more related to Thorazine use (approximately one out of every two hundred taking the medication) than to the other major tranquilizers. It is transient and rarely serious.

3. *Hyperpyrexia*—greatly increased body temperature in hot weather which can lead to heat stroke. This is also extremely rare and related more to Thorazine than to the other major tranquilizers.

4. *Tardive dyskinesias*—persistent movements, usually of the neck and face, particularly continual twisting movements of the mouth or tongue. In the past this syndrome was reported to occur primarily in older people who had been taking the major tranquilizers for many years (up to 56 percent of such individuals in some studies). Recent studies have shown a significant incidence in younger people who have been taking the medication for a relatively short time (less than two years). Though no threat to health, a tardive dyskinesia can be very aggravating and disfiguring and very serious because it is often permanent. The antidote which will stop the abnormal movements hasn't yet been discovered. (Stopping the major tranquilizer will often only make them worse.)

Clinicians now agree that even the very slight risk of this

syndrome occurring makes the prescription of a major tranquilizer *an extremely serious matter.* They agree that the major
tranquilizers should only be prescribed if they are *greatly helpful.* Further, *they should be prescribed at the lowest effective dose
and not one day longer than they are truly needed.* They should
not be prescribed routinely for mild to moderate anxiety or
depression (as they often are).

ADDICTION POTENTIAL

*The major tranquilizers are neither physically nor psychologically
addicting.* Somehow in recent years the impression has arisen
that the major tranquilizers are addicting. Numerous individuals have expressed this concern to me. However, that
impression is totally false. The major tranquilizers are not
drugs which anyone tends to abuse. They are not physically
addicting. In the first place, tolerance does not develop to
them, that is, the dose required to produce a given effect
does not steadily increase with continual use. In the second
place, severe or life-threatening "withdrawal" symptoms do
not occur upon suddenly stopping the medication (some
minor discomfort, e.g. insomnia and restlessness, may occur, but this is far different from the often life-threatening
withdrawal syndrome produced by the addicting drugs).
Further, the major tranquilizers are not psychologically addicting in the same way such drugs as the amphetamines or
cocaine may be. They do not produce the sort of euphoric
"high" that amphetamines, the opiates (for example, heroin
or Demerol), or cocaine do, nor do they produce the mellow,
pleasurable "tranquilization" often associated with the use of
alcohol, marijuana, the minor tranquilizers (for example, Valium or Librium), or various sleeping medications (for exam-

ple, the "downer" barbiturates, Nembutal or Seconal). Like the anti-depressant medications, the major tranquilizers are primarily *stabilizers*. They do not tend to facilitate various avenues of escape from reality; rather they tend to promote more accurate perceptions of reality in individuals prone to severe emotional upsets and disorganized states of mind. As with someone taking insulin, the primary concern of individuals taking the major tranquilizers is when they can stop taking them, not how they can get more. This is quite a different situation from that which occurs with even the minor tranquilizers, such as Valium or Librium, where some individuals have a tendency to become psychologically dependent and to want more and more medication. In short, like insulin and other similar stabilizing medications, the major tranquilizers are not drugs which individuals tend to abuse. There are many problems with the continued use of the major tranquilizers, but, fortunately, addiction is not one of them.

DOSAGE

The usual dose for treating an acute schizophrenic-type disorder is 400 to 600 mg of Thorazine or its equivalent. Occasionally the dose goes as high as 1500 mg. (Doses above about 800 mg should be administered in a hospital setting.)

After several weeks or months the dose is usually tapered off to a maintenance dose of about 100 to 300 mg of Thorazine or its equivalent. For individuals with a single acute schizophrenic-type reaction, the medication should probably be discontinued after six months to a year. If disorganization recurs, then medication is clearly helpful and it should be reinstituted.

OVERDOSAGE

Drug-overdose suicide attempts have become increasingly prevalent in our society. For example, it can be estimated that approximately one out of every twenty individuals in the Boston area will make a drug-overdose suicide attempt over the next years if current rates prevail.[2] Individuals undergoing schizophrenic-type reactions are frequently struggling with an underlying despair, and their suicide-attempt and completed-suicide rates are even higher than those of the population in general. Most suicide attempts, especially those occurring in individuals with schizophrenic-type disorders, are the result of a momentary impulse and not of any elaborate planning. Most people simply reach for the nearest bottle of pills and take whatever is inside. It's important to insure that, for anyone undergoing an acute schizophrenic-type reaction, *only a limited amount of medication is on hand at any one time*. All of those drugs in the medicine cabinet no longer being used should be flushed down the drain, and the drugs being used kept only in a limited supply (for example, for the major tranquilizers, a one-month supply).

ACUTE SCHIZOPHRENIC-TYPE DISORDERS

Who Benefits?

The evidence is overwhelming that the major tranquilizers are enormously helpful in (1) providing relief from the panic and desperation of acute psychosis; (2) normalizing the attendant, often extreme physical hyperarousal (enabling the individual, for example, to get some sleep again) and (3)

217

decreasing the attendant extreme disorganization of thought or the paralysis of thinking capacity.

If you define getting back to your old (prepsychotic) self—no matter how dissatisfied or unhappy with that old self you may be—as a "recovery," then there is no doubt that for most, the major tranquilizers speed up recovery tremendously, enabling people to get back on their feet in a matter of weeks instead of months, as used to be the case. In the same way, most people will recover from a bout of pneumonia eventually on their own, but antibiotics speed up the process of recovery tremendously.

However, you should be aware that recent research, largely stimulated by Laing's pioneering Kingsley Hall work, has shown that, in the proper settings—for example, certain therapeutic communities such as Soteria House[3]—most people can recover from acute schizophrenic-type disorders as well without drugs as with drugs. However, the setting needs to be very special, and recovery usually takes somewhat longer than with appropriate medications.

Who Doesn't Benefit?

Further, you should be aware that there is a small subgroup of individuals with acute schizophrenic-type disorders who do as well without drugs as with them, and that there is probably another subgroup that does *better* without drugs than with them—that is, the drugs *slow* their recovery. Unfortunately, to date there is no way to tell beforehand which individuals fall into which group. To discover who these people might be, researchers need to stop thinking of schizophrenia as a single disease. It's only in recent years that researchers have really begun to consider *schizophrenia* a label which may stand for many types of disorders, some of which may do better, others worse, on medication. Thus, the delineation of differentially responding subgroups is years, if not decades, off.[4]

CHRONIC SCHIZOPHRENIC-TYPE DISORDERS

Who Benefits?

There is little doubt that in general, for many individuals with chronic schizophrenic-type disorders, maintenance doses of the major tranquilizers (1) decrease the frequency and severity of acute disorganized episodes in those prone to recurrent schizophrenic-type reactions; and (2) decrease some of the more troublesome (from the individual's point of view, and not merely the clinician's, or society's, as some critics would have it) chronic symptoms such as hallucinations, delusions, disorganized thinking, emotional paralysis, withdrawal, and apathy.

Who Doesn't Benefit?

Most well-controlled studies have shown that somewhere between 40 and 60 percent of individuals with chronic schizophrenic-type disorders will have an acute episode within a year or so after stopping the major tranquilizers. Only 20 percent of those *continued* on maintenance doses of the major tranquilizers will relapse. Thus, for many, the major tranquilizers are clearly helpful, (if preventing acute psychotic reactions is considered helpful, as it should be).

However, there's another way to look at the above results. Let's take the higher figure and say that 60 percent, or three out of every five individuals, will have an acute schizophrenic-type episode when taken off active medication and given a placebo (an inactive substance). This means that 40 percent, or two out of the five, *don't relapse* and do as well on placebos as on active medication. Put differently, for every five "chronic schizophrenics" taking maintenance major tranquilizers, it appears that there are at least two who don't need to be taking them.[5] How do we know who they are? In general, we don't. Some research has indicated that if you've been taking the major tranquilizers for many years at relatively low doses—300 mg or less of Thorazine or it's equivalent—there's a good chance you'll do as well without medication as with it. Currently, however, the only way to know who may no longer need the medication is *to stop the medication and see who does well and who doesn't.* For most, this should be done at least every several years.

There are two further observations on the above research results which need to be made. First, 20 percent, or approximately one out of every five individuals, relapsed *despite* taking medication. It's perfectly possible that there are subgroups of chronically disorganized individuals who (1) do as poorly with the medication as without it—that is, the medication simply has no effect on *their* type of psychosis of unknown origin; or who (2) are actually made worse by the medication. At present we have no way of identifying beforehand who these individuals might be. *The only way to find out is to stop the medication at some point and see if the individual does either (1) no worse or (2) better without it than with it.*

Second, other studies have shown that some individuals do *better* on placebos than on no pills at all. These are the so-called placebo-responders.[6] Again, we have no way to identify them beforehand.

A way to summarize this section, which may be somewhat confusing, would be as follows: For every five individuals with a *chronic or recurrent* schizophrenic-type disorder (we're *not* talking about acute schizophrenia here):

1. one individual (20 percent) will do *poorly despite* taking major tranquilizers;

2. one individual (20 percent) will do *well* without taking either major tranquilizers *or* a placebo pill;

3. one individual (20 percent) will do *well* without taking a

major tranquilizer *if* a placebo pill is given (which the individual thinks is active medication); and

4. *two individuals* (40 percent) *will benefit* **specifically** *from taking the major tranquilizers.*

OTHER USES OF THE MAJOR TRANQUILIZERS

Drug companies encourage physicians to prescribe the major tranquilizers for all sorts of other conditions, especially for anxiety and depression. For groups of individuals with anxiety or depression the major tranquilizers, the antidepressants, and the minor tranquilizers *all* appear to be equally effective. Most anxious and depressed states improve on their own anyhow. Clinicians may swear by the fact that "80 percent of my anxious patients got better on new wonder drug X." They're not particularly impressed by the fact that 60 or 70 percent of those people would have gotten better anyway. They attribute it all to the wonders of modern pharmacology. There are, however, some who do respond specifically to the minor tranquilizers. There are even some who appear to respond to the major tranquilizers and not to the other antianxiety drugs. We don't know who they are beforehand. The only sensible way to proceed is to take the medications with more limited or less potentially serious side effects first (the minor tranquilizers), and further, to take a major tranquilizer only if there are *very strong* indications for doing so, that is, if the symptoms constitute a *major* handicap.

The major tranquilizers are helpful in acute manic episodes and in severe agitated depressions. They are also helpful for what has been termed "explosive personality disorders" (for example, individuals subject to uncontrollable rage attacks). They are also helpful in blunting the emotional onslaught in anyone subject to overwhelmingly strong emotions—for example, panic, terror, or rage. Finally, they are helpful in reversing the effects of some of the hallucinogens such as LSD.

Thus, the fact that someone is taking a major tranquilizer is not an indication that he or she is "schizophrenic" or has had a schizophrenic-type disorder.

SUMMARY

1. The major tranquilizers can be of great help in relieving the symptoms of schizophrenic-type disorders. They don't "cure schizophrenia," but when used appropriately they can cut down tremendously on suffering and incapacitation.

2. The major tranquilizers are very potent medications with a vast array of troublesome and potentially serious side effects. They should only be taken for very good reasons and under a physician's direction.

3. A certain number of individuals on maintenance major tranquilizers will probably do as well—or in some instances as poorly—without medication as with it.

4. A great deal of research needs to be done to discover which individuals with acute and with chronic schizophrenic-type disorders specifically benefit from the major tranquilizers and which individuals either don't benefit from them or are made worse by them.

15

Megavitamin Therapy

ORTHOMOLECULAR PSYCHIATRY

In a recent issue of *Drug Therapy*, Hoffer has described orthomolecular psychiatry—or megavitamin therapy, as it was once called—as follows:

> Orthomolecular psychiatry is one of the branches of psychiatry currently advocating chemotherapy for schizophrenia. The other branch is toximolecular psychiatry. There are vast conceptual differences between the two and great differences in efficacy for the patient. Toximolecular psychiatry advocates the use of sublethal doses of agents not normally

found in the body. Their use has not significantly improved recovery rate over that occurring naturally. . . .
Orthomolecular psychiatry on the other hand emphasizes a system of treatment, not any one drug or chemical.

He goes on to write:

Most acute and subacute schizophrenics are vitamin dependent and respond best to a megavitamin approach to therapy. . . . Vitamin B_3 dependency is the most common cause of schizophrenic syndromes. About two-thirds of patients who are considered acute and sub-acute schizophrenics respond to megadoses of either nicotinic acid (niacin) or nicotinamide (niacinamide). . . .

Perhaps half the cases of chronic schizophrenia are caused by unrecognized cerebral allergies. . . . Treatment is relatively simple and consists of determining the causative factor (food, airborne or contact allergens) and eliminating it from the diet, if possible, or minimizing contact by another method such as rotation diet.

He summarizes his results as follows:

Patients on orthomolecular treatment, however, have two or three times the recovery rate of the toximolecular group. Failures are rare and usually occur after discontinuance of the program. The principal factor for success is a cooperative patient. About 90% of my patients who complete Phase 1 treatment are recovered or much improved.

Concerning his critics he writes:

Today's debate between orthomolecular and toximolecular psychiatrists is one of methodology. Toximolecularists appear content to use double-blind studies as a control, even though such other more important variables as severity and treatment are uncontrolled. They reject orthomolecular theory on the basis of a handful of studies performed on a few chronic schizophrenics in mental hospitals, and pay no attention to data from double-blind studies on acute and subacute patients.

To date there is not one published attempt to repeat any of our double-blind experiments using combined ECT and vitamin B$_3$ therapy on acute and sub-acute cases. Nor have any critics bothered to see the results of our treatment first hand, spend some time learning how it is done, or even try it on their own patients. (Hoffer, 1977, pp. 79, 83–85)*

THE CRITICS

McGrath, in a study involving individuals with chronic, subacute, and acute schizophrenic-type disorders, concluded:

> In summary, this double-blind collaborative study failed to demonstrate any therapeutic effect of the addition of nicotinamide (3 grams per day for 1 year) in the treatment of a consecutive series of 265 schizophrenic patients. (McGrath, 1972, p. 75)

Concerning the acute and subacute patients, he found that "there is clearly no difference between the two groups."

Concerning the patients who received both electroshock therapy (ECT) and nicotinamide, he found:

> In our series, of those patients with a duration of illness of 1 year or less, 21 patients on placebo and 22 receiving nicotinamide had ECT. . . . Again there is no significant difference between the two groups. (McGrath, 1974, p. 5)

---

*Reprinted by permission of *Drug Therapy*, Biomedical Information Corp., New York.

In recent years extensive studies have been carried out in Canada in an attempt to decide this issue once and for all. The conclusions reached by Lehmann and his group were as follows:

> This collaborative study has been ongoing for 5 years, and 5 of the 12 clinical trials originally contemplated have been completed. . . . The results are summarized below:
>
> The overall therapeutic efficacy of nicotinic acid as the sole medication in newly admitted schizophrenic patients is not superior to the overall therapeutic efficacy of an inactive placebo.
>
> The overall therapeutic efficacy of nicotinic acid as an adjuvant medication (to standard treatment with phenothiazines) in newly admitted schizophrenic patients is inferior to the overall therapeutic efficacy of an inactive placebo.
>
> The overall therapeutic efficacy of nicotinic acid (3,000 mg. day) as an adjuvant medication (concomitant with phenothiazines) in chronically hospitalized schizophrenic patients is inferior to the overall therapeutic efficacy of an inactive placebo. (Autry, 1975, p. 95)

Concerning the evidence for the hypothesis that some schizophrenic disorders may be vitamin-dependent diseases, the conclusions of a National Institute of Mental Health workshop on "Orthomolecular Treatment in Schizophrenia" were as follows:

> Controlled clinical trials of niacin (nicotinic acid) do not substantiate the claims of efficacy by proponents of this treatment approach (although criticism was aimed at the controlled studies on the grounds that they did not replicate the original study). . . .
>
> The theoretical and nutritional rationale for the use of high doses of vitamins as a treatment for schizophrenia remains largely hypothetical. It was pointed out, however, that schizophrenia does not resemble the known vitamin depen-

dent or vitamin deficient diseases. The possibility remains, presently neither substantiated nor refuted, that some small percentage of patients presently diagnosed as schizophrenic have a vitamin-dependent component to their illness. (Autry, 1975, pp. 101–102)

SOME PERSONAL OPINIONS

If the general public picks up almost any popular book on nutrition, "schizophrenia" will be found listed as an example of a vitamin-deficiency disease. Many popular books on mental illness will report "schizophrenia" to be in part due to vitamin deficiency. The investigators who believe in the efficacy of "orthomolecular" psychiatry have engaged in a very vigorous public relations campaign to alert all "schizophrenics" or "borderline schizophrenics" to the efficacy of their treatment. They have published their own journal, the *Journal of Orthomolecular Psychiatry* (formerly *Schizophrenia*) and created self-help groups in many cities known as Schizophrenics Anonymous. In their publications they have presented a plethora of scientific results and conclusions, such as those outlined in the above remarks by Hoffer. They cite an impressive list of references to support each of their conclusions (e.g., that "schizophrenics" are vitamin-dependent, that chronic "schizophrenics" have an allergic disease, that their treatment method is superior and produces an extremely high percentage of cures). The question is: why don't most other researchers accept their established conclusions? Why have the orthomolecular researchers felt they have had to bypass the therapeutic establishment and carry their case directly to the public? Presumably most scientists and clinicians don't have anything against finding out what contributes to the cause and cure of schizophrenic-type disorders. In fact, many are devoting their lives to helping such individuals in every way possible.[1]

My personal opinion is that the orthomolecular psychiatrists are way off base, presenting speculation as fact and misleading the public into thinking that we know the "cause" of "schizophrenia" and that they, the orthomolecular psychiatrists, know the cure, while the "toximolecular" psychiatrists are providing second-rate treatment. The fact that the general public, in my opinion, has been misled (even though with the best of intentions) I find quite intolerable. But there are other things to be said about the orthomolecular psychiatrists which the psychiatric establishment often fails to say.

First of all, many of them are intensely devoting their time and energy to the actual treatment of individuals with schizophrenic-type disorders. I suspect their high cure rate, if valid, is more a function of the extra care and attention given to their patients than to any vitamin supplements. (Most "establishment" psychiatrists don't have any particular interest in, let alone enthusiasm for, treating individuals with schizophrenic-type disorders.)

Second, they have provided the general public with a lot of useful information about "schizophrenia." Despite their belief in a biochemical cause, their efforts, including the formation of Schizophrenics Anonymous, have done much to promote understanding of and empathy for individuals undergoing schizophrenic-type disorders. (Unfortunately, in their zeal to cure "schizophrenics" they have used a very broad definition of *schizophrenia*. Some of their publications have gone so far as to provide a checklist so that you can diagnose the degree of your own "schizophrenia." I've encountered several individuals who have joined Schizophrenics Anonymous under the impression they were suffering from some form of a schizophrenic-type disorder when they clearly weren't. Given current misconceptions, it's my feeling that it doesn't do anyone any good to go around thinking he or she is schizophrenic—not even someone who may be prone to schizophrenic-type reactions, let alone someone who isn't.)

SUMMARY

1. Orthomolecular psychiatrists claim schizophrenia in many instances is caused by vitamin-dependent disorder or an allergy and that schizophrenia can be cured by appropriate vitamin supplements and by appropriate manipulation of the diet.

2. Most other psychiatrists feel the evidence for such claims is woefully lacking.

16

Hospitalization

In the past, if someone were undergoing a psychotic-type reaction, either acute or chronic, the first thought often was: this person should be in the hospital. In the past two decades, however, there has been considerable rethinking on this issue. Hospitalization is no longer considered the only, primary, or best way to help someone undergoing a schizophrenic-type reaction. While there are circumstances where hospitalization may be the most helpful, or the most expedient, alternative, there are other circumstances in which hospitalization may be unnecessary or actually detrimental. Many books have been written on the history of psychiatric hospitalization,[1] the problems of involuntary commitment, the pros and cons of hospitalization versus other types of treatment, and the sociology of "institutionalization."[2] In this chapter my very limited aim is to present a summary of current thinking with respect to the usefulness of psychiatric hospitalization in the treatment of the schizophrenic-type disorders. As the situation is in many respects quite different for someone who's done relatively well and has become acutely disorganized versus someone who's chronically disorganized, the following discussion will deal with each situation separately.

THE ACUTE SCHIZOPHRENIC-TYPE DISORDERS

Over several days or several weeks, you begin acting or talking more and more strangely. You seem out of touch, disorganized, anguished. You can't sleep. You can't concentrate. You make strange comments. You do all sorts of things which let others know something's wrong. Most of the time you yourself know something is radically wrong and you ask for help. Sometimes you're too afraid, too deluded, or too hopeless to ask for any, and your family or friends, feeling utterly distraught and overwhelmed, must seek help for you. If you're disorganized enough, the advice is often that you should be hospitalized. The reasons for hospitalization usually fall in the following areas:

1. *To provide you with a refuge* (an "asylum") from the severe stresses in your life which may have precipitated the "breakdown" (for example, to enable you to get away from home, or from the hated employer, or from the bleak ghetto rented room you live in).
2. *To provide you with "around-the-clock" support, comfort, and understanding.* Often the feeling of isolation while "going

crazy" is the greatest horror of all, and simply having someone there can make a world of difference.

3. *To evaluate more thoroughly what in fact is going on.* Is it in
fact a "psychosis of unknown origin," or rather a disorganized state brought on by any number of physical disorders
(for example, hyperthyroidism or bromide intoxication)?

4. *To enable vigorous treatment with medication, if appropriate,*
to be undertaken at once in a controlled hospital setting
where the medication can be adjusted from hour to hour if
need be and side effects monitored.

5. *To provide relief for family, friends, and so on* who may be
feeling overwhelmed and "at their wit's end."

6. *To protect you in your disorganized, more or less deluded state
from hurting yourself* (for example, from walking out a
second-story window to prove you can walk on air.)

7. *To protect you from hurting others.* This is rarely a consideration, but those undergoing an acute schizophrenic-type
reaction may have hostile impulses, just like the rest of us,
and such impulses may be exacerbated by their confusion or
delusions, just as some people intoxicated with alcohol may
be more prone to act on their hostile impulses (while others
may be less prone!).

Currently however, most psychiatrists are beginning to
realize that most individuals undergoing an acute "psychotic
break" can be helped out of their misery without hospitalization. It's clear that if someone is in great danger of hurting
himself or herself or others, there is less risk with the individual under twenty-four-hour observation in the hospital.
But apart from that, most of what a hospital provides can be
provided outside the hospital.

For example, several research projects have shown that,
with the proper use of major tranquilizer medication, symptoms of disorganization can be reduced dramatically in many
individuals within a matter of hours. With the more dramatic
"crazy" symptoms no longer dominating (i.e., with the person feeling tremendously more comfortable, organized, and

calm), there is often no longer any pressing need for hospitalization.[3]

Mendel in summarizing his experience has written:

> I have lived with 500 patients ("schizophrenic") from ages twenty to forty. . . . many of my patients spent no time in the hospital even during the most severe crisis; all of the problems could be handled in an out-patient setting, in a day-care center, in the home, in a social recovery station, or with intensive contact in the office, by mobilizing social support in the community, the family, and their circle of acquaintances. Others spent two or three days in the hospital, between one and three times in their lives. Each time the hospitalization was a result not of their illness but of the disorganization of support forces, or an inability on my part to muster the necessary resources of caring for the patient at the very moment when he needed it. (Mendel, 1976, pp. 112, 123–124)*

My experience is in full agreement with his.[4] In sum: *Psychiatric hospitalization is not necessary to help most individuals overcome their acute disorganized state (acute psychotic reaction) if appropriate intensive community support is available.*[5]

However, most of the time appropriate intensive community support is not available, and hospitalization then becomes the most helpful alternative.

THE DISADVANTAGES OF PSYCHIATRIC HOSPITALIZATION

In discussing the disadvantages of hospitalization, first let's assume we're talking about *good* psychiatric hospitals. (I'll save my comments on bad psychiatric hospitals for later.) A

---

*Reprinted by permission of the author and Jossey-Bass, Inc.

good psychiatric hospital should be a positive experience for anyone undergoing an acute psychotic episode. Why, then, it may be asked, go to all the extra time and trouble of trying to avoid hospitalization? Is there something so terrible about all psychiatric hospitals, even the good ones? My answer would be that there is nothing "terrible" about a good psychiatric hospital, but there are disadvantages which need to be taken into account. Many psychiatrists unfortunately very lightly make the decision to hospitalize without wrestling with the very real disadvantages to such a course.

Psychiatric hospitalization for mental illness is a social curse. On almost every application form for the rest of your life you'll be faced with the question: Have you ever been hospitalized for a mental illness? If you have been and you answer truthfully, you may as well forget about the job. No one wants a "crazy person" as an employee when there are so many "noncrazy people" to choose from—unless, of course, the employer is a bit "cracked" also, or has read this book or a similar book and has gotten over his or her prejudices about what "craziness" is all about. In most people's minds, being psychiatrically hospitalized—and even more so, being labeled "schizophrenic"—means there's some kind of monster inside you. They don't want you around. They don't want you doing anything requiring responsibility and mature judgment. They don't trust you. Who wants to get involved with an unpredictable "crazy" when you can find a nice "normal," sane person?

Maybe by this point you can see what I mean. It all makes good sense—even though it's perfect rubbish. Rabkin, in an excellent review of public attitudes toward mental illness, summarized the situation of the ex–mental hospital patient as follows:

> Upon their return [from the psychiatric hospital], they often find that being an ex–mental patient is more of a liability than being an ex-criminal in the pursuit of housing, jobs, and

friends. Mental patients have for years been regarded with more distaste and less sympathy than virtually any other disabled group in our society, and in fact their handicaps are partly attributable to public attitudes of rejection and avoidance. . .

The four disabilities that were consistently ranked lowest by all respondents were ex-convict status, mental retardation, alcoholism, and mental illness in last place of all. (Rabkin, 1974, pp. 10, 16)

When ex–mental hospital patients ask me how they should answer questions concerning psychiatric hospitalization and treatment, I tell them to lie. It's none of their employer's damn business. The question shouldn't be there in the first place. I tell them it's the last thing their friends should know, not the first. There is a very subtle process which goes on even among the closest of friends if someone has been adjudged "crazy" or "mentally ill." For example, if some disagreement arises, in an infinitely subtle but unmistakable way the "sane" person discounts the logical processes of the "mentally unstable" person. The person who tells someone else he or she had a schizophrenic-type disorder never gets treated quite the same, is never taken quite as seriously, is never listened to quite as carefully . . . all very subtle, but a curse the size of Everest when it comes to the lives of those who have been psychiatrically hospitalized.

To have been psychiatrically hospitalized is a social curse which can, and often does, affect to a greater or lesser extent much of the individual's future life. [6] If you don't believe that, ask Senator Eagleton.

A further serious disadvantage to psychiatric hospitalization is that *psychiatric hospitalization for mental illness often becomes a permanent blow to the individual's own self-esteem.* As many have written, (e.g., Goffman, Scheff), psychiatric hospitalization is like an official initiation into the ranks of the "mentally ill." It is a sort of baptism or bar mitzvah. You may

have been as odd or daffy as they come prior to hospitalization and thought of yourself only as a "character," an "original," an "eccentric," or whatever. But once psychiatrically
hospitalized, the stigma of being a "mental patient," of being
certifiably "mentally ill," becomes part of your own self-
image. Since many who have undergone schizophrenic-type
reactions have utterly miserable self-images to start with,
this added insult can sometimes be the blow from which
their self-esteem never recovers. For the rest of their lives
they go around feeling hopelessly flawed and inferior.

An even more serious disadvantage of hospitalization is
that some individuals, as a result of being hospitalized, accept the fact they are "sick" and use this as an excuse for
their failure to overcome their failings in life. Psychiatric
hospitalization for a "psychosis of unknown origin," with
the usual accompanying label *schizophrenic*, gives them official license to tell themselves, "Why try?—I'm schizophrenic." It gives someone who feels overwhelmed by growing up a perfect excuse not to grow up.

Finally, being in a psychiatric hospital enables you to
see all sorts of other ways of being mentally disturbed. You
may actually learn a few new ways of not coping. If you're
there long enough, in an environment dominated by emotionally disturbed behavior, you may come to see such disturbed behavior as more and more "normal."

*Hospitalizing someone in a psychiatric hospital for the first
time, given the current prejudices in our society, is, or should be, a
momentous decision. There are many compelling reasons for avoiding it if at all possible.*

With respect to bad psychiatric hospitals—ones with
inadequate staff, or poorly trained staff, or inappropriate
treatment (e.g., hospitals which "snow" their patients with
medication, or use electroshock therapy extensively, or keep
their patients for inordinately long times)—the best that can
be said of them is that they really are a "last resort," a dis-
graceful last resort, of the same ilk as some of our utterly dis-
graceful last-resort nursing homes.

SHORT-TERM VERSUS LONG-TERM
HOSPITALIZATION

In an ideal world, if you're undergoing an acute schizo-phrenic-type reaction, you could be treated without hospitalization. In the real world, for lack of a viable alternative (for example, of a therapist with the time and interest—whom you can afford), you may well end up being hospitalized. Decades ago, before the advent of the major tranquilizer medications, individuals with acute "psychotic breaks" would be hospitalized for six months to a year or longer. Often there would be recurrent episodes of severe disorganization during this period, making release home inadvisable. Currently, most psychotic episodes, with the use of appropriate medication, will resolve to a great extent within a week to several weeks, and with appropriate low-dose maintenance medication the recurrence of disorganized episodes can be to a great extent prevented. Consequently, most hospitals in recent years have come to view themselves as centers for short-term "crisis intervention," with an average stay varying from three to six weeks. There are still some old-line hospitals where it's believed that someone who has undergone an acute psychotic episode can best be helped by long-term hospitalization (six months to two years). They are not content to help the person over his or her psychotic symptoms, but believe there are many areas of personality change which need to be promoted and which can be accomplished best away from home in an intensive hospital setting. Many studies have shown longer-term hospitalization, in various settings, to be no more beneficial in the long run than shorter-term hospitalization. But a few studies have shown that, for some individuals, a longer-term stay in the hospital after the acute symptoms have abated may be more helpful in some respects.[7] The debate continues currently.

In general, most individuals who have undergone an acute disorganized episode, if hospitalized, only need to be hospitalized for a short time (two to six weeks).

Numerous studies have shown that the reason an individual is hospitalized in the first place, and the reason he or she remains in the hospital, often has more to do with the social situation than with any symptoms—that is, will the family take the person back? Is there a place to live? Any income? A job? And so on.[8]

If someone has undergone an acute psychotic episode and ends up staying in the hospital for month after month, serious questions should be raised about the treatment (or lack of treatment) the person is receiving.

TYPES OF PSYCHIATRIC HOSPITALS

Approximately one out of every 150 individuals is hospitalized for psychiatric reasons each year. Since approximately half of these are first admissions, it can be estimated that roughly one out of every ten individuals (or 10 percent) will end up psychiatrically hospitalized at some time in their lives (calculations based on data given in Keith, 1976 and National Institute of Mental Health, 1973). Thus, you should be well aware of the differences between psychiatric hospitals, if for no other reason than there's a good chance that you, or one of your acquaintances, may end up in one someday.

There are three major categories of psychiatric hospitals: state, private, and psychiatric units in general hospitals. If you have a considerable amount of money or private health insurance, you'll be accepted at a private psychiatric hospital. If you don't have any savings, or are on welfare, you'll have to accept hospitalization at a specific state psychiatric hospital or, if you're fortunate, in the psychiatric unit of a general hospital which "accepts" welfare.

State Hospitals. State hospitals earned a terrible reputation in the first half of this century as places where the "insane" were locked up and subjected to every variety of indignity (restraints, enforced seclusion, wet packs, electroshock, insulin coma, brain surgery, etc.) and as places where they were ultimately forgotten about and left to rave on back wards for the rest of their lives with the other "incurable maniacs." All of this was luridly portrayed in the film *Snake Pit*. Unfortunately, there were some elements of truth to this shocking picture of life in the warehouses of the overcrowded, disgracefully understaffed state mental hospitals. But there were also many state hospitals which were doing their best to provide enlightened, compassionate, humane care. Today state hospitals in general are in the process of transforming themselves radically. Their main interest now is in discharging patients as soon as possible to be followed up by treatment in an out-patient clinic. Most of the criticism these days is leveled at the hospitals' discharging their patients too soon and their failure to provide custodial care for those individuals who can't make it on the outside. The back ward is fast disappearing, and the kind of pathetic "incurably schizophrenic" individual, who was a product of the back wards and not of any schizophrenic-type disorder per se, is being seen less and less frequently. Further, I might add that most of the abuse of patients in the past was based on hostile staff reaction to the patients' uncontrollable "crazy" symptoms. With the appropriate use of medications most of the more dramatic symptoms of schizophrenic-type disorganization have disappeared. The fact is that you could walk onto most psychiatric hospital wards today and talk to whoever is there and not encounter anything particularly unusual at all, merely a lot of sad, troubled, perhaps angry human beings, the same as you would find almost anywhere. The film *One Flew over the Cuckoo's Nest* presents a picture of the kind of problems state hospitals currently run into. They're still very understaffed, which means the patients get very little attention. The staff is often poorly trained because there isn't enough senior staff to train them. Staff morale is often quite low, because there is no prestige (and often not much salary either) associated with working at a state hospital. Medication is often overused to tranquilize patients when some caring human interaction would do as well. If the state hospital is associated with a university or medical school training program (and many are), then it's likely to be a bit more mindful of its good image and less likely to lapse into a *One Flew over the Cuckoo's Nest* form of dehumanized institutional care. Many other state hospitals not connected with any teaching centers may also provide adequate (to excellent) care. But the fact remains that many state hospitals are still disgracefully understaffed and underfinanced, with all the reprehensible *Cuckoo's Nest* consequences which follow.

Private Hospitals. There is usually no choice about state hospitals. You either go to the one in your area or you don't go at all. With private hospitals you have a choice. And just as with the state hospitals, there are good private hospitals and bad ones. The bad ones will eagerly hospitalize you, regardless of whether the situation can be perfectly well handled on an out-patient basis or not, and regardless of whether hospitalization would actually be detrimental to you or not. The bad ones will keep you long past the time hospitalization is doing you any good. They will keep you, in fact, until your insurance runs out. The bad ones will indiscriminately use the same treatment techniques on you and everyone else (e.g., electroshock therapy, antidepressant or major tranquilizer medication, intense confrontational group therapy). Most private hospitals are profit-making organizations; the bad ones are very-high-profit-making organizations, keeping overhead at a minimum and patients' fees at a maximum. Money, money, money, a lot of hypocrisy (because just as in the nursing home business, no one admits they're more interested in profits than in providing their patients with the best, most appropriate care), and a lot of unnecessary pain and suffering for the "patients" put through the money mill.

How does one avoid bad private hospitals? Well, how

does one avoid bad nursing homes? Or bad doctors? Unfortunately, there are no consumer guides. It's all by word of mouth. Contacting an academic center, a medical school or associated teaching hospital, a university psychology department, or mental health clinic are some of the ways of getting some reasonable advice (but no guarantees!).

Hospital-based Psychiatric Wards. One of the newest approaches to in-patient psychiatric care is to set aside a ward in a general hospital for psychiatric problems. The wards are usually small (fifteen to twenty beds), are often well staffed, are usually geared toward brief hospitalization, and have the decided advantage of giving you the feeling you have simply entered the local hospital for a week or two of rest and recovery from an emotional strain. This is worlds away from the sort of feeling you're likely to get if you're spirited off to some institution for "crazies," sequestered, as is often the case, behind high brick walls and, as often as not, a forest to boot. By its very smallness, its human scale, and its high visibility as part of a general hospital environment, many of the problems of the psychiatric institution are obviated. For most people who need to be hospitalized for an acute schizophrenic-type disorder, a small psychiatric ward in a good general hospital can usually provide all that's needed to get them over their disorganized state as quickly as possible.

CHRONIC SCHIZOPHRENIC-TYPE DISORDERS

As indicated in an earlier chapter, there are some people who remain chronically disorganized, who simply can't get their thoughts together, who can't find the motivation to face the ridicule and rejection of the world, who retreat into themselves, into their fantasies, fears, and suspicions, who indeed have a crippling emotional disorder (as often as not diagnosed chronic undifferentiated or simple schizophrenia), and who need all the help we can give them.

These are the people who in prior decades would have ended up forgotten on the back wards. In isolation, their emotional and mental state would deteriorate terribly until, in their bizarreness and primitiveness, they would begin to approximate the general public's mad notions of "madness."

Today there is no desire to chronically hospitalize anyone. Since the early 1960s the state hospitals have been emptying out their back wards and moving patients into the community, into foster homes, halfway houses, boarding homes, and so on. The number of patients in state hospitals has fallen drastically. In 1963 there were approximately five hundred thousand patients in state hospitals, many of them chronic patients. In 1973 there were approximately two hundred fifty thousand.[9] In some states (Massachusetts and California) a number of state hospitals have closed down altogether. Others have moved their quarters from fortresslike buildings far from the city to smaller clinics within the community.

In general, all of this has been of enormous benefit to those chronically disorganized individuals who in prior times would have been locked away from public view for life. Their fears and sufferings should never have set them apart, but drawn them closer to us, since their fears and sufferings were the same as ours, only more extreme, more crippling. The "us" and "them" should never have come into being, only a more troubled, less fortunate "us."

Many studies have shown that when "they"—the chronic schizophrenics—are returned to the community in a way which permits them to live with a modicum of dignity, to do some meaningful work, to maintain some self-determination, and to be, to some extent, freed from the curse of the label *chronic schizophrenic*, they manage much better than would have been predicted on the basis of their helplessness in the hospital. They have some disability, of course, but in general with the proper support they can lead self-respecting, if troubled, lives like the rest of us.[10]

Without proper support after leaving the hospital, however, many such individuals will be worse off than when they were in the hospital. The titles of two recent articles should convey the picture: "The Chronically Mentally-Ill Patient Shuffles to Oblivion" and "Foster Homes—the New Back Wards?"[11] It has been discovered that if you're a chronic hospital patient, it can sometimes be cheaper to maintain you outside the hospital. So you're put on welfare, set up in a shabby room somewhere, and told to take your medication and keep your weekly (or monthly) clinic appointments. That's it. The world can be a brutal, ugly, loathsome place as seen from the single window of a rented room in the middle of some bleak inner city, especially for someone who's frightened to death of life. Under such circumstances, some people are better off in a decent hospital. So there remains a place for long-term care for some individuals—at least, until we as a society can get together and *accept* and *support* those whom we have cast out and rejected.

The hospital is a better place for some people until we can learn to be better people ourselves.

SUMMARY

1. "All of the services that we traditionally provide in the hospital can be better provided, less expensively, and with fewer side-effects in other kinds of settings. The only reason we continue to use hospitals as centers for crisis intervention is because they are there. Thus suitable alternatives have not been developed in many communities." (Mendel, 1976, p. 124)*

---

*Reprinted by permission of the author and Jossey-Bass, Inc.

2. Since most of the time intensive community support is not available, hospitalization then becomes the most helpful alternative.

3. Psychiatric hospitalization for a schizophrenic-type disorder is a curse which can seriously affect a person's self-image, personal relationships, social interactions, and job opportunities.

4. Hospitalizing someone in a psychiatric hospital for the first time is, or should be, a momentous decision, given current prejudices. There are many compelling reasons for avoiding it if at all possible.

5. In general, most individuals who have undergone an acute disorganized episode, if hospitalized, only need to be hospitalized briefly (two to six weeks).

6. If someone who has undergone an acute psychotic episode ends up staying in the hospital for month after month after month, serious questions should be raised concerning the treatment, or the lack of treatment, the person is receiving.

7. Many state hospitals still have serious shortcomings in the quality of care they provide. Private hospitals, as state hospitals, may be relatively good or relatively bad. Psychiatric wards in good general hospitals have many advantages for the short-term treatment of an acute schizophrenic-type disorder.

8. Most chronically disorganized individuals will do relatively well outside the hospital if the community accepts and supports them adequately.

9. A good hospital is a better place for some chronically troubled people until we can learn to get over our own prejudices and be better people ourselves.

17

Psychotherapy

Does someone who has undergone an acute schizophrenic-
type disorganized episode (psychosis of unknown origin)
need to sit down with an individual or group psychothera-
pist one, or two, or three hours a week for one, or two, or
three years in order to prevent a recurrence? Or, put differently, is psychotherapy helpful for individuals with schizophrenic-type disorders? If so, what kind (psychoanalytic or
supportive, individual or group) and for how long?

PSYCHOTHERAPY IN GENERAL

Someone who's undergone a disorganized episode is not a
"schizophrenic" but a person like the rest of us with problems like the rest of us. The fact that he or she occasionally

becomes disorganized is a problem added to all the others. If psychotherapy could help with the "other problems" in the rest of us, it should help with the other problems that occur in someone prone to schizophrenic-type reactions.

So a more basic question would be: Is psychotherapy helpful for the rest of us? The answer, unfortunately, is not clear. There are a number of investigators who have looked carefully at the studies comparing various types of psychotherapy with "no-therapy" and have concluded that many of the studies are seriously flawed in the way they were designed or carried out. They have also noted that in many of the better-designed studies the individuals who received "no-therapy" or the briefest kind of supportive contact often did about as well as those receiving intensive psychotherapy. Also, it was noted in some studies that psychotherapy may have made some people a lot better, but others a lot worse, than if they hadn't had any therapy at all.

The above may seem somewhat incredible in the light of the widespread acceptance of psychotherapy as *the* way to solve our neurotic (or worse) problems. For the past forty years or so, ever since the start of Americans' love affair with psychoanalysis, an enormous number of books, popular and technical, have poured forth telling of the wonders of this or that type of psychotherapy. There has been no end to the claims. They still go on, proliferating as fast as the mind of man can fantasize new versions of life's "basic problem." It has only been relatively recently that psychotherapy has been asked to "prove itself." And the impetus for this came not from the clinicians, but from certain experimental psychologists (later to evolve into "behavior therapists") and, even more forcefully, from the increased funding of mental health services in the 1960s and the demand for cost-accountability.

This is not to say that individual or group psychotherapy is not helpful. It is merely to say that the evidence to date is not overwhelmingly convincing. And this is primarily because a properly designed study of psychotherapy is almost overwhelmingly difficult to carry out. My personal opinion is that for certain kinds of problems certain kinds of psychotherapy are very helpful. But to definitely establish this, in a rigorously controlled fashion, is extremely difficult. Until the claims of certain schools of psychotherapy (psychoanalysis, Rogerian, gestalt, etc.) are definitely established to be valid for treating such and such types of problems, then our scepticism is warranted, and our belief that this or that approach (e.g., primal scream) is *the* way to resolve this or that problem (depression, anxiety, etc.) should be clearly accepted as such—as a belief, or an act of faith, based on our own personal experience. Over the next decades we may expect the claims to continue to proliferate, with self-proclaimed experts rushing in to fill the evidential void with new revelations as to the fundamental way to cure man of his emotional ills.[1]

STUDIES OF PSYCHOTHERAPY IN SCHIZOPHRENIA

Only a handful of well-controlled studies have in fact been carried out on the effectiveness of individual psychotherapy in the schizophrenic-type disorders. One was carried out in Wisconsin by a group led by Carl Rogers. Chronically hospitalized "schizophrenics" were offered individual psychotherapy. They did only slightly better, on some measures, than the individuals who had received no such therapy. Another elaborate study was carried out in California by May in which forty-eight "schizophrenics" receiving drugs alone did much better than forty-six receiving no drugs and two hours of psychotherapy per week for up to a year. (Another forty-four individuals who received both psychotherapy *and* drugs did as well as, but no better than, the forty-eight receiving *only* drugs.) This meticulously carried-out study is cited again and again in the literature as proving that drugs are the most helpful approach in treating schizophrenic-type disorders and that psychotherapy adds little or nothing to what's provided by drugs alone (plus a generally supportive environment). However, the psychotherapy was carried out by first-year residents in psychiatry or relatively inexperienced junior staff. The severest blow to the claim that intensive psychoanalytic-type psychotherapy is helpful in the treatment of individuals with a chronic schizophrenic-type disorder was a study carried out by Grinspoon and others at the Massachusetts Mental Health Center. Twenty individuals received intensive psychotherapy (two hours a week for two years) by a group of psychoanalysts, many of whom were considered outstanding therapists and several of whom were considered authorities on the psychotherapy of "schizophrenia." Their conclusion, succinctly put, was:

> Psychotherapy alone (even with experienced psychotherapists) did little or nothing for chronic schizophrenic patients in two years. (Grinspoon, Ewalt, and Shader, 1977, p. 154)

Finally, it should be mentioned that in a study by Karon in Michigan, twenty-four individuals with a first-admission acute schizophrenic-type disorder appeared to receive definite benefit from intensive psychotherapy for one year, and the more experienced the therapist, the more the benefit. However, the study had many methodological shortcomings which have led others to question this interpretation of its results.

This recitation of the only well-controlled studies of the psychotherapy of "schizophrenia" may seem dull and uninteresting to a general public schooled in the colorful writings of any number of clinicians who have all found a way to "cure schizophrenia." Most of the books written about schizophrenic-type disorders in the past fifty years are either reports by individuals with schizophrenic-type disorders of their psychosis and cure, or the reports of clinicians, most often psychoanalysts, describing their approach to the therapy and cure of "schizophrenia." All of this makes for interesting and valuable reading, but the question must always be asked: Would this person have done as well, or better, with no therapy, or with a different kind of therapy? And we can only begin to answer that question by carrying out the kind of relatively dull, plodding, uninspiring studies such as those cited above.[2]

The best evidence to date, from the studies cited above, indicates that, so far as individual, almost-always psychodynamic psychoanalytic-type therapy is concerned:

> **1.** For individuals hospitalized for several years with a *chronic* schizophrenic-type disorder, intensive individual psychotherapy for up to two years doesn't appear to be greatly helpful in enabling the individual to become more functional.

> **2.** For individuals with an *acute* schizophrenic-type disorder, individual psychotherapy during the acute episode may be somewhat helpful, but far less helpful than medication appears to be.

SOME QUALIFICATIONS

Freud felt individuals with schizophrenic-type disorders couldn't be treated by psychoanalysis. Their "egos" were too defective; therefore, they couldn't form a working relationship with the therapist. Most therapists didn't want a working relationship with "schizophrenics" anyhow, and Freud's dictum gave them justification for their reprehensible neglect of this great segment of suffering humanity. "Schizophrenics" were considered "therapeutically hopeless," and thus were consigned to state hospital warehouses to be treated by institutional psychiatrists (whom, incidentally, the reigning analytic academic establishment looked down upon with scorn as second-class citizens). All this is part of the sad history of American psychiatry. What is also part of the history of American psychiatry is that while in Europe "schizophrenics" were thought of as essentially hopelessly brain-damaged, there were a handful of courageous, committed individuals who broke with both the orthodox analysts and the "hopelessly brain-damaged" theorists and decided "schizophrenics" were human beings who could be reached and touched and helped by caring fellow human beings and who devoted their lives to helping them. Harry Stack Sullivan, Frieda Fromm-Reichman, Harold Searles, John Rosen, and Silvano Arieti are the names of a few of these pioneers who, by their individual crusades in the service of "treating the untreatable," managed to restore some reason and humanity to our dealings with the "hopelessly insane." In their writings (and in those of some of the European existentialist psychiatrists such as Minkowski and Binswanger) they tore away the "madman's" mask (a mask *we* had put there) from the face of someone undergoing a schizophrenic-type reaction and showed us someone like ourselves, only more frightened, more vulnerable. We're still gathering the fruits of their humanizing efforts. More and more we see how great a difference our understanding and our acceptance and our human caring makes in whether someone else acts or thinks "crazy" or not. I have no doubt that their efforts, and the efforts of many others who have followed in their path since, have been of inestimable value in helping individuals through their schizophrenic-type reactions. There are things involving human dignity and decency and compassion, things such as simply being there with someone while they go through a hell too deep for words, which are not so easily measured, but which, in the very deepest sense, may make all the difference in the world.

SCHOOLS OF PSYCHOTHERAPY

Once you begin to read in the area of "schizophrenia" you'll be confronted with a very confusing array of recommendations for the successful psychotherapy of schizophrenia. Based on the current state of our knowledge, the most reasonable way to approach the whole situation is probably to say the following:

1. Most respectable theories derive from careful observations of some individuals and as such are probably valid for some individuals.
2. Most respectable approaches to the therapy of schizophrenia are probably successful for some individuals but certainly not for all.

A certain type of therapy may be helpful for some individuals, but not all. So when you sit down and read, for example, *I Never Promised You a Rose Garden,* you're reading about a technique of therapy—Frieda Fromm-Reichmann's—which was helpful for one young lady. We don't know if it would be helpful for someone else, and, as the critical reader will conclude, we don't even know if the young lady would have gotten well without any therapy, since, in many respects, she fell within the good-prognosis category. Only the rare therapist writes about his or her failures, even though, given the recalcitrant nature of some schizophrenic-type disorders, there probably have been any number of failures. Therapists, however, write books about their successes, not their failures.

Thus for one person Laing's approach may be the most effective, for someone else Fromm-Reichmann's. Because the theoreticians have felt compelled to generalize—overgeneralize, in my view—concerning the nature of "schizophrenia," this doesn't mean the rest of us need to go along with their speculations. For all we know, "schizophrenia" may have many different causes—and many different cures.

Despite the differing theories, however, there is one point about which most therapists agree. They all tend to see individuals with chronic, or recurrent, schizophrenic-type disorders as having failed to grow up. They see the person as, in many ways, still emotionally stuck at the level of a child—according to some theorists (for example, Klein), at the level of a newborn. This has very important implications for therapy, because we don't grow up overnight. No matter what you do, you can't transform a two-year-old into a mature adult in five years, and you can't transform an emotionally immature person into an emotionally mature one overnight either. Most experienced therapists don't talk in terms of one or two years of therapy for the more pervasive schizophrenic-type disorders. It takes fifteen to twenty years to raise a child properly. There are no magical shortcuts. Most therapists feel individuals with chronic schizophrenic-type disorders need the same kind of year-in and year-out, sustained, almost parental concern, attention, and guidance. The fact that, in the studies cited, up to two years of intensive psychotherapy failed to make much difference would not be surprising to many therapists who have worked with individuals with schizophrenic-type disorders. Hymen Spotnitz, one among many "experts" on the therapy of "schizophrenia," has said it takes two years to convince the person to even get *started* in therapy. After five years he only expects to *begin* to see some fundamental changes taking place. We very much want to believe in instant transformations, but unfortunately we aren't put together that way, and despite all the promises held out to us by the latest miracle worker, the road to emotional maturity is a long, painful, and arduous one.[3]

In sum: *For certain individuals with great adjustment difficulties and a recurrent, or chronic, schizophrenic-type disorder, very-long-term individual therapy may well prove helpful, though how helpful and whether it would be more helpful than other approaches (e.g., group therapy) remains to be established.*

GROUP THERAPY

Some recent studies have indicated that certain types of group psychotherapy may be more helpful than individual psychotherapy for individuals after the acute episode. These kind of results fall in line with much of what has been learned over the past thirty years concerning the effects of isolation and neglect on individuals prone to recurrent schizophrenic-type disorders. The disorganization is often an expression of becoming overwhelmed by people and the world (see Chapter 6). "Craziness" perpetuates itself because it helps to keep the world and other people at a safe distance. Such individuals are not likely to reach out to us. We have to reach out to them and prove to them that the world need not be such a hurtful place. The more that those with chronic schizophrenic-type problems become involved with caring, empathetic people, the less they're forced into their own disorganization or "craziness." The same holds true for those still-vulnerable individuals recovering from an acute psychotic episode. Individual therapy tends to focus their attention in upon themselves; group therapy and various kinds of supportive group counseling and social activities tend to turn their attention away from themselves and out "into the world" of other people. If the others seem to be clearly "with you" and not "against you," then you're on the way to restoring some confidence in yourself and the possible good intentions of other people. (The problem, however, which all too frequently arises is that many individuals with schizophrenic-type disorders will insist on seeing others as "against them," even when they're not, and this is where the special skills of the group leader or counselor are called for.)[4]

FAMILY THERAPY

Many theories of the nature of "schizophrenia" see the causes of such disorders as residing within the family. (Laing, Lidz, and Haley are three among many theorists in this area.) Consequently, a great deal of attention has been focused in recent years on "treating the schizophrenic family" and not merely the "sick" or "schizophrenic" individual. Many varieties of family therapy have been tried. Though the whole area is enormously interesting, the best one can conclude currently, in my view, is what Massie and Beels concluded in their review of the effectiveness of family therapy:

> In summary, we can conclude that outcome studies of the family therapy of schizophrenia are relatively limited and inadequate in scope. . . . There is a clear need for more systematic evaluation of results in this area. Nonetheless family techniques do give indications of effectiveness in treating schizophrenia. . . . while the expenditure of time and effort with family techniques is modest compared to that of other forms of therapy, neither the durability of beneficial change associated with family therapy nor the frequency of need for retreatment has been tested with a sufficient number of cases and sufficient length of follow-up. (Massie and Beels, 1972, p. 35)

It's almost always the case that family or friends are doing things to make someone's schizophrenic-type disorder worse. Most people simply don't know how to deal with such an event. At the very least, the family itself often needs some good advice on how best to weather the storm. More often than not, it turns out they're doing a great many things which could be changed to the advantage of all concerned. Family therapy may help them make these difficult changes. If the family won't change, then family therapy may help the individual undergoing a schizophrenic-type reaction finally make the break from an impossible situation. For many young adults with a schizophrenic-type disorder, making the decision to begin an independent existence can often be of decisive importance.

BEHAVIOR THERAPY

Behavior therapy is an approach to changing other people's behavior, and indirectly their ideas and attitudes, by quite consciously rewarding certain kinds of behavior and failing to reward or punishing certain other (undesirable) behaviors. Much of the early research on the application of behavior-therapy techniques to humans involved chronically hospitalized, severely disturbed "schizophrenic" patients. (I reiterate at this point that most of the disturbed behavior of such individuals was due to neglect and not to any "schizophrenia" per se.) By rewarding someone for using the toilet, changing clothes, sweeping the floor, talking to other people, and so on, it was found, not too amazingly, that such appropriate behaviors would increase. Reading many of the early studies now, one cannot help but feel repelled by the way patients were manipulated like pigeons in a cage, with little respect for their human dignity. The argument went that someone who sits all day mute, smearing his own feces on the wall, doesn't have much dignity left, and the end (restoration of self-respect) justifies the means (manipulation). The twentieth century is all too familiar with such arguments.

Despite the reservations some might have about such "operant conditioning" techniques, the fact is they do work to some extent in encouraging, or forcing, a person to alter his behavior. Behavior-therapy approaches have become much more sophisticated in recent years, and immeasurably more humane. (For example, the therapists pay much more attention to what the individual wants to change about himself or herself, rather than to what the institution feels should be changed.) In dealing with acute schizophrenic-type disorders, behavior therapy techniques and wards set up on behavior-therapy principles (e.g., a "token economy") have not been demonstrably more effective than other types of therapy. In dealing with individuals with chronic schizophrenic-type disorders, behavior therapy has proven somewhat helpful in a hospital setting. One review, by a leading exponent of behavior therapy, concludes:

> Behavior modification technology has been applied to a wide variety of schizophrenic behaviors, including social interaction, delusions, hallucinations, self-help and grooming skills and instrumental work behavior. The token economy, a systematic and consistent use of reinforcement principles to [alter] patients' behaviors in a ward milieu, has been shown to be effective in increasing the adaptive repertoire of institutionalized schizophrenics. . . . Generalization of treatment effects to new situations, such as the community, has not yet been shown to occur regularly as a result of behavior modification efforts. (Liberman, 1972, p. 47)

I would add further that a ward set up on behavior-therapy principles is a small totalitarian state in which human rights are drastically curtailed. The individual quite literally is treated like a two-year-old child. The line between helping such individuals and degrading and exploiting them is perilously thin.

Anyone hospitalized on such a ward should have the right to leave or at least to change wards. If they don't have that right, somebody should introduce them to a good lawyer. There's a great difference between being confined to an institution and being confined to an institution and treated like a guinea pig. We may have the right to do the former, but I don't think we have, or at least we shouldn't have, the right to do the latter.

SOME RECOMMENDATIONS

I've cited the "best evidence" with respect to the effectiveness of various forms of therapy in treating "schizophrenia." Quite candidly, the recommendations below are based on the "best evidence" tempered by a great deal of personal experience.

Medication seems to decrease the vulnerability of some individuals to disorganized or schizophrenic-type episodes. But beyond whatever relief medication may afford, there is still someone who has led a more or less satisfying life, who is filled, as the rest of us, with his or her own very unique hopes, joys, anxieties, and despairs. Does *that* person need help? Is *that* person lost and floundering, dispirited or desperate, embittered or paralyzed with fear? Has a unique crisis temporarily overwhelmed a relatively stable person, or has the person been adrift for years on a sea of anguish and despair? The fact that an individual had an acute schizophrenic-type episode tells me almost nothing about how stable, or vulnerable, the person is. As Orwell portrayed in his novel *1984*, and as has been subsequently demonstrated by sadists (e.g., POW camp officials and police interrogators) the world over, everyone has something he or she simply can't bear. If you're clever enough, you'll find it. Some individuals who have had an acute psychotic episode have "cracked" under a very unique constellation of stresses which are highly unlikely to recur. These are the good-prognosis individuals who never have recurrences. There may be no pressing indications for extended psychotherapy at all (except in the eyes of some therapists who think almost everyone is maladjusted and in need of therapy). On the other hand, there are those chronically disordered individuals who are exquisitely vulnerable to even the slightest stress. The kind of support given by a group or group activities appears to be the best way to help them over their fears. In between these extremes, there are people who have or have had an acute schizophrenic-type disorder and who, to put it simply, have a great many additional difficulties. For some of these, certain types of group therapy appear to be helpful, and for others, certain types of family or long-term individual therapy may be of great help.

SUMMARY

1.   For individuals with a *chronic* schizophrenic-type disorder, intensive individual psychotherapy for up to two years doesn't appear to be greatly helpful in enabling such individuals to become more functional. (Psychotherapy, however, may be helpful in other as-yet-undetermined ways; for example, it may decrease such an individual's sense of estrangement, or emptiness, or hopelessness.)

2.   Some clinicians feel individuals with *chronic* schizophrenic-type disorders need to be in therapy for many years before significant change occurs. However, no controlled

studies have been done on the efficacy of individual therapy for periods of longer than two years.

3. For individuals with *acute* schizophrenic-type disorders, there is some evidence that individual psychotherapy during the acute episode may be somewhat helpful (but less helpful than medication appears to be).

4. Following an acute schizophrenic-type episode, there is some evidence that group therapy or supportive counseling is beneficial for some individuals.

5. Family therapy appears to be helpful at times; however, properly controlled studies need to be done to determine if in fact it is as helpful, or more helpful, than other treatment approaches.

6. Behavior-therapy techniques appear to offer little in the treatment of acute schizophrenic-type disorders. They may be helpful in promoting change in some individuals with chronic schizophrenic-type disorders. Behavior-therapy techniques, however, invite abuse, especially in an institutional setting. Special measures should be taken, by the individual or the individual's family or friends, if not by the staff, to ensure that individual rights and prerogatives are meticulously respected.

Notes

These notes are intended primarily (1) to provide references supporting statements made in the text and (2) to indicate reviews or studies which may be usefully consulted to provide further analyses of issues discussed in the text. I have also added some comments on research methodology and on the interpretation of certain research results.

(Consult the References section directly for names cited in the text but not cited here.)

Preface

1. See B. Fish (1977) for an excellent recent review of the literature on the relationship between childhood and adult schizophrenic-type disorders.

2. See Broen (1968) and Chapman and Chapman (1973) for two superb summaries of the literature on cognitive and psychophysiologic functioning in the schizophrenic-type disorders. See also Maher (1977) for an anthology of summary papers by various outstanding researchers. Chapman and Chapman (1973) contains a detailed summary of the methodological reasons why so much of the extensive research on cognitive and perceptual disturbances in the schizophrenic-type disorders has proven of equivocal value. It should be required reading for all graduate students before the next avalanche of theses is loosed upon the world. Cromwell (1972) has also written an article, "Strategies for Studying Schizophrenic Behavior," which should be required reading, especially the section "Schizophrenic-Normal Comparisons" (pp. 124–27). Suffice it to say here that very few practically useful findings are going to emerge from such investigations until research concentrates on (a) differences between individuals, or groups of individuals, with schizophrenic-type disorders (or "psychoses of unknown origin"), (b) differential performance and functioning of the same individual over time (for example, during and after an acute disorganized episode), and (c) correlations between any differences found and differential outcome, biochemical markers, or response to various interventions.

Chapter 2

1. Concerning the great overuse of the diagnostic label "schizophrenia" in the United States, see also Koehler and Jacoby (1978) who compared hospital admission diagnoses in three countries. 86 percent of hospital psychiatric admissions were diagnosed as schizophrenic in New York, whereas in London and Homburg/Saar (West Germany) only 41 percent and 34 percent respectively were so diagnosed.

2. See Jaspers (1976) for an account of Swedenborg as "schizophrenic" (he also discusses Van Gogh, Strindberg, and the German poet Holderlin).

Chapter 3

1. For a review of the depersonalization-derealization syndrome see Sedman (1970).

2. For descriptions of the manic and depressive psychoses see Mendels (1970) and standard textbooks of psychiatry and abnormal psychology.

3. Concerning the Nazi war criminals see Fest (1970). For a particularly harrowing biography of an "ordinary man" (Stangl, Commandant of Treblinka), see Sereny (1974).

4. Concerning mental illness and violent crimes in general see Lunde (1976). ("The incidence of psychosis among murderers is no greater than the incidence of psychosis in the total population. Furthermore, the percentage of murderers among former mental patients is actually slightly lower than that among persons who have never been in a mental hospital."—Lunde, 1976, p. 93)

5. For a general theoretical overview of the hallucinogens see Snyder (1974). For the effects of chronic LSD use see Blacker et al. (1968), Bowers (1971), and Breakey et al. (1974). For a comprehensive review of the effects of marijuana see Grinspoon (1977).

Chapter 4

1. Concerning the shift from one subtype to another see Janzarik (1961).

2. Concerning schizoaffective illness as a variant of manic-depressive illness see McCabe (1975 and 1976) for two reviews with further references.

3. For a review of European conceptions of "schizophrenia" see F. Fish (1962).

4. The criteria of Feigner et al. (1972) detailed in the text are research criteria designed to identify a small group of indi-

viduals whom almost everyone would agree have had a schizophrenic-type disorder.

5. Schneider (1959) several decades ago identified a set of symptoms supposedly diagnostic (in the absence of organic illness) of "schizophrenia." See also F. Fish (1962) and Taylor (1972). Though useful, they have proven to be far from pathognomonic; see, for example, Carpenter et al. (1973).

6. Numerous other investigators have defined "schizophrenic" subtypes in terms of good versus poor premorbid adjustment. For example, see Klein and Davis (1969), who define three types of schizophrenic reactions (childhood asociality, fearful paranoid, and schizoaffective), or Forrest and Hay (1973), who define three similar types (the schizophrenic syndrome of young adults, the paranoid psychoses of middle life, and the schizophreniform psychoses).

7. See Vaillant (1964b) for a review of some of the earlier diagnoses, such as "benign stupor," used to label acute good-prognosis schizophrenic-type disorders.

Chapter 5

1. Concerning good-prognosis "schizophrenia" see Stephens (1970) for a general review; see also Langfeldt (1969) and McCabe (1975 and 1976).

2. See Gittleman-Klein and Klein (1969) for a classic study of premorbid adjustment and outcome; see also Strauss and Carpenter (1977).

3. See Vaillant (1964) and Stephens (1970) for two classic American studies of prognostic factors. See Strauss and Carpenter (1977) for a study which failed to confirm many of the classic prognostic factors (though, not surprisingly, chronic maladjustment predicted continued maladjustment in their study for all types of psychiatric in-patients).

4. Concerning M. Bleuler's observations it should be mentioned that he goes on to make two less encouraging state-

ments: "My statistics do not indicate that the number of permanent full recoveries has increased since the improvement of therapeutic methods.

". . . The statistics do not show that the number of severe chronic psychoses is diminished by therapy" (M. Bleuler, 1970, p. 214).* (It should be reiterated that M. Bleuler is using a very narrow definition of "schizophrenia,"—i.e., those schizophrenic-type disorders with a relatively poor prognosis.)

Chapter 6

1. Concerning the bombing of Coventry see Stevenson (1977, p. 165). Concerning psychiatric casualties in intelligence work see McGarvey (1973, p. 7) or Stevenson (1977, p. 211).

2. Stress psychoses are also termed *reactive* or *psychogenic psychoses;* see McCabe (1975) for a detailed study with extensive references.

3. Concerning the types of hysterical psychoses see Hirsch and Hollender (1969). Many clinicians are unaware of the important concepts developed in this paper (that is, they continue to diagnose hysterical-type psychoses as schizophrenic reactions).

4. Concerning schizophrenic-type psychoses occurring "out of the blue" Bowers has written: "Patients often initially said that 'It came out of the blue'; however, on further questioning one could essentially always discover a state of mind characterized by conflict and impasse. . . . 'There was no way out' " (Bowers, 1974, p. 176–77).

5. Concerning the early stages of psychotic reactions see Conrad (1958), Bowers (1974), and Donlon and Blacker (1973). Their stages compare to those in the text in the following table.

---

*Reprinted from *Behavioral Science*, Vol. 15, No. 3, 1970, by permission of James G. Miller, M.D., Ph. D., and the author.

Text	Conrad	Bowers	Donlon and Blacker
Generalized Anxiety	Trema	1. Destructuring of perception and affect a) Heightened awareness	1. Denial and anxiety 2. Depression
Altered sense of self	Apophany	b) Ideas of reference and influence	3. Panic and primitive fantasies
Psychosis	Apocalypse Consolidation	2. Destructuring of the sense of self a) Identity dissolution b) Delusions	4. Psychotic disorganization

See also Detre and Jarecki's textbook of psychiatry (1971) for a detailed analysis of early signs and McGhie and Chapman (1961) for a classic description of early perceptual changes. Docherty, et al. (1978) have recently summarized many studies of the early stages of the psychotic disorders, and their review should be consulted for additional references.

6. Concerning the relationship of acute schizophrenic disorders to manic-depressive illness see McCabe (1976).

7. For an incisive reply to some of Szasz's arguments see Moore (1975).

8. Concerning inconsistency see Kolakowski (1969): "The race of inconsistent people continues to be one of the greatest sources of hope that possibly the human species will somehow manage to survive. . . . total consistency is tantamount to fanaticism, while inconsistency is the source of tolerance" (p. 213).

Chapter 7

1. Concerning the "end-stage" classification see Leonhard (1959), summarized in F. Fish (1962).

2. Concerning the average citizen's tolerance for "craziness," or resistance to seeing deviant behavior as mentally disordered, see Gove (1970).

3. Concerning the ability of individuals with schizophrenic-type disorders to recognize normal word associations see Fuller and Kates (1969), Lisman and Cohen (1972), Moran et al. (1964), and O'Brien and Weingartner (1970).

4. Concerning Binswanger's central metaphor of losing one's (existential) way in the world see Binswanger (1968, p. 342) for his essay on *"Verstiegenheit"* ("extravagance").

5. For an unforgettable portrait of one of life's eccentrics (or "chronic schizophrenics") see Peter Wilson's *Oscar: An Inquiry into the Nature of Sanity* (1974). Knut Hamsun's novel *Hunger* (1967), written in 1890, remains the most sensitive and accurate portrayal I know of in literature of the daily despairs and triumphs of someone struggling with what we would call a chronic schizophrenic-type disorder.

Chapter 8

1. For summaries of the literature and two operational definitions of the borderline condition see Grinker et al. (1968) and Gunderson and Singer (1975).

2. See Kernberg (1967) for an example of the broad definition of the borderline disorders. Concerning the use of the term to describe "egotists" see Kohut (1971) for an extremely technical analytic exposition of the "narcissistic character." Concerning the borderline condition and the existentialists see Libowitz and Newman (1967) and Chessick (1972).

3. Concerning the genetics of the "schizophrenic spectrum disorders" see Kety et al. (1975).

4. Concerning individuals diagnosed as borderline remaining "borderline" see Werble (1970) and Gunderson et al. (1975) for two of the few follow-up studies to date.

5. Grinker et al. (1968) in their comprehensive study derived four basic overall characteristics of borderline states:

1. *Anger,* which constituted the main or only affect.

2. *A deficit in affectional relationships,* which were "anaclitic, dependent or complementary, but rarely reciprocal."

3. *An absence of indications of consistent self-identity* and "vacillating behavior associated with a confused view of the self . . . 'as if I were watching myself playing a role.' "

4. *Depression*—"not the typical guilt-laden, self-accusatory remorseful 'end of the rope' type, but more a loneliness as the subjects realize their predicament of being unable to commit themselves in a world of transacting individuals" (pp. 90, 91).

6. Borderline Personality Disorders will be included in the new psychiatric nomenclature as an official diagnosis. "Operational criteria" for diagnosing someone as having a borderline personality disorder are as follows:

The following are characteristic of the individual's long-term functioning and are not limited to episodes of illness. At least five of the following are required:

1. Impulsivity or unpredictability in at least two areas which are potentially self-damaging . . .

2. A pattern of unstable and intense interpersonal relationships . . .

3. Inappropriate intense anger or lack of control of anger . . .

4. Identity disturbance . . .

5. Affective instability . . .

6. Problems tolerating being alone . . .

7. Physically self-damaging acts . . .

8. Chronic feelings of emptiness or boredom. (APA, 1978, pp. K21–22)*

Chapter 9

1. For a short review of the currently more popular theories see Chodoff and Carpenter (1975).

*American Psychiatric Association Task Force on Nomenclature and Statistics, *Diagnostic and Statistical Manual of Mental Disorders* (3rd ed., draft 1/15/78), Washington, D.C.: APA, 1978. Reprinted with permission of APA.

2. See Gardiner (1961) for a discussion of the nature of historical explanation; see also McGuire (1971) for an interpretation of psychoanalytic reconstructions and Frank (1963) for a classic analysis of the interrelationships between belief, explanation, and personal change.

3. For a prime example of dialectical thought gone wild see Laing's *Knots* (1970). See also Foucault (1965), Kolakowski (1969), and Jacoby (1975) for several dazzling (and therefore relatively blinding) examples of dialectical cognitive style.

4. For a comprehensive presentation of the "high-risk" strategy, see the review by Garmezy and Streitman (1974), which should be required reading for anyone interested in investigating the schizophrenic-type disorders. B. Fish (1977) has also written an important review, focusing on the antecendents of childhood "schizophrenia." See also Cancro (1976) for a compilation of several related articles.

5. Concerning the "schizophrenogenic malevolent mother" Chodoff and Carpenter (1975) note in their review that "a prominent feature in current thinking has béen a withdrawal from these formulations" (p. 68).

6. Concerning infamous infancies and the theories of Klein, Fairbairn, and Winicott see Guntrip (1971) for a summary overview. See Stierlin (1968) for a variant interpretation. See Hill (1955) for a more traditional analytic perspective.

7. Concerning ferocious families, for one of the earliest and most influential formulations see Sullivan (1962). See Weakland (1960) for an exposition of the double-bind; see also Haley (1963) for a variant, and Laing and Esterson (1971). (But note: "The intriguing Bateson-Jackson concept of the double-bind seems to have suffered something of the fate of the malevolent schizophrenogenic mother."—Chodoff and Carpenter, 1975, p. 69) Lidz (1973) and Wynne et al. (1975) have also developed influential family interaction theories of "schizophrenia" which emphasize pathological communication patterns.

8. Concerning cruel worlds see, for example, the later Laing (1967), or, for a much subtler statement, Foucault (1965).

Much of the currently popular (in Europe, if not here) Marxist-socialist-oriented analysis of deviant behavior in general, and "schizophrenia" in particular, is based on this perspective.

Chapter 10

1. For two comprehensive reviews of current knowledge of the genetics of schizophrenic-type disorders see Rosenthal (1970) and Gottesman and Shields (1976). The latter review is followed by the commentaries of several other authorities, including Lidz (1973) (who essentially finds the genetic evidence inconclusive: "Of course, I am disappointed that the adoption studies, which held such great promise, have as yet settled so little"—p. 410) and Kety (1969), who replies with a critique of Lidz's own research (on interactions within the families of "schizophrenics") "which may displease him even more than have our findings" (p. 422).

2. See Rosenthal (1970, pp. 104–8), for a review of some representative incidence studies; see also Babigian (1975). See Torrey (1973) for a discussion of the "Western technological society" hypothesis.

3. See Kohn (1973) for a review of the relationship between social class and the occurrence of schizophrenic-type disorders.

4. Results of the Danish adoption study cited in the text are presented in Rosenthal (1970) and Kety et al. (1968); see also Kety et al. (1975).

5. Concerning the finding by the Danish study that borderline (or "schizophrenic spectrum") disorders occurred with increased frequency in the families of individuals with chronic schizophrenic-type disorders, consider the following paradigm:
Four different schizophrenic-type disorders (A, B, C, and D) and four different borderline-type disorders (d, e, f, and g), where d is a milder form of D, but the types e, f, and g are unrelated to A, B, C, or D. If such were the case, then a study

such as the Danish study would find the borderline disorders "genetically related" to the schizophrenic-type disorders when in fact only one subtype of the schizophrenic disorders (i.e. subtype D) is related to one subtype of the borderline disorders (i.e. subtype d) and most borderline disorders have no such relationship to the schizophrenic disorders at all. (When one reads sweeping conclusions concerning biochemical disorders or every variety of perceptual or cognitive or psychophysiological dysfunction being "associated" with schizophrenia, the above paradigm for analyzing the results should prove equally useful, since in almost all such studies it is only a subgroup of the "schizophrenic" individuals who show disordered functioning.)

6. Concerning IQ, a number of studies have shown a slightly decreased IQ associated with groups of individuals with schizophrenic-type disorders. It's clear that schizophrenic disorganization interferes with efficient thinking. One of the well-known signs of "schizophrenic" performance on IQ tests is an erratic inconsistent performance. For example, on a vocabulary test incorrect answers may be given to the simplest items and the most difficult answered correctly, thus indicating interference with the expression of a relatively normal intelligence. Interference, transient or chronic, with the development or expression of normal intelligence, however, is quite different from a genetically determined limited intellectual capacity.

7. Concerning the roughly 90 percent of individuals with chronic schizophrenic-type disorders who have no relatives with a similar disorder Wynne has said: "What has been more interesting to me than the question of how ten percent of the offspring of schizophrenics become schizophrenic has been how come ninety percent do not" (L. C. Wynne, quoted in *Psychiatric News*, Oct. 21, 1977, p. 33).

Chapter 11

1. A great number of articles appear every year reviewing the latest biochemical research on the schizophrenic-type

disorders. Usually it's enough to know who the reviewer is to know which biochemical studies will be emphasized (those even remotely related to the reviewer's own biochemical hypothesis) and which will be relatively neglected. Despite the claims to objectivity, at the very forefront of scientific research balanced, unbiased reviews are as difficult to come by as balanced, unbiased views (see Kuhn, 1970). Snyder's (1974) book, though heavily weighted in favor of the dopamine hypothesis, is one of the best general presentations of the biochemical theories available. See Himwich (1970) and the *Schizophrenia Bulletin*, vol. 2, no. 1, 1976, for two excellent compilations of review articles by leading proponents of the various biochemical theories.

2.   See Kety (1969) for a classic review of the methodological deficiencies in many of the earlier biochemical studies. Concerning the pink and mauve factors see also the review by Wyatt et al. (1971).

3.   See Snyder (1974) for a detailed exposition of the topics covered in the sections on the disordered-transmitter hypothesis and the effects of amphetamines, hallucinogens, and the major tranquilizer drugs.

4.   The adenochrome hypothesis was advanced by, among others, Hoffer and Osmond, who subsequently became two of the leading exponents of megavitamin therapy. As discussed in Chapter 15, the megavitamin theory and the experiments supporting it have run into much the same criticisms from the scientific "establishment" as did the adenochrome experiments. This is not surprising, since megavitamin therapy is a logical extension of the adenochrome hypothesis of "schizophrenia." Suffice it to say here that neither the hypothesized action of adenochrome nor the hypothesized (reversing) action of vitamin B_3 (as a methyl-group acceptor) have been satisfactorily demonstrated by other researchers, making the experimental underpinnings for the megavitamin hypothesis appear to many singularly unimpressive.

5.   See Meltzer and Stahl (1976) for a detailed review of the dopamine studies and, in particular, studies of dopamine–major tranquilizer interactions.

6. See Brown and Herrnstein's (1975) textbook of psychology, pp. 642–51, for a superb discussion, using the experiments involving "Tarexin" as an example, of the way to properly analyze and evaluate experimental "discoveries" and scientific "breakthroughs."

7. See Durrell and Archer (1976) for a brief review, with extensive references, of recent research on the autoimmune hypothesis. Their conclusion: "The weight of evidence, therefore, does not support an auto-immune hypothesis for schizophrenia" (p. 154).

8. Studies of the DMT-bufotenin and related hypotheses of endogenous hallucinogen formation are reviewed briefly by Rosengarten and Friedhoff (1976). The viral hypothesis is presented by Torrey and Peterson (1976).

9. See Villet (1978) for a popularized account of the endomorphins. Despite the hyperbole of its title ("Opiates of the mind: The biggest medical discovery since penicillin") the article is an extremely well-informed and informative survey of an exciting, if somewhat confused, area of new research.

Chapter 12

1. See Bridges and Bartlett (1977) for a recent review (with extensive references) and apologia for the use of psychosurgery in certain conditions (predominantly nonschizophrenic). See May (1974) or May (1975b) for a review of the few controlled studies of the effects of psychosurgery. (Note: The four studies May singles out as adequately controlled occurred before or during the introduction of the major tranquilizers. No satisfactory comparison of psychosurgery versus drugs is cited.) Concerning the traditional leucotomy (or lobotomy) May concludes: "The original operation did have therapeutic value in certain cases, but was abandoned because of its adverse secondary effects and because of the introduction of phenothiazines." He goes on to say: "The newer operations reported to be more effective and less associated with secondary effects have simply not been evaluated in any scientific

experiment. At most, there has been an attempt to follow up the results of occasional cases without comparison with a control group" (May 1975b, p. 978).

Breggin, a prominent critic of psychosurgery, has stated, "Most thorough reviews of the subject of psychosurgery, pro or con, have admitted that there is little or no empirical evidence that psychosurgery 'works' and that one must rely upon the authority of the psychosurgeons themselves" (Breggin 1977, p. 26). There is, however, certainly some empirical evidence that it sometimes "works"; what is lacking are good controlled studies comparing it to other treatment approaches (my personal opinion is that we can dispense with such studies in particular and psychosurgery in general).

Concerning the "attempt to follow up the results of occasional cases" and the relying upon the word of "authority," there is the instructive case of Thomas R. "suffering from paranoia and uncontrollable outbursts of rage and violence" who was subjected to psychosurgery. His outcome was reported in the literature, in part, as follows: "Four years have passed since the operation, during which time, Thomas has not had a single episode of rage."

Breggin did his own follow-up and reported that the patient was unable to care for himself and had to be hospitalized periodically for violent and psychotic behavior. Eight years after the operation a neurologist was reported to have stated that "the patient would never be able to function in society" (related in Sutherland, 1976, p. 193, from an original report in Chorover, 1974).

I cite this as one particularly appalling example (if Breggin's follow-up is to be believed) of what is not that uncommon in medical research: a combination of limited observation and self-serving distortion of what is observed (a sort of tunnel vision through rose-colored spectacles). This is why throughout this book I have emphasized the importance of rigorously designed, controlled research. It is one of the few relative safeguards we have against our own vanity and credulity. (Consider the above example: For several years the research received wide publicity for having established an effective treatment for some forms of violent behavior. The next step in a society plagued with violent behavior and obsessed with law-and-order solutions? . . . I leave you to ponder the solutions some societies might have decided upon based on such "findings.")

Chapter 13

1.   Concerning the treatment of relatively severe "endogenous" depressions, most studies have shown a 40–50 percent improvement rate with placebo (some as high as 65 percent—for example, see Greenblatt, 1977), a 60–70 percent improvement rate with antidepressant medication, and an 80–90 percent improvement rate with ECT. See Lehmann (1968) for a summary statement and Klein and Davis (1969) for a detailed review. See Smith et al (1969) for an instructive analysis of antidepressant drug studies which demonstrates, among other things, how the efficacy of the drug varies with the design of the study (for example, single- versus double-blind, fixed-dose versus unregulated-dose, in-patient versus out-patient population, etc.). See Raskin (1974) for a discussion of another crucial variable, the type of depression. (These same concerns need to be brought to bear in evaluating any studies on the efficacy of drugs in schizophrenic-type disorders.)

2.   The Royal College of Psychiatrists (1971) in Britain has recently come out with the following summary statement concerning the indications for the use of ECT: "These findings suggest that in the treatment of schizophrenia ECT has no general value comparable to neuroleptic medication. The question arises whether there are specific features which respond to ECT" (p. 263).

3.   May has carefully evaluated the studies comparing ECT with other modes of treatment for the schizophrenic-type disorders and has concluded: "The balance of the relatively few controlled studies can be taken as establishing that ECT is

superior to milieu therapy alone but less effective and more hazardous than drug therapy" (May, 1975a). That, I think, is a fair conclusion, but to give you a further insight into the sometimes puzzling nature of scientific conclusions, I might add that in a related report May (1975b) reviews the few studies comparing ECT to no treatment (or general-milieu treatment) and, out of what appear to be six relevant studies, concludes that "5 studies . . . indicate that ECT was not better than a placebo." The one study which showed ECT better than milieu was his own! Nonetheless, he concludes above that "the balance of the relatively few well-controlled studies can be taken as establishing that ECT is superior to milieu . . ." (pp. 936, 975).

That conclusion may seem rather baffling to someone who considers five greater than one. What May unwittingly has done, however, is to administer a master lesson in the nature of "scientific objectivity." He quite simply decided his one study was a better study than the other five studies. But it doesn't quite come out that way. Why did he feel compelled to state his conclusion in the peculiar, "scientifically objective" way he did? A worthwhile point to ponder.

4. Kalinowsky, another leading proponent of ECT, also finds himself concluding that ECT is most helpful where it's needed least (i.e., in patients with "acute onset of illness" and "duration of illness less than one year"). He recognizes that "all this corresponds to the spontaneous prognosis of untreated schizophrenics," but his conclusion that "reliable statistics have shown convincingly that the results with shock treatments, both convulsive and insulin, double the figures of spontaneous remissions in a mixed group of schizophrenics" (Kalinowsky, 1975, p. 1974) is quite misleading, since reliable statistics do not show that ECT is more effective than drugs for such a group. But he leaves that part out. (You perhaps are beginning to appreciate why you should not let yourself be seduced by scientific authority and objectivity. Everyone has biases, and if you're going to see through the veneer of "scientific objectivity" to the authoritative biases, you've got to

do the thinking for yourself. There's no other way if, as in the above example, you don't want to be victimized by half-truths.)

5.   See Friedberg (1977) for a review of studies of cellular damage after ECT.

6.   See Squire (1977) for a recent study (with extensive references) of memory function after ECT.

7.   Concerning ECT and the insurance companies, consider the fact that, for example, in Massachusetts most Blue Shield policies pay a maximum of five hundred dollars for out-patient psychiatric services per year. For ECT, however, there is no limit. The psychiatrist, quite literally, is rewarded for choosing ECT. This, as you may imagine, is not exactly what you would call an ideal arrangement.

8.   Both of the above cited papers (notes 5 and 6, and Greenblatt, 1977) are contained in a recent issue of the *American Journal of Psychiatry* which devoted a special section to papers on ECT. That a special section was devoted to ECT (whereas, for example, another leading research publication, the *Archives of General Psychiatry,* had published no article on ECT in the prior two years) is perhaps an indication of how anxious the rank and file of the psychiatric establishment have become over current legislative threats to limit the use (and abuse) of ECT. Frankel's paper in the same issue is particularly notable for the level of ad hominem vitriol expended in reply to Friedberg's "not only inaccurate and careless, but also somewhat indiscriminate" review of the literature (Frankel, 1977, p. 1016).

Similar vitriolic replies were generated by a recent article by Viscott in the *Psychiatric News* outlining the abuses of ECT as he had noted them in the Massachusetts area (which, based on my experience, appeared to be, if anything, a somewhat understated account). (See Viscott's chapter "Quacks; or, Nobody's Perfect But . . . " in his autobiographical account *The Making of a Psychiatrist* (1972) for a portrait of the local "shock shops" in action.)

Chapter 14

1. Baldessarini (1977) has written an excellent book on psychopharmacology which provides a thorough review of the topics discussed in this chapter. Klein and Davis (1969) wrote an earlier exhaustive review which remains an invaluable reference. An excellent short guide to the use of drugs in psychiatry is the book by Honigfield and Howard (1973)— though directed at mental health workers, it should prove equally useful to the general public as well.

2. Concerning the great increase in drug overdoses see O'Brien (1977).

3. Concerning the nondrug treatment of schizophrenic-type disorders see Mosher et al. (1975).

4. Concerning the few studies which have attempted to characterize subgroups of individuals with acute schizophrenic-type disorders who will do as well (or better) on placebo as on drugs see Carpenter, et al. (1977) and Evans (1976) and Goldberg and Mattson (1968). For two papers on the related topic of which individuals with chronic schizophrenic-type disorders will do as well on placebo as on drugs see Prien and Klett (1972, p. 66) for an early summary and Hogarty et al. (1974). Some ongoing projects are summarized in Keith et al. (1976, pp. 552–53). Research in both of these areas is vitally needed and will probably mark the next significant advance in the drug treatment of the schizophrenic-type disorders.

5. See Prien and Klett (1972) and Davis (1975) for two reviews of the literature concerning relapse rates upon the withdrawal of maintenance medications in individuals with chronic schizophrenic-type disorders. In my discussion I have simplified the actual situation somewhat. *Relapse* is usually defined as a moderately severe exacerbation of symptoms, frequently as a florid exacerbation requiring hospitalization. Some of the approximately 40 percent who aren't counted as "relapses" after withdrawal of medication may, in

fact, do less well off the medication (they may feel more anxious, more preoccupied, more irritable, etc.). In other words, they may not become psychotic when the medication is withdrawn, but it still may have been benefiting them considerably.

6. The distinction between those who relapse on placebo and those who don't relapse on placebo, but do if the placebo is stopped (so-called "placebo responders"), is not emphasized enough either in research reviews or clinical recommendations. Only a few studies have addressed themselves to this important issue (i.e., relapse rate upon stopping placebo). See Prien and Klett's (1972) review. My estimate that 20 percent of individuals with chronic schizophrenic-type disorders are placebo responders is based on Caffey's and on Whittaker and Hay's reports (cited in Prien and Klett, 1972) in which 30 percent and 31 percent respectively were found to be placebo-responders. (Due to the short-term follow-up of each study, I have somewhat arbitrarily considered a low estimate of 20 percent as probably a more realistic long-term relapse estimate.) Further research is obviously needed in this area.

Chapter 15

1. Reports of studies on megavitamin, or orthomolecular, therapy appear in the *Journal of Orthomolecular Psychiatry*. See also the anthology edited by Hawkins and Pauling (1973). For two succinct critiques of research on the orthomolecular treatment of the schizophrenic-type disorders see Autry (1975) and Lipton (1976).

Chapter 16

1. Two influential books which have dealt with the history of the development of psychiatric hospitals (in the West) should be mentioned. Foucault's *Madness and Civilization* (1965) is written in a fascinatingly contorted style which is only surpassed by his doubly contorted conclusions (which

fall in line with biases that have only become explicit in his later writings on penal institutions). For a trebly contorted view see Szasz's *The Manufacture of Madness: A Comparative Study of the Inquisition and the Mental Health Movement* (1970). Both books are monuments to synecdochical thinking (taking the part for the whole) and to the half-truth and should be consulted by anyone interested in the refinements of the art of dialectical rhetoric.

2. Concerning the sociology of institutionalization see Goffman (1959) and Scheff (1966).

3. Concerning the rapid relief of psychotic symptomatology see Anderson et al. (1976) and Carter (1977).

4. Concerning hospitalization, Scott in England, among others, echoes Mendel's sentiments: "Mental illness is not a myth, but coming to the hospital because of illness is a myth. Patients wanting help can secure it as out-patients; we have no treatment available in the hospital that is not also available outside" (Scott, 1974, p. 70).

5. See Langsley et al. (1971) and Stein et al. (1975) for two representative studies of hospital versus nonhospital treatment of the acute schizophrenic-type disorders.

6. See Scheff (1966 and 1975) for a discussion of the stigma associated with mental illness. See Rabkin (1974) for an excellent review of the literature with extensive references.

7. See Hargreaves et al. (1977) for a recent study which found some advantage to longer-term hospitalization for a subgroup of individuals with schizophrenic-type disorders (those with good premorbid functioning). They comment, however, upon their finding as follows: "This is not to say that the long-term group would not have functioned just as well with extended partial day care or intensive out-patient intervention. Experimental evidence regarding these other comparisons suggests this may be so . . ." (pp. 310–11).

8. For a recent study, with further references, of the factors involved in the decision to admit, see Rose et al. (1977).

9.   Figures on the fall in the population of state hospitals are taken from Schmidt et al. (1977). The title of their report is instructive; "The Mentally Ill in Nursing Homes: New Back Wards in the Community."

10.   For a classic study of the rehabilitation of chronically hospitalized, presumably "hopelessly schizophrenic" individuals see Fairweather et al. (1969), summarized in Sanders (1972). For a recent excellent study see Linn et al. (1977).

11.   See Reich and Siegel (1973) for the report "The Chronically Mentally-Ill Patient Shuffles to Oblivion" and Murphy et al. (1972) for the report "Foster Homes—the New Back Wards?"

Chapter 17

1.   Concerning the effectiveness of psychotherapy in general see Bergin (1971) for a comprehensive review of the literature up to 1970. See Sloan et al. (1975, pp. 15–48) for a more recent overview of the literature; their superb study should be consulted by anyone interested in evaluating the outcome of psychotherapy. In their study of individuals with moderately severe neurotic symptoms they found that, after four months, "93% of the patients treated by behavior therapy were considered improved while 77% of both psychotherapy and wait-list patients were either improved or recovered" (p. 101). The very high spontaneous (or no-treatment) improvement rate is why anyone can go out and invent a new form of "psychotherapy" and claim it's effective in "80% or 4 out of every 5 individuals," and it's why you end up believing that all sorts of ridiculous things have "cured" you of your emotional upsets, when, in fact, more often than not, you would have cured yourself anyway. Some types of therapy do help, but it takes some exquisitely designed research, such as that done by Sloan et al., to show that they do.

2.   For the four cited studies of psychotherapy in schizophrenia see Grinspoon et al. (1972), Karon and VandenBos (1972), May (1968), and Rogers (1967). For an excellent review

of such studies see Feinsilver and Gunderson (1972); see also May (1975b).

3. For a useful outline of the various schools of psychotherapy of the schizophrenic-type disorders see Auerbach (1961). For several of the classic texts on the psychotherapy of the schizophrenic-type disorders see Sullivan (1962), Fromm-Reichmann (1960), and Searles (1966). See Arieti (1974), Scheflen (1961), and Spotnitz (1968) for additional variants on the analytic approach. The British school (see Guntrip, 1971, for a review) and the existentialist school (see Binswanger, 1968, and Minkowski, 1953) have also contributed helpful perspectives.

For a Rogerian approach, there is a modest paper by Gendlin, "Therapeutic Procedures in Dealing with Schizophrenics" (in Rogers, 1967, pp. 369–400), which, I must say, has more to say, and in a more concise, direct, and readily understandable fashion, than most lengthy volumes I've read on the subject—which typically, following Freud's unfortunate example, labor under a monstrous load of jargon, prolixity, obfuscation, and gratuitous metapsychological complexification—the paradigm apparently being: the more obscure, the more profound (which, of course, is true when applied to the bottoms of wells, but less so when applied to human thought).

4. See O'Brien et al. (1972) for a recent study which found group therapy more helpful than individual therapy following an acute schizophrenic-type reaction. See also Hogarty et al. (1974) for a study which indicated the value of supportive counseling.

References

Adorno, T. W. Sociology and Psychology. *New Left Review*, 46, 1972.

American Psychiatric Association Task Force on Nomenclature and Statistics. Diagnostic and Statistical Manual of Mental Disorders (3rd ed., draft 1/15/78). Washington, D.C., 1978.

American Psychiatric Association. *Diagnostic and statistical manual of mental disorders* (2nd ed.). Washington, D.C., 1968.

Anderson, W. H., Kuehnle, J. C., and Catanzano, D. M. Rapid treatment of acute psychosis. *American Journal of Psychiatry*, 133:1076, 1976.

Arieti, S. *Interpretation of schizophrenia* (2nd ed.). New York: Basic Books, 1974.

Arnold, O. H., *Die Therapie der Schizophrenie.* Stuttgart: Hippokrates, 1963.

Auerbach, A. H. A survey of selected literature on psychotherapy of schizophrenia. In A. E. Scheflen, (ed.), *A psychotherapy of schizophrenia: Direct analysis.* Springfield, Ill.: Charles C. Thomas, Publisher, 1961.

Autry, J. H. Workshop on orthomolecular treatment of schizophrenia: A report. *Schizophrenia Bulletin,* 12:94, 1975.

Babigian, H. M. Schizophrenia: Epidemiology. In A. M. Freedman, H. I. Kaplan, and B. J. Sadock (eds.), *Comprehensive textbook of psychiatry—II* (2nd ed.). Baltimore: Williams and Wilkins Co., 1975.

Baldessarini, R. J. Frequency of diagnosis of schizophrenia versus affective disorders from 1944 to 1968. *American Journal of Psychiatry,* 127:59, 1970.

Baldessarini, R. J. *Chemotherapy in psychiatry.* Cambridge: Harvard University Press, 1977.

Bergin, A. E. The evaluation of therapeutic outcome. In A. E. Bergin and S. L. Garfield, *Handbook of psychotherapy and behavior change.* New York: Wiley, 1971.

Bernhard, T. *Gehen.* Frankfurt am Main: Suhrkamp Verlag, 1971. (Excerpts translated by P. O'Brien).

Bernhard T., *The Lime Works* (translated by S. Wilkins). New York: Alfred A. Knopf, 1973.

Bernhard, T. Rede, in Botond, A. (ed.) Uber Thomas Bernhard. Frankfurt am Main: Suhrkamp Verlag, 1970. (Excerpt translated by P. O'Brien and S. Wilkins)

Binswanger, L. *Being-in-the-world: Selected papers of Ludwig Binswanger* (trans. J. Needleman). New York: Harper Torchbooks, 1968.

Blacker, K., et al. Chronic users of LSD: The acidheads. *American Journal of Psychiatry,* 125:341, 1968.

Bland, R., and Parker, J. Prognosis in schizophrenia. *Archives of General Psychiatry,* 33:949, 1976.

Bleuler, E. *Dementia praecox; or, the group of schizophrenias* (trans. Zinkin) Monograph Series on Schizophrenia: No. 1. New York: International Universities Press, 1966.

Bleuler, M. Some results of research in schizophrenia. *Behavior Science*, 15:3, 1970. (Reprinted in Cancro, 1971.)

Bleuler, M. Chronische Schizophrenie. *Wien Zeitschrift fur Nervenheilkunde*, 29:177, 1971.

Bowers, M. Psychoses precipitated by psychotomimetic drugs: A follow-up study. *Archives of General Psychiatry*, 34:832, 1971.

Bowers, M. *Retreat from sanity: The structure of emerging psychosis.* New York: Human Sciences Press, 1974.

Breakey, W. R., Goodell, H., Lorenz P. C., and McHugh, P. R. Hallucinogenic drugs as precipitants of schizophrenia. *Psychological Medicine* 4(3):255, 1974.

Breggin, P. R. If psychosurgery is wrong in principle . . . ? *Psychiatric Opinion*, 14:23, 1977.

Bridges, P. K., and Bartlett, J. R. Psychosurgery: Yesterday and today. *British Journal of Psychiatry*, 131:249, 1977.

Broen, W. E., Jr. *Schizophrenia; Research and theory.* New York: Academic Press, 1968.

Brown, B. In Lyons, R.D., 20 million people or more need mental care, U.S. panel asserts. *New York Times*, Sept. 16, 1977.

Brown, G., et al. *Schizophrenia and social care.* London: Oxford University Press, 1966.

Brown, R., and Herrnstein, R. J. *Psychology.* Boston: Little, Brown, and Co., 1975.

Cancro, R. (ed.). *The schizophrenic syndrome: An annual review.* Vol 1, 1971; vol. 2, 1972; vol. 3, 1973; vol. 4, 1974–1975. New York: Brunner/Mazel 1971, 1972, 1973, 1976.

Carpenter, W. T., Jr., McGlashan, T. H. and Strauss, J. S. The treatment of acute schizophrenia without drugs: An investigation of some current assumptions. *American Journal of Psychiatry*, 134:14, 1977.

Carpenter, W. T., Jr., Strauss, J. S., and Muleh, S. Are there pathognomic symptoms in schizophrenia? An empiric investigation of Schneider's first-rank symptoms. *Archives of General Psychiatry*, 28:847, 1973.

Carter, R. G. Psychotolysis with haloperidol: Rapid control of the acutely disturbed psychotic patient. *Diseases of the Nervous System*, 38:237, 1977.

Castenada, C. *A separate reality: The teachings of don Juan, a Yaqui way to knowledge.* New York: Pocket Books, 1968.

Chapman, L. J., and Chapman, J. P. *Disordered thought in schizophrenia.* Englewood Cliffs, N.J.: Prentice-Hall, 1973.

Chessick, R. D. *How psychotherapy heals.* New York: Science House, 1969.

Chessick, R. D. Externalization and existential anguish. *Archives of General Psychiatry,* 27:764, 1972.

Chodoff, P., and Carpenter, W. T. Psychogenic theories of schizophrenia. In E. Usdin (ed.), *Schizophrenia: Biological and psychological perspectives.* New York: Brunner/Mazel, 1975.

Chorover, S. L. Psychosurgery: A neuropsychological perspective. In Boston University Law Review and Center for Law and Health Science, *Psychosurgery: A multidisciplinary symposium.* Lexington, Mass.: Lexington Books, 1974.

Conrad, K. *Die beginnende Schizophrenie.* Stuttgart: Thieme, 1958.

Cooper, D. *Psychiatry and anti-psychiatry.* New York: Ballantine Books, 1967.

Cottman, S., and Mezey, A. Community care and prognosis in schizophrenia. *Acta Psychiatrica Scandanavica,* 53:95, 1976.

Cromwell, R. L. Strategies for studying schizophrenic behavior. *Psychopharmacologia,* 24:121, 1972.

Davis, J. M. Overview: Maintenance therapy in psychiatry—I: Schizophrenia. *American Journal of Psychiatry,* 132:1237, 1975.

Detre, T. P., and Jarecki, H. G. *Modern psychiatric treatment.* Philadelphia: J. B. Lippincott Co., 1971.

Docherty, J. P., Van Kammen, D. P., Siris, S. G., and Marder, S. R. Stages of onset of schizophrenic psychosis. *American Journal of Psychiatry,* 135:420, 1978.

Donlon, P. T., and Blacker, K. H. Stages of schizophrenic decompensation and reintegration. *Journal of Nervous and Mental Diseases,* 157:200, 1973.

Donnelly, J. Incidence of psychosurgery in the United States, 1971–1973: Summary. In *Scientific Proceedings in Summary Form: The 130th Annual Meeting of the American Psychiatric Association.* Washington, D.C.: American Psychiatric Association, 1977.

Durrell, J., and Archer, E. G. Plasma proteins in schizophrenia: A review. *Schizophrenia Bulletin*, 2:147, 1976.

Evans, J. R., Rodnick, E. H., Goldstein, M. J., and Judd, L. L. Premorbid adjustment, phenothiazine treatment, and remission in acute schizophrenics. *Archives of General Psychiatry*, 27:486, 1972.

Evans, R. I. *R. D. Laing: The man and his ideas*. New York: E. P. Dutton and Co., 1976.

Fairweather, G. W., Sanders, D. H., Cressler, D. L., and Maynard, H. *Community life for the mentally-ill: An alternative to institutional care*. Chicago: Aldine Publishing Co., 1969.

Feighner, J., et al. Diagnostic criteria for use in psychiatric research. *Archives of General Psychiatry*, 26:57, 1972.

Feinsilver, D. B., and Gunderson, J. G. Psychotherapy for schizophrenics—is it indicated? A review of the relevant literature. *Schizophrenia Bulletin*, 6:11, 1972.

Fest, J. *The face of the Third Reich: Portraits of the Nazi leadership* (trans. M. Bullock). New York: Pantheon Books, 1970.

Fish, B. Neurobiologic antecedents of schizophrenia in children: Evidence for an inherited, congenital neurointegrative defect. *Archives of General Psychiatry*, 34:1297, 1977.

Fish, F. *Schizophrenia*. Bristol, England: John Wright and Sons, 1962.

Forest, A., and Hay, A. The schizophrenias: Operational definitions. *British Journal of Medical Psychology*, 46:337, 1973.

Foucault, M. *Madness and civilization: A history of insanity in the Age of Reason* (trans. R. Howard). New York: Random House, 1965.

Frank, J. D. *Persuasion and healing: A comparative study of psychotherapy*. New York: Schocken Books, 1963.

Frankel, F. H. Current perspectives on ECT: A discussion. *American Journal of Psychiatry*, 134: 1014, 1977.

Frankl, V. *The doctor and the soul: From psychotherapy to logotherapy*. New York: Random House, 1973.

Freedman, A. M., Kaplan, H. I., and Sadock, B. J. (eds.). *Comprehensive Textbook of Psychiatry—II* (2nd ed.). Baltimore: Williams and Wilkins Co., 1975.

Friedberg, J. Shock treatment, brain damage, and memory loss: A neurologic perspective. *American Journal of Psychiatry*, 134:1010, 1977.

Fromm-Reichmann, F. *Principles of intensive psychotherapy*. Chicago: Phoenix Books, 1960.

Fuller, G. D., and Kates, S. L. Word association repetoire of schizophrenics and normals. *Journal of Consulting and Clinical Psychology*, 33:497, 1969.

Gardiner, P. *The nature of historical explanation*. London: Oxford University Press, 1961.

Garmezy, N., and Streitman, S. Children at risk: The search for the antecedents of schizophrenia. *Schizophrenia Bulletin*, 8:14 (part 1), 9:55 (part 2), 1974.

Gittelman-Klein, R., and Klein, D. Premorbid asocial adjustment and prognosis in schizophrenia. *Journal of Psychiatric Research*, 7:35, 1969. (Reprinted in Cancro, 1971.)

Goffman, E. *Asylums: Essays on the social situation of mental patients and other inmates*. Garden City, N.Y.: Anchor Books, 1959.

Goldberg, S. C., and Mattson, N. B. Schizophrenic sub-types defined by response to drugs and placebo. *Diseases of the Nervous System*, 29, suppl.: 153, 1968.

Gottesman, I. I., and Shields, J. A critical review of recent adoption, twin, and family studies of schizophrenia: Behavioral genetics perspectives. *Schizophrenia Bulletin*, 2:360, 1976.

Gove, W. R. Societal reaction as an explanation of mental illness: An evaluation. *American Sociological Review*, 35:873, 1970.

Green, H. *I never promised you a rose garden*. New York: Holt, Rinehart, and Winston, 1964.

Greenblatt, M. Efficacy of ECT in affective and schizophrenic illness. *American Journal of Psychiatry*, 134:1001, 1977.

Grinker, R. An essay on schizophrenia and science. *Archives of General Psychiatry*, 20:1, 1969. (Reprinted in Cancro, 1971.)

Grinker, R., Werble, B., and Drye, R. *The borderline syndrome*. New York: Basic Books, 1968.

Grinspoon, L. *Marijuana reconsidered* (rev. ed.). Cambridge; Harvard University Press, 1977.

Grinspoon, L., Ewalt, J. R., and Shader, R. I. *Schizophrenia: Phar-*

macotherapy and psychotherapy. Baltimore: Williams and Wilkins Co., 1972.

Gross, G., and Huber, G. Zur Prognose der Schizophrenie. *Psychiatrica Clinica* (Basel), 6:1, 1973.

Gunderson, J. G., Carpenter, W. T., and Strauss, J. S. Borderline and schizophrenic patients: A comparative study. *American Journal of Psychiatry*, 132:1257, 1975.

Gunderson, J. G., and Singer, M. T. Defining borderline patients: An overview. *American Journal of Psychiatry*, 132:1, 1975.

Guntrip, H. J. S. *Psychoanalytic theory, therapy, and the self.* New York: Basic Books, 1971.

Gurland, B. J., et al. Cross-national study of diagnosis of mental disorders: Hospital diagnoses and hospital patients in New York and London. *Comprehensive Psychiatry*, 11:18, 1970. (Reprinted in Cancro, 1971.)

Haley, J. *Strategies of psychotherapy.* New York: Grune and Stratton, 1963.

Haley, J. *The power tactics of Jesus Christ and other essays.* New York: Discus Books, 1971.

Hamsun, K. *Hunger* (trans. R. Bly). New York: Noonday Books, 1967.

Hargreaves, W. A., Glick, I. D., Drues, J., Showstack, M. P. H., and Feigenbaum, E. Short versus long hospitalization: A prospective controlled study. *Archives of General Psychiatry*, 34:305, 1977.

Hawk, A. B., et al. Diagnostic criteria and five-year outcome in schizophrenia: A report from the International Pilot Study of Scmizophrenia. *Archives of General Psychiatry*, 32:343, 1975.

Hawkins, D. R., and Pauling, L. (eds.). *Orthomolecular Psychiatry.* San Francisco: W. H. Freeman, 1973.

Heston, L. L. Psychiatric disorders in foster home reared children of schizophrenic mothers. *British Journal of Psychiatry*, 112:819, 1966.

Hill, L. B. *Psychotherapeutic intervention in schizophrenia.* Chicago: University of Chicago Press, 1955.

Himwich, H. E. *Biochemistry, schizophrenias, and affective illnesses.* Baltimore: Williams and Wilkins Co., 1970.

Hirsch, S. J., and Hollender, M. H. Hysterical psychosis: A clarification of the concept. *American Journal of Psychiatry*, 125:909, 1969.

Hoffer, A. Orthomolecular psychiatry in theory and practice. *Drug Therapy*, August 1977, p. 79.

Hogarty, G. E., Goldberg, S. C., Schooler, N. R., and Ulrich, R. F. Drug and sociotherapy in the after-care of schizophrenic patients: Two-year relapse rates. *Archives of General Psychiatry*, 31:603, 1974.

Hogarty, G. E., and Ulrich, R. F. Temporal effects of drugs and placebo in delaying relapse in schizophrenic out patients. *Archives of General Psychiatry*, 34:297, 1977.

Honigfield, G., and Howard, A. *Psychiatric drugs: A desk reference.* New York: Academic Press, 1973.

Jacoby, R. *Social amnesia: A critique of conformist psychology from Adler to Laing.* Boston: Beacon Press, 1975.

Janzarik, W. Die Typologie schizophrener Psychosen im Lichte der Verlaufsbetrachtung. *Archiv für Psychiatrie und Zeitschrift für d. ges. Neurologie*, 202:140, 1961.

Jaspers, K. *Stringberg und Van Gogh: Versuch einer pathographischen Analyse unter vergleichender Heranziehung von Swedenborg und Holderlin* (2nd ed.), Berlin: J. Springer, 1926.

Kafka, F. *The diaries of Franz Kafka, 1910–1913* (ed. M. Brod, trans. J. Kresh). New York: Schocken Books, 1965.

Kalinowsky, L. B. The convulsive therapies. In A. M. Freedman, H. I. Kaplan, and B. J. Sadock; (eds.), *Comprehensive textbook of psychiatry—II* (2nd ed.) Baltimore: Williams and Wilkins Co., 1975.

Karlsson, J. L. Inheritance of schizophrenia. *Acta Psychiatrica Scandanavica*, suppl. 247, 1974.

Karon, B. P., and VandenBos, G. R. The consequences of psychotherapy for schizophrenic patients. *Psychotherapy: Theory, Research, and Practice*, 9:111, 1972.

Keith, S. J., Gunderson, J. G., Reifman, A., Buchsbaum, S., and Mosher, L. R. Special report: Schizophrenia, 1976. *Schizophrenia Bulletin*, 2:509, 1976.

Kernberg, O. Borderline personality organization. *Journal of the American Psychoanalytic Association*, 15:641, 1967.

Kety, S. S. Biochemical hypotheses and studies. In L. Bellak and L.

Loeb (eds.), *The schizophrenic syndrome.* New York: Grune and Stratton, 1969.

Kety, S. S., et al. The types and prevalency of mental illness in the biological and adoptive families of adopted schizophrenics. In D. Rosenthal and S. S. Kety (eds.), *The transmission of schizophrenia.* Oxford: Pergamon Press, 1968.

Kety, S. S., Rosenthal, D., Wender, P. H., Schulsinger, F., and Jacobsen, B. Mental illness in the biological and adoptive families of adopted individuals who have become schizophrenic: A preliminary report based upon psychiatric interviews. In R. Fieve, D. Rosenthal, and H. Brill (eds.), *Genetic research in psychiatry.* Baltimore: Johns Hopkins University Press, 1975.

Klein, D., and Davis, J. *Diagnosis and drug treatment of psychiatric disorders.* Baltimore: Williams and Wilkins Co., 1969.

Koehler, K., and Jacoby, C. Schneider-oriented psychiatric diagnosis in Germany compared with New York and London. *Comprehensive Psychiatry,* 19:19, 1978.

Kohn, M. L. Social class and schizophrenia: A critical review and a reformulation. *Schizophrenia Bulletin,* 7:60, 1973.

Kohut, H. *The analysis of the self.* New York: International Universities Press, 1971.

Kolakowski, L. *Toward a Marxist humanism: Essays on the left today* (trans. J. Peel). New York: Grove Press, 1969.

Krupp, M. A. and Chatton, M. J. *Current medical diagnosis and treatment.* Los Altos, Calif.: Lange Medical Publications, 1976.

Kuhn, T. S. *The structure of scientific revolutions* (2nd ed.). Chicago: University of Chicago Press, 1970.

Laing, R. D. *The divided self: A study of sanity and madness.* London: Tavistock Publications, 1960.

Laing, R. D. *The politics of experience.* New York: Pantheon Books, 1967.

Laing R. D. *Knots.* New York: Pantheon Books, 1970.

Laing, R. D., and Esterson, A. *Sanity, madness, and the family* (2nd American ed.). New York: Basic Books, 1971.

Langfeldt, G. Schizophrenia: Diagnosis and prognosis. *Behavioral Science*, 14, 1969. (Reprinted in Cancro, 1971.)

Langsley, D., Machotka, P., and Flomenhaft, K. Avoiding mental hospital admission: A follow-up study. *American Journal of Psychiatry*, 127:1391, 1971.

Lehmann, H. E. Clinical perspectives on anti-depressant therapy. *American Journal of Psychiatry*, 124 (11), suppl.:12, 1968.

Leonhard, K. *Aufteilung der endogenen Psychosen* (2nd ed.) Berlin: Akademie Verlag, 1959.

Levenson, A. J., et al. Acute schizophrenia: Efficacious outpatient treatment approach as alternative to full-time hospitalization. *Diseases of the Nervous System*, 38:242–45, 1977.

Liberman, R. P. Behavioral modification of schizophrenia: A review. *Schizophrenia Bulletin*, 6:37, 1972.

Libowitz, N. A., and Newman, K. M. Borderline personality and the theatre of the absurd. *Archives of General Psychiatry*, 16:268, 1967.

Lidz, T. *Origin and treatment of schizophrenic disorders.* New York: Basic Books, 1973.

Linn, M. W., Caffey, E. M., Klett, J., and Hogarty, G. Hospital versus community (foster) care for psychiatric patients. *Archives of General Psychiatry*, 34:78, 1977.

Lipton, M. A. The pharmacological treatment of schizophrenia with special emphasis on megavitamin therapy. In L. J. West and D. E. Flinn (eds.) The treatment of schizophrenia: Progress and prospects. New York: Grune and Stratton, 1976.

Lisman, S., and Cohen, B. Self-editing deficits in schizophrenia: A word-association analogue. *Journal of Abnormal Psychology*, 79:181, 1972.

Lunde, D. *Murder and madness.* San Francisco: San Francisco Book Co., 1976.

McCabe, M. S. Reactive psychoses: A clinical and genetic investigation. *Acta Psychiatrica Scandanavica*, suppl. 259:1, 1975.

McCabe, M. S. Reactive psychoses and schizophrenia with good prognosis. *Archives of General Psychiatry*, 33:571, 1976.

McGarvey, P. *CIA: The myth and the madness.* Baltimore: Penguin Books, 1973.

McGhie, A., and Chapman, J. Disorders of attention and perception in early schizophrenia. *British Journal of Medical Psychology,* 34:103, 1961.

McGrath, S. D. Nicotinamide treatment: An addendum. *Schizophrenia Bulletin,* 10:5, 1974.

McGrath, S. D., O'Brien, P. F., Power, P. J., and Shea, J. P.: Nicotinamide treatment of schizophrenia. *Schizophrenia Bulletin,* 5:74, 1972.

McGuire, M. T. *Reconstructions in psychoanalysis.* New York: Appleton-Century-Crofts, 1971.

Maher, B. A. (ed.) Contributions to the psychopathology of schizophrenia. New York: Academic Press, 1977.

Malcolm, N. *Ludwig Wittgenstein: A memoir.* London: Oxford University Press, 1958.

Massie, H. N., and Beels, C. C. The outcome of the family treatment of schizophrenia. *Schizophrenia Bulletin,* 6:24, 1972.

Masterson, J. F. *Treatment of the borderline adult: A developmental approach.* New York: Brunner/Mazel, 1976.

May, P. R. A. *Treatment of schizophrenia.* New York: Science House, 1968.

May, P. R. A. Treatment of schizophrenia, III: A survey of the literature on prefrontal leucotomy. *Comprehensive Psychiatry,* 15:375, 1974.

May, P. R. A. Schizophrenia: Overview of treatment methods. In A. M. Freedman, H. I. Kaplan, and B. J. Sadock (eds.), *Comprehensive textbook of psychiatry—II* (2nd ed.). Baltimore: Williams and Wilkins Co., 1975a.

May, P. R. A. Schizophrenia: Evaluation of treatment methods. In A. M. Freedman, H. I. Kaplan, and B. J. Sadock (eds.), *Comprehensive textbook of psychiatry—II* (2nd ed.), Baltimore: Williams and Wilkins Co., 1975b.

Meltzer, H. Y., and Stahl, S. M. The dopamine hypothesis of schizophrenia: A review. *Schizophrenia Bulletin,* 2:19, 1976.

Mendel, W. *Schizophrenia: The experience and its treatment.* San Francisco: Jossey-Bass, 1976.

Mendels, J. *Concepts of Depression*. New York: John Wiley and Sons, 1970.

Minkowski, E. *La schizophrenie*. Paris: Desclee de Brouwer, 1953.

Moore, M. S. Some myths about "mental illness." *Archives of General Psychiatry*, 32:1483, 1975.

Moran, L. J., Mefferd, R. B., and Kimble, J. P. Idiodynamic sets in word associations. *Psychological Monographs*, 78(2), whole no. 579, 1964.

Mosher, L. R., Menn, A., and Matthews, S. Soteria: Evaluation of a home-based treatment for schizophrenia. *American Journal of Orthopsychiatry*, 45:455, 1975.

Murphy, H. B. M., Pennee, B., and Luchins, D. Foster homes: The new back wards? *Canadian Mental Health*, 20, suppl. 71:1, 1972.

National Institute of Mental Health. *Utilization of mental health resources by persons diagnosed with schizophrenia*. DHEW publication no. (HSM) 73-9110. Washington, D.C.: U.S. Government Printing Office, 1973.

Niskanen, P., and Achte, K. A. The course and prognosis of schizophrenic psychoses in Helsinki: A comparative study of first admissions in 1950, 1960, and 1965. *Monographs from the Psychiatric Clinic of the Helsinki University Central Hospital*, no. 4, 1972.

Noyes, A., and Kolb, L. *Modern clinical psychiatry* (6th ed.). Philadelphia: W. B. Saunders Co., 1963.

O'Brien, C. P., Hamm, K. B., Ray, B. A., Pierce, J. F., Luborsky, L., and Mintz, J. Group versus individual psychotherapy with schizophrenics. *Archives of General Psychiatry*, 27:474, 1972.

O'Brien, J. P. Increase in suicide attempts by drug ingestion: The Boston experience, 1964–1974. *Archives of General Psychiatry*, 34:1165, 1977.

O'Brien, J. P., and Weingartner, H. Associative structure in chronic schizophrenia. *Archives of General Psychiatry*, 22:136, 1970.

Odier, C. *Anxiety and magic thinking*. New York: International Universities Press, 1956.

Prien, R. F., and Klett, C. J. An appraisal of the long-term use of tranquilizing medication with hospitalized chronic schizophrenics: A review of the drug discontinuation literature. *Schizophrenia Bulletin*, 5:64, 1972.

Professional Staff of the United States–United Kingdom Cross-National Project. The diagnosis and psychopathology of schizophrenia in New York and London. *Schizophrenia Bulletin*, 11:80, 1974.

Rabkin, J. Public attitudes toward mental illness: A review of the literature. *Schizophrenia Bulletin*, 10:9, 1974.

Raskin, A. A guide for drug use in depressive disorders. *American Journal of Psychiatry*, 131:181, 1974.

Reich, R., and Siegel, L. The chronically mentally ill shuffle to oblivion. *Psychiatric Annals*, 3:35, 1973.

Research Task Force of the National Institute of Mental Health. Research in the services of mental health. DHEW Pub. No. (ADM) 75-236. Washington, D.C.: U.S. Government Printing Office, 1975.

Rogers, C. R. (ed.). *The therapeutic relationship and its impact: A study of psychotherapy with schizophrenics.* Madison: University of Wisconsin Press, 1967.

Rose, S. O., Hawkins, J., and Apodaca, L. Decision to admit: Criteria for admission and readmission to a Veterans Administration hospital. *Archives of General Psychiatry*, 34:418, 1977.

Rosengarten, H., and Friedhoff, A. J. A review of recent studies of the biosynthesis and excretion of hallucinogens formed by methylation of neurotransmitters or related substances. *Schizophrenia Bulletin*, 2:90, 1976.

Rosenhan, D. On being sane in insane places. *Science*, 179:250, 1973. (Reprinted in Scheff, 1975.)

Rosenthal, D. *Genetic theory and abnormal behavior.* New York: McGraw-Hill Book Co., 1970.

Royal College of Psychiatrists' memorandum on the use of electroconvulsive therapy. *British Journal of Psychiatry*, 131:261, 1971.

Sanders, D. H. Innovative environments in the community: A life for the chronic patient. *Schizophrenia Bulletin*, 6:49, 1972.

Sartorius, N., et al. The International Pilot Study of Schizophrenia. *Schizophrenia Bulletin*, 11:21, 1974.

Sartre, J. P. *Existential psychoanalysis.* South Bend, Ind.: Gateway Editions, 1962.

Scheff, T. J. *Being mentally ill: A sociological theory.* Chicago: Aldine, 1966.

Scheff, T. J. (ed.). *Labeling madness.* Englewood Cliffs, N.J.: Prentice-Hall, 1975.

Scheflen, A. E. A psychotherapy of schizophrenia: Direct analysis. Springfield, Ill.: Charles C. Thomas, Publisher, 1961.

Schmidt, L. J., Reinhardt, A. M., Kane, R. L., and Olsen, D. M. The mentally ill in nursing homes: New back wards in the community. *Archives of General Psychiatry*, 34:687, 1977.

Schneider, K. *Clinical Psychopathology* (trans. M. Hamilton). New York: Grune and Stratton, 1959.

Scott, R. D. Cultural frontiers in the mental health service. *Schizophrenia Bulletin*, 10:58, 1974.

Searles, H. F. *Collected papers on schizophrenia and related subjects.* New York: International Universities Press, 1966.

Sedman, G. Theories of depersonalization: A re-appraisal. *British Journal of Psychiatry*, 117:1, 1970.

Sereny, G. *Into that darkness: From mercy killing to mass murder.* New York: McGraw-Hill Book Co., 1974.

Sloane, R. B., Staples, F. R., Cristol, A. H., Yorkston, N. J., and Whipple, K. *Psychotherapy versus behavior therapy.* Cambridge: Harvard University Press, 1975.

Smith, A., Traganza, E., and Harrison, G. Studies on the effectiveness of anti-depressant drugs. *Psychopharmacology Bulletin*, March 1969.

Snyder, S. *Madness and the brain.* New York: McGraw-Hill Book Co., 1974.

Spotnitz, H. *Modern psychoanalysis of the schizophrenic patient.* New York: Grune and Stratton, 1968.

Squire, L. R. ECT and memory loss. *American Journal of Psychiatry*, 134:997, 1977.

Stein, L. I., Test, M. A., and Marx, A. J. Alternative to the hospital: A controlled study. *American Journal of Psychiatry,* 132:517, 1975.

Stephens, J. Long-term course and prognosis in schizophrenia. *Seminars in Psychiatry,* 2:464, 1970. (Reprinted in Cancro, 1972.)

Stevenson, W. *A man called Intrepid.* New York: Ballantine Books, 1977.

Stierlin, H. *Conflict and reconciliation: A study in human relations and schizophrenia.* New York: Anchor Books, 1968.

Stone, A. A. *Mental health and the law.* New York: Jason Aronson, 1977.

Strauss, J. and Carpenter, W. Prediction of outcome in schizophrenia, III: Five-year outcome and its predictors. *Archives of General Psychiatry,* 34:159, 1977.

Sullivan, H. S. *Schizophrenia as a human process.* New York: W. W. Norton and Co., 1962.

Sutherland, S. *Breakdown: A personal crisis and a medical dilemma.* London: Weidenfeld and Nicolson, 1976.

Szasz, T. *The manufacture of madness: A comparative study of the inquisition and the mental health movement.* New York: Colophon Books, 1970.

Szasz, T. S. *Schizophrenia: The sacred symbol of psychiatry.* New York: Basic Books, 1976.

Taylor, M. Schneiderian first-rank symptoms and clinical prognostic features in schizophrenia. *Archives of General Psychiatry,* 26:64, 1972.

Torrey, E. F. Is schizophrenia universal? An open question. *Schizophrenia Bulletin,* 7:53, 1973.

Torrey, E. F., and Peterson, M. R. The viral hypothesis of schizophrenia. *Schizophrenia Bulletin,* 2:136, 1976.

Vaillant, G. Prospective prediction of schizophrenic remission. *Archives of General Psychiatry,* 11:509, 1964a.

Vaillant, G. An historical review of the remitting schizophrenias. *Journal of Nervous and Mental Disease,* 138:48, 1964b.

Villet, B. Opiates of the mind: The biggest medical discovery since penicillin. *The Atlantic Monthly,* 241 (no. 6):82, 1978.

Viscott, D. S. *The making of a psychiatrist.* New York: Arbor House, 1972.

Watt, N. F. Childhood and adolescent routes to schizophrenia. In D. Ricks, et al. (eds.), *Life history research in psychopathology,* vol. 3. Minneapolis: University of Minnesota Press, 1974.

Weakland, J. H. The double-bind hypothesis of schizophrenia and three-party interaction. In D. D. Jackson (ed.), *The etiology of schizophrenia.* New York: Basic Books, 1960.

Weiner, H. Schizophrenia: Etiology. In A. M. Freedman, H. I. Kaplan and B. J. Sadock (eds.), *Comprehensive textbook of psychiatry—II* (2nd ed.). Baltimore: Williams and Wilkins Co., 1975.

Weiss, P. *The persecution and assassination of Jean-Paul Marat as performed by the inmates of the asylum at Charenton under the direction of the Marquis de Sade.* New York: Atheneum Publishers, 1965.

Werble, B. A second follow-up study of borderline patients. *Archives of General Psychiatry,* 23:3, 1970.

Wilson, P. J. *Oscar: An inquiry into the nature of sanity.* New York: Random House, 1974.

Wyatt, R. J., Termini, B. A., and Davis, J. Biochemical and sleep studies of schizophrenia: A review of the literature, 1960–1970—Part I: Biochemical studies. *Schizophrenia Bulletin,* 4:10, 1971.

Wynne, L. C., Singer, M. T., Bartko, J. J., and Toohey, M. L. Schizophrenics and their families: Recent research on parental communication. In J. M. Tanner (ed.), *Psychiatric research: The widening perspective.* New York: International Universities Press, 1975.

Yeats, W. B. *The Collected Poems of W. B. Yeats.* New York: Macmillan Co., 1956.

Index